Sobel argues that Americans' tendency to seek solutions from experts has caused economists such as John Kenneth Galbraith, Milton Friedman, Paul Samuelson, and William Simon to be thrust into the popular limelight. In this book, he candidly discusses their personalities and translates some of their ideas and thoughts into language accessible to the layman who is affected daily—and inevitably—by the economy's twists and turns. Sobel devotes a chapter to each economist, and presents two chapters that deal with the ongoing economic debate in Washington from the late 1960s to the beginning of the 1980s. He provides clear statements on complex economic theories, discusses their evolution, and identifies the exponents of these theories.

No other book discusses these men, their ideas and personalities, and the policies with which they have been associated in such a clear, understandable manner. For the individual with an interest in current economic policy, in how government actually functions, and in the economist as an activist symbol in today's popular culture, *The Worldly Economists* offers an inside look at the people who predict, analyze, and may even help solve, today's economic crisis.

ROBERT SOBEL is Professor of Business History at Hofstra University. A syndicated columnist for *Newsday* ("Knowing the Street"), he is the author of numerous books, most of which deal with business and economics, including *Inside Wall Street, The Age of Giant Corporations, The Money Manias* and *The Last Bull Markets*. Currently, Sobel is working on a history of ITT.

THE
WORLDLY
ECONOMISTS

BY THE SAME AUTHOR

They Satisfy
Inside Wall Street
The Fallen Colossus
The Manipulators
N. Y. S. E.
Herbert Hoover at the Onset of the Great Depression
The Entrepreneurs
The Money Manias
For Want of a Nail . . .
The Age of Giant Corporations
Conquest and Conscience: the 1840s
Machines and Morality: the 1850s
Amex
The Curbstone Brokers
Panic on Wall Street
The Great Bull Market
The Big Board
The Origins of Interventionism

THE
WORLDLY
ECONOMISTS

Robert Sobel

THE FREE PRESS
A Division of Macmillan Publishing Co., Inc.
NEW YORK

Collier Macmillan Publishers
LONDON

The Free Press
A Division of Macmillan Publishing Co., Inc.
866 Third Avenue, New York, N.Y. 10022

Collier Macmillan Canada, Ltd.

Library of Congress Catalog Card Number: 80-66129

Printed in the United States of America

printing number
1 2 3 4 5 6 7 8 9 10

Library of Congress Cataloging in Publication Data

Sobel, Robert
  The worldly economists.

  Bibliography: p.
  Includes index.
  1. Economists—United States—Biography. I. Title.
HB119.A3S64   330'.092'2 [B]   80-66129
ISBN 0-02-929780-X

Thanks are due the following sources for permission to reprint the photographs included in a separate section: 1. Copyright © 1979 Don Perdue, New York; 2. Massachusetts Institute of Technology photo by Margo Foote; 3. Photo by Frank Wolfe, courtesy of the Lyndon Baines Johnson Library; 4. Photo by Paul Conklin; 5. Wide World Photos; 6. Department of the Treasury photo; 7. Wide World Photos; 8. National Archives, White House Photo Collection; 9. Official Department of Defense photo by R. D. Ward; 10. Photo by David Kennerly, courtesy of the Gerald R. Ford Library; 11. Photograph courtesy of Cornell University; 12. National Archives, White House Photo Collection; 13. Photo by Yoichi Okamoto, courtesy of the Lyndon Baines Johnson Library; 14. U.P.I. photo; 15. Department of the Treasury photo; 16. Photo by Yoichi Okamoto, courtesy of the Lyndon Baines Johnson Library.

for
Dorothy and Larry Stessin

If economists could manage to get themselves thought of as humble, competent people on the level with dentists, that would be splendid.

John Maynard Keynes

CONTENTS

PREFACE

Ours is surely an age for economists. No generation in American history has been so involved in economic debate or so curious regarding the theories and personalities of the profession's leading practitioners. Such individuals enjoy fame, wealth, and, if they desire, political power and influence, while even the lesser lights often can combine a satisfying academic career with government or business service.

The reasons for this are fairly obvious. We live in a period when economic crises have become chronic, difficult to comprehend, and, for some, almost impossible to cope with. At the same time the level of educational attainment has reached a point where millions of Americans have at least a smattering of economic knowledge and perhaps feel a need to take stands on theoretical issues and practical policies. Hence, intelligent and informed citizens engage more often in discussions revolving around such issues than at any time since the Great Depression.

This is an era of political and social activism. After a decade of Vietnam and Watergate, Americans found themselves mired in stagflation. More even than nuclear power and ecological concerns, this economic issue has provided them with a focus for interest, further study, reflection and political action.

Their curiosity regarding the major economists is a product of crisis and technology. Americans tend to seek solutions from experts, and so these individuals have been thrust into the limelight. They present their theories to a public conditioned by television, a medium better suited to exploiting personalities than interpreting abstract concepts. It does not suffice today for major economists to develop new ideas or even solutions to problems. They must also be able to translate their constructs into everyday English, not only for the masses, but for their political leaders, who also lack more than a modicum of knowledge in this field.

Yet even when this is done, many otherwise literate and astute citizens harbor an inner suspicion that they really don't understand the terms of economic debate. They have no problem following Milton Friedman's discussions regarding freedom of the marketplace, for example, but are lost once he delves beneath the surface of monetary theory. Such people can digest Paul Samuelson's 750-word essays in *Newsweek* with comparative ease, but have difficulties plowing through his textbook when they take freshman economics in college.

This book has been written with such individuals in mind, in the hope that after finishing it they will know more about the ideas of these men and will understand the nature of contemporary conflicts within the profession and the government. In the process, the readers should come to appreciate the enlarged role professional economists play in modern politics, which is one of the more striking but little discussed developments of the postwar era.

Finally, the project was undertaken to satisfy the needs of students in my classes in economic theory, many of whom wonder how the ideas of Adam Smith, Alfred Marshall, and John Maynard Keynes can be applied to modern problems. These students have been weaned on Robert Heilbroner's classic *The Worldly Philosophers,* in which are explored the ideas and programs of giants in the field. *The Worldly Economists* (which clearly has been inspired by the Heilbroner work) is concerned with living practitioners who have made an important impression on public policy, especially as it emerges from Washington.

The following chapters have been based on an exhaustive reading of the works of these political economists, articles and reports concerning them, and published interviews. Whenever possible I discussed the men and their ideas with individuals who were associated with them at one time or another and knew them and their works. I corresponded with several of the economists and spoke with them over the telephone. I saw them in action at conventions and public forums, and being grilled on television interview and discussion programs. But I deliberately avoided interviewing them for this work, or even meeting them, though most were quite willing and some even eager for the experience.

This approach is somewhat contentious and old-fashioned. Proximity certainly can lead to new insights, but the author may also become too involved with his subject and tend to become blind to faults or to exaggerate errors. It can also transform a search for understanding into a conclusion for advocacy, masked or open. Others have interviewed these

men, and I have had access to their work. All of the economists have set
down their ideas in clear and complete fashion. Any questions I might
have had regarding their ideas and careers have been asked, answered,
or avoided on many occasions. All that remained to be explored were
matters of motivation, and my experiences with other interviews conducted for my previous books have led me to believe that answers to
such questions would tend to be self-serving, rehearsed, and, for the most
part, of little use. Whether or not this has been a wise decision for this
book is for the reader to decide.

Many of my colleagues at various institutions have read parts of or
complete individual chapters, offering criticisms, objections, and recommendations, all of which have been taken into consideration. Two of
them—Jake Weissman and Lynn Turgeon—have gone through several
of the chapters and have expended efforts beyond the call of friendship
and collegiality, for which they have my profound gratitude.

1

AN AGE
FOR ECONOMISTS

ONE CAN LIVE A PERFECTLY FRUITFUL LIFE, and one can even prosper, without having much formal knowledge of economics. Millions of Americans do. This is not to suggest they overlook means of maximizing incomes or that they fail to appreciate the impacts of inflation and recession. Every day such people make economically based decisions and do so without having heard of Adam Smith, David Ricardo, or John Maynard Keynes. In much the same way as people don't need physicians to tell them they feel ill, so they can see their situations improving or worsening without recourse to the wisdom of John K. Galbraith or Milton Friedman.

But what holds true for individuals does not obtain for society as a whole. In a complex environment there are barriers to trade that prevent the smooth workings of economic laws, attempts to stifle competition, regulations that make little economic sense but that nonetheless have to be obeyed, and a wide variety of social and political demands that confound economic intelligence. Furthermore the interests of society as perceived by its elected leaders often clash with the desires and values of individual citizens, who have to be coerced into actions they find distasteful. The physician who has to prescribe a single treatment for an entire ward may wind up helping a goodly number of his patients, but some of them may be killed by the therapy.

Although many economists specialize in advising businessmen and consumers, those who have achieved celebrity status prescribe for entire societies. They are on call at the White House to assist Presidents, most of whom had been ignorant of the complexities of modern economic doctrines. They provide services that bear some resemblance to those afforded King Arthur by Merlin the Magician. Such men are practitioners of the often obscure science of economics, who by means of their prescriptions promise to make a gross national product expand, an inflation rate decline, and unemployment shrink.

To continue with the medical analogy, the President will ask his economist-in-residence to recommend therapies to alleviate distress and mitigate problems. In his responses the economist will warn against side effects, estimate how long the treatment must continue before results are seen, and discuss the costs. He would then have to convince the President that his medicine should be taken. Often this is a difficult task, requiring high political and personal talents, for there are other practitioners with different therapies, all promising to do the job faster, better, and with fewer sacrifices.

An individual can be treated for a malady without understanding its pathology, but the wise patient selects his physician carefully, and within limitations learns all he can about the illness and the recommended treatment. This same person will observe the workings of an economic policy with an incomplete understanding of why certain programs have been initiated or dropped, what benefits will accrue, and what actually is being done. Presidents will take great care to explain in clear, nontechnical terms, offer slogans, and make exhortations. But such actions rarely have been successful. Americans now understand that Presidents have the benefit of advice from professional economists, and they know who these people are. Occasionally one reads articles about the economists and their ideas in the press, and some of them appear often on television interview programs. But most people, most of the time, remain in what might be called a half-dark when it comes to economics. They know, however, that when the economy is in distress—and even when it's not—Presidents turn to their economic soothsayers for advice and prescriptions.

Although economics as a science and profession emerged comparatively recently, almost all the Presidents have employed advisors on the subject. Alexander Hamilton, the first Secretary of the Treasury, clearly was the first of them. His four financial reports, produced over a period of two years, provided George Washington with a workable philosophy, a program to realize it, and a direction toward which to head. Furthermore, it was politically feasible. Hamilton gave Washington what White House economists today attempt to offer their chiefs. Yet he was not a professional economist but instead a soldier, lawyer, pamphleteer, and politician.

Throughout the nineteenth century most Presidents relied upon Cabinet members, legislators, bankers, and cronies for economic advice, but seldom did they feel the strong need for it. With the exceptions of transportation policy in the early part of the century and a wide range of programs during the Civil War, the federal government remained aloof from direct intervention in the economy. The three great and lasting economic issues of the second half of the century—the tariff, the money issue, and internal improvements—were dealt with by interactions between businessmen, farm organizations, and politicians. Some of them employed economic arguments derived from academia, but the economists themselves more often than not remained far from the scene of battle. This was an age dominated by practical men of affairs. When financial panic struck, Presidents looked to Wall Street bankers for help; they did not put in hurried calls to Harvard, Yale, or some other gathering place for professional economists.

Toward the end of the century some state governments, most of them in the Middle West, employed economists in technical posts. Woodrow Wilson utilized their services during World War I, and afterwards Secretary of Commerce Herbert Hoover called upon professional academic economists for assistance in planning for government action in the event of a depression. Several respected economists, most notably Wesley Clair Mitchell, Frank Taussig, and William Z. Ripley, traveled to the capital to help frame policies and influence legislation. Julius Klein, formerly a member of the Harvard faculty, served as Assistant Secretary of Commerce under Hoover and played a role in developing programs to deal wth the Great Depression.

Franklin Roosevelt brought dozens of economists to Washington, where they helped staff New Deal agencies and also draft legislation. Many of those who served in the capital during this period still recall the heady experience of seeing their theories being translated into policies. Yet Roosevelt showed little interest in abstract thought. When Keynes visited Washington in mid-decade he noted with approval the advanced thinking of many government economists, a number of whom had accepted his formulations and were trying to put them into practice. But he left a meeting with Roosevelt amazed at his ignorance of basic doctrines. He perceived that the men around the President were politicians, not professionals. The situation changed somewhat during World War II, when additional hundreds of economists came to the capital, but few of them had much in the way of real power, and, even then, economic advice was dispensed by individuals who were relative amateurs.

Initially it appeared that Harry Truman would continue in this vein. The new President showed little inclination to seek the advice of professional economists in dealing with the problems of reconversion. Rather, he relied upon holdover figures from the Roosevelt Administration and close friends he made while a senator. But this would not do. A botched attempt to ease the way to a civilian economy and growing fears that the nation was about to slip into another depression helped change Truman's mind. Furthermore, an important segment of the New Deal contingent in Congress and the Administrative branch started to doubt Truman's dedication to liberalism and insisted he take an activist role in guaranteeing economic stability and low unemployment. The President was pushed by the course of events and pulled by those around him to accept the Employment Act of 1946, arguably the most important piece of domestic legislation in the three decades between Franklin Roosevelt's hundred days and Lyndon Johnson's first months in office.

This measure, written in large part by New Deal economist Leon Keyserling, required the President to assume direct responsibility for the economy's performance, to make certain there would be no new depression, and by implications guard against runaway inflation as well. There would be constant supervision of the economy in the future; intervention would not be limited to periods of deep distress, as had been the case under Hoover and Roosevelt. As economic historian Edward Flash put it, acceptance of the Employment Act "transformed the issue of conscious governmental intervention from 'whether' to 'how.'"

Passage of the legislation all but guaranteed that additional economists would be employed in the White House—but with what powers? To a large degree that depended upon the personalities and abilities of the economists and the ways Presidents reacted to them and their advice. These men would have to be political economists in the Hamilton mold and not disinterested economic scientists. There was some doubt that those practitioners of the old generation would be able to perform well in such a setting, and some of them, including the first Chairman of the Council of Economic Advisors, Edwin Nourse, failed in this regard.

Attention was immediately focused on the Council, whose task it would be to assist and advise the President in molding policies and in preparing an annual Economic Report. This document was to be an "economic state of the union message" and in addition was an agenda, an apologia, and a treatise on Administration economic philosophy. It could not be prepared by amateurs, politicians, or bureaucrats, though on occasion such individuals could influence its contents. Nor was it supposed to be an objective text, which meant that technical economists would be of little use except in advisory capacities. Rather, the President would require the services of professionals who also possessed a social vision, one similar to his own. The *Wall Street Journal* grasped some of the implications of the Employment Act when it called it a "Magna Carta for economists," and so it proved to be. From that time to the present no chief executive has lacked resident economic soothsayers, and candidates for high office employ the talents of such individuals in their campaigns. But at first they were a rare breed.

Initially it appeared such economists would issue their pronouncements from the Council; whenever the President required an analysis, wanted to discuss problems, or hoped to peer into the future, he would call in his Chairman, ask his questions, and be tutored in one or another aspect of the discipline. Such was Nourse's conception of his role. But Truman wanted more: he required political loyalty, partisanship, and, most of all, a defender for his policies before Congress and in public forums. He found such a person in Keyserling, who set the pattern for those who followed. Arthur Burns, a man of strikingly different personality, tried at first to remain in the background, but in time he put on the armor and fought for Dwight Eisenhower's programs and approach to inflation and depression. Walter Heller had a similar relationship with John Kennedy.

By the mid-1950s, however, as economic issues and debate became more important and familiar—and as some leading economists came to accept their political roles and learned how to communicate better with an informed public—several practitioners achieved influence in their own rights and spoke from independent pulpits. One of the profession's most lucid and original commentators, John K. Galbraith, was a best-selling author prior to entering the Kennedy government, where he served as Ambassador to India, not as CEA Chairman. Although Galbraith hasn't exercized influence in the White House for more than a decade and a half, his grip upon the liberal imagination is as strong as ever; he remains the consummate political economist. Paul Samuelson, more of a mainstream economist than Galbraith, refused an official post at the capital, in part because he rejected the political role; but his advice has been sought by Presidents and candidates, and no one within the profession has achieved higher status. Furthermore, several generations of students were introduced to the discipline by means of his text, the most successful work of its kind ever written. A third independent political economist, Milton Friedman, has like Samuelson offered advice and even advocacy to Presidents and candidates but has served under none of them. Yet his ways of looking at the economy have affected the approaches and programs of the last three Administrations. In varying degrees Paul McCracken, George Shultz, and William Simon attempted to deal with inflation, recession, and economic instability by recourse to Friedmanesque ideas and programs. In more recent times Alfred Kahn has created a blend of microeconomic techniques and elements of Friedmanism to create a synthesis that is neither liberal nor conservative and may prove a prelude to a new stage in the economic debate.

The personalities, philosophies, and prescriptions of these men have had a profound impact upon the way Americans perceive their government and economy and how the former deals with the latter. At no previous time in the nation's history have professional economists been so prominent in the political debate or their ideas so hotly discussed, both in and out of government. As the informed public developed a taste for economic knowledge, the major economists attempted to cast their doctrines in terms that were readily comprehensible. In the process, the concepts have become simplified and distorted, their contributions to theory and basic assumptions trivialized, while the men themselves often have been elevated or reduced (depending on how one considers such things) to the status of celebrities and symbols.

Where did their ideas come from? As has been indicated, the attitudes, interests, and objectives of most of the major soothsayers either were fashioned or influenced by the twin impacts of the Great Depression and the arrival in America of Keynesian doctrines. These men were not only faced with the most traumatic event in American economic history but also a revolutionary doctrine that appeared to some to offer a way to deal with it. Keynesianism had its greatest impact on students, especially those prepared to discard the old, discredited theories. Some rushed to embrace the ideas, while others rejected them; but few could ignore them. Friedman was born in 1912, Samuelson and Heller three years later, and McCracken and Kahn in 1917; all were students in the 1930s. "Bliss was it in that Keynesian dawn to be alive," wrote Samuelson later on. "But to be young was very Heaven!" They were both.

Keyserling and Galbraith were 25 years old in 1933 and so less susceptible to that intellectual virus. Keyserling became a prominent figure in New Deal Washington, where his ideas were shaped less by abstract theories than by his innate pragmatism and a devotion to a set of social objectives. Galbraith served in that city in a minor capacity toward the end of the 1930s and in more important posts during the war, all the time developing his own approaches to social and economic problems. With these men the Keynesian influence was indirect. Such was the case too for Arthur Burns, 29 years old at the time of Roosevelt's inauguration. His ideas already were fixed and his career developing; Burns would not be bitten by the Keynesian bug until much later. As for George Shultz and William Simon, both came from moderately well-to-do families, were younger men who did not have vivid memories of the Great Depression, and neither developed a strong interest in economic thought until years after the Keynesian wave had crested.

Shultz, Simon, and to a lesser degree McCracken, were more concerned with curbing inflation than with preventing a recession. While Keynes had written on both subjects, most of his followers had concentrated on matters of growth and not rising prices. With the arrival of the Nixonians in the late 1960s, it would appear that the Keynesian generation had passed from the scene, to be replaced by post-Keynesians and non-Keynesians of various persuasions. Yet the monument remains. In different ways Galbraith, Friedman, and even Simon are rebels. The orthodoxy they are contesting is Keynesianism.

None of these men has tasted independent political power. Galbraith once hoped for a Senate seat, while Simon stands prepared to accept a political bid. While in the White House, however, these men and the others functioned as teachers and sounding boards, as publicizers and propagandists.

The teachers gained as much as their students. Most economists emerged from the experience with a deeper appreciation of the processes of government and the workings of the economy, and they profited greatly from their exercizes in political economy, an art that they helped to recreate. Several of them derived enhanced professional status and celebrity from their White House careers. Paul McCracken might be known today only to a small circle of business economists were not for his services on the Council, and to a lesser degree the same might be said of Walter Heller. Neither Shultz nor Kahn had any great public recognition prior to arriving at the White House. Had he not been tapped for service in the Eisenhower Administration, Arthur Burns, in some respects the most effective political economist of them all, would be known today within the profession as one who carried on the work started by Wesley Clair Mitchell at the National Bureau and would not be the person whose pronouncements cause the prices of stocks and gold to shoot upward or decline. Yet, in terms of contributions to theory, Mitchell was by far the more important person.

Although their public roles had a major impact on these economists' careers, the effect on the nation has been far more important. No person who hopes to understand the political process can afford to ignore the ideas and policies these men and their acolytes present and defend, for during the past three-and-a-half decades their advocacies have formed the basis for programs that have transformed the nation.

Their weapons were ideas, which they used in attempts to influence chief executives. This is not to suggest that they were Svengalis. Rather, the most successful of them understood how best to appeal to their Presidents. Keyserling convinced Truman the economy could expand and the nation have full employment with only minor inflation. Burns believed the economy as a whole could be tracked, that there were early warning signals for recessions and inflations, and that armed with this knowledge leaders could employ a variety of weapons to alleviate and mitigate their impacts; his style and philosophy were in tune with Eisenhower's. Samuelson and Heller told Kennedy there need be no more recessions and that with prompt and continual intervention the nation's economic performance could be vastly improved. This appealed to the man who had campaigned on the promise to get the nation moving again. Without an appreciation of Heller's new economics, few major New Frontier and Great Society programs can be understood, for both Kennedy and Johnson counted on economic growth to provide the funds to pay for them. Some might even say that the new economics provided them with the means of obtaining the financing for the Vietnam War.

While the new economists proclaimed the dawn of an era of continued growth and prosperity in which social and racial differences would be dissolved, Galbraith entered a demurrer. He claimed the society was so structured as to all but guarantee persistent, chronic, and debilitating inflation. The only way to deal with this, he said, was to impose wage and price controls, and this belief eventually would lead him to espouse a form of native socialism. Milton Friedman also saw inflation as a major threat, but his solution was radically different. Where Galbraith would enlarge government, he would diminish its role. The debate between the Galbraithians and Friedmanites intensified in the late 1960s, when inflation replaced recession as the nation's most serious economic problem. The new economists were in disarray, and for a while it appeared America was in for a period of conservative economic policies and doctrines.

It was then, almost without warning and certainly without precedent, that stagflation struck. Classical economists said it couldn't happen, while modern ones thought it was a temporary aberration. But in the early 1970s America experienced both inflation and recession—the worst in more than a generation—simultaneously. Three Presidents and their economic advisors struggled with the malady, using a variety of approaches, some of them Galbraithian, others generated by the Friedmanites. Nothing seemed to work. Economic science itself seemed to have reached some kind of dead end. The soothsayers, whose reputations and status had reached their pinnacle in the early 1960s, were now partially discredited. But they had not lost their audiences. Their words were listened to and read, their prescriptions analysed and evaluated. Friedmanites and Galbraithians continue to argue that their systems would work, if only given a proper chance by the right political leader, while others within the spectrum set forth combinations and mixtures that they too claim would perform the task.

That some form of therapy is required cannot be denied—but which one? In order to choose, one must first know the physicians and their treatments. The function of this book is to provide both.

2

LEON KEYSERLING

SHORTLY BEFORE CHRISTMAS 1978, the *New York Times* published a letter from Leon Keyserling in which was set forth a series of objections to President Carter's programs aimed at defending the dollar and containing inflation. The writer opposed higher interest rates and scheduled increases in Social Security taxes and spoke out forcefully against what he termed "no growth" federal budgets that could cause a recession. Keyserling did not think the defense of the dollar had "higher priority than protecting the economy and people at home." In any case, the Administration was going about the task in the wrong way. The best method to insure the soundness of the currency and halt inflation would be to release the full power of the American economy. As Keyserling saw it, various attempts over the past quarter of a century to hold down inflation by cutting into production have resulted in the forfeiture of more than $5.5 trillion dollars in goods and services and $1 trillion in tax revenues. Had these been available the standard of living for all Americans would have been much higher and the currency secure. Economic stimulation, and not a dampening of the fires, was the proper economic medicine, and Keyserling implied that there were people around capable of dispensing it. "What we need now is a new Department of Experience to guide those not yet profiting by experience," he concluded.

Like much of Keyserling's writings this letter was forceful, direct, blunt, and clear. It gave one the feeling of hearing a tart, perhaps humorless, schoolmaster lecturing a group of not overly bright students. Those who read his articles and pamphlets over the years, or who recall seeing him in television interviews, had no trouble recognizing the tone and cadence of the words. Even the message was familiar, for Keyserling's ideas today are what they were in the late 1940s and early 1950s, when he was often in the public eye. At that time he was an important Washington figure, a veteran who knew his way around and from whom great things were expected. Perhaps more than anyone else in the Truman Administration Keyserling possessed a clear and realistic view of the nation's economic potential, and he had a set of plans that seemed capable of realizing it. Also, he became a "media figure," one of the first economists to present his ideas to the general public over radio and television regularly.

But even then he was something of a loner, a man with few close friends within the "economics establishment" in academia, who was more at ease with labor leaders, enlightened businessmen, lobbyists, and journalists than with professors. Due in part to an intellectual arrogance forged decades earlier and a knack he always seemed to have of alienating people, Keyserling became one of that rare breed of Washingtonians—a political insider with few close allies. In the nature of things such individuals usually have short lives in the central arena. So it was with Keyserling.

He was one of the original members of the Council of Economic Advisors and served as its second Chairman from 1950 to 1953. More than anyone else he had been responsible for the framing of the Employment Act of 1946 which had established the Council, and Keyserling was its most energetic and influential figure during the Truman years. But when Truman left office there was no place for Keyserling to go. He lacked the kinds of connection needed to provide him with an important podium. Council members after Keyserling would return to visible and secure posts as professors in prestigious universities or to honored places at major foundations; Keyserling had made no secret of his scorn for full-time academics, and he had more enemies than friends at the leading "think tanks." All he knew was politics, and now he was out in the cold.

So he remained in Washington, where he hoped to become a
rallying point for those who rejected the Eisenhower brand of economics. There were articles in the *New York Times* and analyses in
the *New Republic* and other liberal magazines. Keyserling opened
an office for legal work and consulting. He also organized a minor
research operation of his own, the Conference on Economic Progress, of which he became president and from which he published
a steady stream of pamphlets on important issues. Clearly he is
ready for a job of some kind where he can help shape public policies
once again, and so his call for a Department of Experience. But
none has been offered, and it is unlikely Keyserling will ever again
serve in a government post.

Washington society is still dotted with former New and Fair
Dealers who operate out of major law firms, public relations operations, and lobbying organizations. They have become the heart of
an "old boy" network in the city. Keyserling sees these people at
parties and lunches, but he functions away from the center in a corner of his own. Perhaps this is because of his own inclination. Whatever the reason he is not a very visible or especially newsworthy
figure. But the record remains, and it shows that Keyserling was the
first major economic soothsayer of the modern era. As such, he
helped establish the ground rules under which future economists
would operate in the White House, and in the process he also provided much of the substance for what later came to be known as the
New Economics.

Keyserling was born in Charleston, South Carolina, in 1908, the
son of moderately well-to-do parents. After graduating from the
local high school in 1924 he traveled to New York to enter Columbia
College, where he majored in the liberal arts. From the first he was
interested in social sciences in general and economics in particular.
The teacher who had the most profound effect upon Keyserling was
Rexford Tugwell, who already was considered a rising star in the
field, a charismatic individual who attracted several acolytes from
among the brighter students. Soon thereafter Tugwell came to look
upon Keyserling as a disciple and future colleague, but the young
man didn't want an academic career, which in that period was
about the only way most economists could make their livings. Instead, with Tugwell's approval, he opted for law. Aggressive and
ambitious, he set out to win acceptance at Harvard, which like most
prestigious institutions of the time had a small Jewish quota. Knowing what was required of him, Keyserling became a grind, which

won him a Phi Beta Kappa key and admission to Harvard but few
close friends at Columbia. Those who remember him from this
period speak of a brilliant, arrogant, and aloof intellectual, who had
become radicalized by Tugwell. He impresed his Harvard class-
mates the same way; there, too, he was an odd man out.

Keyserling was at Harvard when the Great Depression struck,
and that cataclysm moved the center of gravity of American thought
and politics several degrees leftward. At the Graduate School, Alvin
Hansen and others were on their way to embracing Keynesianism;
in the 1930s Harvard would become the incubator for a generation
of economists who would occupy strategic positions in the profession
and in Washington during the 1960s—men like John K. Galbraith,
Robert Triffin, James Tobin, Robert Gordon, Henry Wallich, and a
slew of others. But there was no corresponding change at the Law
School, where the majority of faculty members hewed either to the
old conservatism or antique Wilsonian liberalism. Keyserling found
the atmosphere there stodgy and his teachers for the most part un-
imaginative. Although he studied with Felix Frankfurter—considered a giant even then—Keyserling was unimpressed with the man
and his ideas. Law continued to interest him, but increasingly he
sought to combine it with economics so as to form the foundation
of a reform philosophy and program.

Keyserling received his LL.B. in 1931 and was admitted to the
New York bar soon after. With Tugwell's help he obtained an appointment as an assistant in economics at Columbia and registered
for the Ph.D. program in that subject. Now he took classes with
such luminaries as William Z. Ripley and John Bates Clark and
through it all moved more closely to Tugwell. The disciple had become the colleague.

In order to understand Keyserling in this period when his ideas
were being fashioned, it is necessary to appreciate the position of
his mentor. Tugwell was an institutionalist, as were Clark and Ripley. In fact, Columbia was a center for economists of this persuasion
and approach. The institutionalists believed there was no such thing
as "economic man." Rather, individuals and society as a whole had
to be studied with an awareness of the complexities of life, the role
played by irrational forces and large, often impersonal aggregations
of power. Thus, the economist required a deep understanding and
appreciation of sociology, psychology, ethics, and history in order
to function well.

Most institutionalists believed there was no true harmony in

society. Rather, these large forces were constantly in the process
of fighting one another. Big business sought to dominate small; la-
borers organized so as to gain advantages over employers; the farm
interests were at odds with those of manufacturing, and both were
in conflict with consumers.

It was the role of government, they thought, to harmonize these
differences and do so in the light of common, shared beliefs. At his
core each institutionalist was a moralist. He *knew* what was good
for his fellow men and wanted to use government to achieve objectives. These economists operated out of bases in universities, but
their true areas of concern were city halls, state houses, and Washington. Ripley helped mold national transportation policies; Mitchell was a government advisor on business cycles; Commons had
been a key figure in Robert LaFollette's government in Wisconsin.
Rex Tugwell, 40 years old in 1931, had ambitions for a central position in any reform administration that might lead the nation during
the Great Depression.

The following year Tugwell became an advisor to Democratic
presidential candidate Franklin Roosevelt and soon thereafter
served as member of the famous "brain trust." At the same time
he completed work on a book, *The Industrial Idea,* which was published in 1933. In it he called for the creation of an Industrial Integration Board, which would coordinate all aspects of the economy,
using as a model the War Industries Board of World War I. As he
saw it, the various aggregations of power in America were pulling
against one another in such a way as to make recovery impossible.
What was needed was a strong government acting to end wasteful
competition and encourage a sense of shared interest—the industrial
idea of the title. In particular the businessmen had to be assured
that Roosevelt was not a radical and that he would cooperate with
them in an effort at business revival. He urged suspension of the
antitrust laws; creation of White House-sponsored codes of conduct
under which industries would operate; and central planning by a
consortium of political leaders, intellectuals, and important businessmen.

In some respects Tugwell's ideas resembled those put forth by
leading businessmen, and for this reason he was classified as a conservative. Nothing was further from the truth. In fact, Tugwell did
not trust the business leaders, and blamed much of the depression
upon them. For the time being, however, their cooperation and
good will were important, and so he courted them.

The Industrial Idea became the basis for the National Industrial Recovery Act, the centerpiece of the New Deal in its first year. Roosevelt's acceptance of Tugwell's plans offered a clear indication that the Columbia University professor had become an important figure in Washington.

Tugwell was a whirlpool who drew many bright young men from academia to Washington, and one of these was Leon Keyserling. In 1932 Keyserling had worked with Tugwell on a study of education in America, funded by the Rockefeller-supported General Education Fund. He had also served as part of a group at Columbia that studied the value of education in general and, more specifically, the role played by the social sciences. All of this was put aside in 1933 when Tugwell invited Keyserling to come to Washington and offered him a position as attorney for the Agricultural Adjustment Administration. Keyserling was 25 years old at the time, barely out of law school, with only a minor foothold in academia, but of course he accepted. Now he found himself close to the centers of real power during what was perhaps the most exciting period of political reform in American history. This, and not the graduate seminar, was the true focus of interest for an institutional economics. Keyserling suspended his Ph.D. studies and never returned to them.

In 1934 Tugwell and Keyserling edited a book entitled *Redirecting Education*, the vestigial remains of their work at Columbia. Keyserling's contribution was an essay, "Social Objectives in the American College." It was his first significant publication and offers important clues as to his thinking then and later on.

Keyserling was critical of American colleges, which, he said, offered students neither a realistic view of society nor a philosophy to cope with the problems of the day. In particular he noted "the artificial dichotomy between education and politics," which was perhaps "the chief barrier to educational reconstruction." To Keyserling, politics was an integral part not only of education but all aspects of life. "It is a branch of ethics dealing with the ethical duties of states. It is concerned with an evaluation of relationships among men in organized society. There can be no promise in democracy until politics is a passion with most men. The greatest danger to free government lies in a craven withdrawal which leaves politics to the incompetent or the vicious, or envisages it as a pastime of men of independent means fearful of innocuous ease." Clearly these are the words of an impassioned young man, excited with the prospects of using power and eager to see his ethical concepts realized in law and public policy. Keyserling was an economist by this time, but in addition he burned with a strong set of moral convictions, among which was the belief that government must act to help the weak, correct injustices, and provide a high minimum standard of living for all citizens. He attacked academic economists who were seeking a value-free discipline that in some ways could be deemed "scientific" and who remained above the battle on their tenured perches in colleges. "The present trend in the social sciences, whatever rationalization may be made, is due to the fact that they are regarded primarily as instrumentalities for description and analysis, rather than for experimental control." According to him, "every ethical judgement involves an ethical bias, and for this reason the dichotomy is not so much between economics and ethics as between two types of economics." Keyserling was committed to an ideal and functioned in the political world; other economists were busily constructing models out of abstract mathematical formulas and seemed more interested in the approval of their colleagues than the betterment of mankind. He had the scorn of a practical man of affairs for an abstract idealist and would retain this for the rest of his life.

This is the key to understanding Keyserling, not only during the 1930s and early 1940s but later on as well. He saw little value in abstract theories that could not be applied directly to resolve problems. At a time when the Keynesian revolution was percolating through the economics departments of graduate schools, he was involved with framing much of the legislation of the early New Deal. Later on, scholars would claim that part of the inspiration for Roosevelt's programs could be found in the works of Keynes. Keyserling emphatically denies this, tracing the roots to the pragmatic and practical institutionalists, men like Tugwell and himself.

Keyserling soon caught the attention of his next patron, Senator Robert Wagner of New York, who by this time had emerged as a major leader of the New Deal coalition on Capitol Hill and one whose ideas meshed well with those of Tugwell. Wagner's secretary and legislative assistant, Simon Rifkind, was about to leave Washington to take charge of the Senator's private law practice in New York. Wagner offered the post to Keyserling, who after consultation with Tugwell and AAA chief Jerome Frank, accepted.

In this way the young, relatively inexperienced lawyer-cum-economist became an important link between the White House and Congress, while at the same time participating in the drafting of most of the significant legislation on the reform agenda of the mid-

1930s. His hand could be seen in the NIRA, the National Housing Act and the Railroad Retirement Act of 1934, the Social Security Act and the National Labor Relations Act of 1935, and subsequent legislation. He also wrote most of Wagner's speeches, at a time when the Senator was the most vocal proponent of New Deal measures, and he collaborated with Wagner in helping draw up the Democratic platform in 1936. While academic economists were polishing their Ph.D. dissertations and writing articles for journals so as to win appointments at major universities, Keyserling was involved in helping mold an altered economic framework for government-business relations.

Four decades later he would claim that he "was a major initiator and developer of at least two-thirds of the New Deal economic and social legislation." This was hyperbole. Even Tugwell hardly mentions Keyserling in his several histories of the New Deal, and at no point was he singled out by journalists as a member of the inner circle. But even after allowing for exaggeration, it seems clear that Keyserling was one of the relatively significant staff men of the period and that he was a source of ideas and programs for Wagner and others. More to the point, he was receiving an education in economics and politics that was far more complete than any he might have had at Columbia. In the process he became a "practical idealist."

At no point in his career would Keyserling set down his ideas in any theoretical fashion or even make an attempt at erecting a system of one kind or another. References to theory rarely appear in his writings. Rather, he preferred to testify before congressional committees on specific pieces of legislation or write on topical matters for newspapers and magazines. At a time when the path to professional status among economists rested upon the triad of a Ph.D., the ability to use sophisticated theory and construct complex models, and the approval of one's academic peers, Keyserling clearly was an outsider. In fact, even Washingtonians were confused as to his niche. Was he a lawyer or an economist? Throughout the 1930s he was identified as one or the other but rarely as both.

But he did find a specialty though almost by accident. Senator Wagner was interested in sponsoring legislation providing for low-cost housing, and Keyserling prepared a draft bill for such a measure in 1935. It failed to win passage that year but did manage to get through in 1937, one of the last gasps of New Deal reformism. Now there would be a United States Housing Authority, capitalized at more than $500 million, with a mandate to make loans to other agencies so as to provide more than a billion dollars worth of construction by 1941.

Nathan Straus was named as USHA Administrator, and Keyserling left Wagner's staff to become his general counsel. Insofar as his development and career were concerned, this was a good move. The war in Europe would soon begin, and Wagner would play only a minor role in it. The USHA, on the other hand, became involved with defense procurement and military housing, and this enabled Keyserling to work closely with leading military as well as civilian leaders. When Straus left the agency under fire in late 1941, Keyserling, only 33 years old, became its acting chief and now was more visible than ever. Recently married to government economist Mary Dublin, he also became a more sociable, less pugnacious individual. Clearly he had found a niche in Washington as a top bureaucrat and had that city's version of academic tenure. Keyserling thus became one of that modern breed of political economists who outlasts administrations and make careers in government service.

He served in a variety of posts during the war, most of them involved with housing and procurement. Out from under the shadows of Tugwell and Wagner and more or less on his own, he became involved in several intra-agency squabbles in which he polished his political skills. Keyserling had his share of setbacks but in the process gained new allies. One of these was Senator Harry Truman, who in his investigations of the war effort gave him high praise.

By then Keyserling had spent more than a decade in Washington and had seen most of his compatriots of 1933 leave the scene. He had been involved in fighting the depression and the war and in the process refining his economic ideas and ideology, selecting problems he hoped to resolve.

One of the more important of these was the issue of postwar planning. Most economists seemed to agree there would be a return to depression after the war. Clearly some approach had to be devised to meet this challenge. Acting in this spirit, the Pabst Brewing Company sponsored a competition among economists, who were invited to submit recommendations for government action. There were close to 36,000 entries, and Keyserling's won the $10,000 second prize. (The first prize of $25,000 went to War Production Board economist Herbert Stein).

"The American Economic Goal—A Practical Start Toward Post-

war Full Employment" was published and widely circulated. In it
Keyserling wrote of the need for tax incentives for businessmen,
government aid for housing, encouragement of world trade, and,
where necessary, public works programs. It was a generalized statement of intent rather than a specific agenda for action, but in it
Keyserling implied that in his view the key to prosperity was in
increased production of goods and services. If the American economic machine would be stimulated in peacetime as it had been
during the war, an avalanche of products would come to market, to
be purchased by the very workers who turned them out. Later on,
in a series of magazine articles inspired by the Pabst essay, he elaborated upon this theme: "Our unrivaled American aptitude for technological advance, spurred on by the depression years and since
driven harder by the impulse of total war, has exceeded the most
fanciful expectations." Taking a cue from suggestions made by Vice
President Henry Wallace, Keyserling sketched a plan by which 60
million jobs could be had. As a foundation there would be "an inte-
grated economic policy based on combined judgement of industry,
agriculture, labor, and government." Maximum employment in private enterprise would be encouraged by proper fiscal and monetary
policies as well as special tax incentives, and further stimulation
would result from government-sponsored research. Where they
were needed and could be justified, special loans would be made
available to private businesses. Finally, a public works program similar to that of the New Deal would be in place.

    This program would be coordinated by "an American Economic
Committee," comprising members of Congress, the Cabinet, and
representatives from labor, industry, and agriculture. Its tasks
would be to define objectives and make recommendations to the
President. Keyserling wrote rhapsodically of this group. "For each
of these performers to take a proper part in our national symphony
of productive effort, there must be a score. Clearly each of them
should play the instrument for which his gifts are greatest; yet if all
of them are to keep clear of discord, someone must wield a baton."

    Keyserling would later claim that his Pabst essay and related
writings provided the inspiration for the Employment Act of 1946
and the creation of the Council of Economic Advisors. While it may
have been true that his work contributed toward both, others also
played important roles, and in any case the concepts were being discussed throughout the war. The need for centralized planning was
the subject of papers emanating from the Treasury Department, the

National Farmers Union, the National Planning Association, and the
National Resources Planning Board. By then the Keynesian doctrines had found roots throughout the nation, and they seemed to
demand some kind of government-directed program to maintain employment. Practical politicians, who perhaps had never heard of
Keynes, felt the government would have to take charge of the conversion effort after the war. Others, who believed the nation would
return to the hard times of the 1930s after wartime spending ended,
thought there would be a second act for the New Deal in the late
1940s. A year before the Keyserling essay, Alvin Hansen, probably
the most important American Keynesian, wrote that "The Government cannot escape responsibility. To fulfill its responsibility it
needs the hearty cooperation of business, labor, farmers, and the
professions in the great task of developing a vigorous, expanding,
and prosperous society." Other economists, among them the young
Paul Samuelson, said as much.

A few months before the end of the war Senator James Murray
of Montana introduced what he called "the Full Employment Act of
1945," which was cosponsored by several of his colleagues, one of
whom was Robert Wagner. The original measure was strong, specific, and clearly in the New Deal tradition. After a year of debate
and amendment it was watered down, reshaped, and finally accepted as "the Employment Act of 1946." This was not what the
liberals in Congress had wanted. Nor did it go as far as Keyserling
had hoped it would. Still, it did bear his stamp. In fact, he was the
leader of the team that framed the measure and then revised it.

In its final version, the Act stated that it would be "the continuing policy and responsibility" of the federal government to help
create "conditions under which there will be afforded useful employment opportunities . . . and to promote maximum employment production, and purchasing power." To assist the President in
his work, the Act provided for the establishment of the Council of
Economic Advisors, to be composed of three members,

> each of whom shall be a person who, as a result of his training,
> experience, and attainments is exceptionally qualified to analyze
> and interpret economic developments, to appraise programs and
> activities of the Government in light of the policy declared . . .
> and to formulate and recommend national economic policy to pro-
> mote employment, production, and purchasing power under free
> competitive enterprise.

No one seemed quite certain of the role the Council would play other than that sketched in the legislation. It was not as though President Truman lacked economic advisors. Secretary of the Treasury John Snyder was an old friend and confidant. John Steelman, who had held a variety of top level posts including that of Economic Stablizer, already considered himself the "house economist" and resented the creation of this new office. The Bureau of the Budget had several capable economists on presidential call and one of them, Gerhard Colm, was a leading expert in the field of national income accounts. Truman gave no indication that he considered the Council an important agency. He waited six months before announcing the appointments and then did so in a diffident fashion. The three men he selected appeared to owe more to political and related considerations than to any special knowledge they might bring to the White House.

The first chairman was to be Edwin Nourse, who at the age of 63 was past president of the American Economic Association and a leader at the Brookings Institution. A mild Keynesian, though of the previous academic generation—Nourse had received his Ph.D. from the University of Chicago in 1915—he at one time had presented strong views on a variety of subjects. By 1946, however, he had little new to contribute and in any case made it clear that he took a limited view of his post. The Council was to advise the President and do little else. In Nourse's opinion the Council should be a nonpolitical body, above advocacy and politics, on hand to provide answers to questions of a technical nature and lead in the preparation of the annual report. Clearly such a person would pose no threat to Snyder, Steelman, and others in the presidential family.

John Clark, the second member, was 62 years old in 1946. A lawyer who had made a fortune as vice president of Standard Oil of Indiana, Clark had returned to academic life in 1929 and two years later received his Ph.D. in economics from Johns Hopkins. He later taught at the University of Denver and at the time of his appointment was dean of the business school at the University of Nebraska. Clark lacked distinction within the profession and indeed was barely known to the upper echelon of economists at the Ivy League and other prestigious places. But he had served in the Wyoming legislature and was considered close to Senator Joseph O'Mahoney of that state, a Washington fixture, a cosponsor of the Employment Act, and a person Truman wanted to please. The Clark appointment was viewed as a sop to the business community and a compliment to O'Mahoney.

Keyserling was to be vice chairman. He was 38 years old at the time, of a different generation than Nourse and Clark, and also of a strikingly different temperament and background. He had more experience as a government economist than almost anyone else in Washington. As previously indicated, Truman knew and respected him. Wagner recommended him highly in a clever letter to John Steelman, implying that Keyserling would prove invaluable in lobbying efforts. "Mr Keyserling is universally well regarded by many members of both the Senate and the House, particularly members of those committees which deal with economic and employment matters," and was "well liked and highly regarded not only by those up here who share his liberal views, but likewise by those with different political viewpoints." At a time when many New Dealers were troubled by what they perceived as Truman's innate conservatism, Keyserling's appointment would demonstrate that reformism was still intact in the White House. In general, then, he was seen as a link between the New Deal tradition and the Trumanites, the executive and the legislative branches of government, and even between lawyers and economists, since he was both. One journal noted that Nourse was an economist and Clark a politician. Keyserling would serve as the expert in political economy and so form a bridge between them.

Congressional liberals applauded the selection. Later on political moderate C. Harley Grattan observed that Keyserling "somehow typifies the thinned ranks of the reserve formation of New Deal brain-trusters, the men who did a job but never enjoyed the dubious fun of being conspicuous to the public." Now he might have that opportunity. "Mr. Keyserling is the most dynamic member of the Council, running on a full head of steam of conviction, and therefore also the one most likely to bring down conservative lightning on his head—and indeed he already has done so." Yet criticisms from that quarter were fairly uncommon, perhaps because Senator Robert Taft spoke highly of Keyserling. Rather, congressional conservatives wondered whether he could work in harmony with the placid Nourse and the mild Clark. Keyserling was known as having a short fuse and not suffering fools and philosophers gladly. His contempt for academics was known, and now he was supposed to work with two of them. Also, he had a conception of the Council far different from that of Nourse. Keyserling expected it to become an in-

tegral part of the White House operation. Nourse opposed the idea
and in fact on several occasions categorized the CEA as an experiment that might have to be disbanded. Conservatives generally
expected the Nourse position to prevail and believed he would be
able to hold the other two members in check. "No one has suggested
that Leon Keyserling ever used his power for selfish ends," wrote
Nation's Business shortly after the appointments were announced.
"Many have regarded him as a person who holds very unpleasant
opinions," and then, in a preview of what would come later on, the
magazine added, "But no one, in fact, has ever suggested that he is
a Communist."

Keyserling's essential economic philosophy at this stage of his
career was far from being communistic and for that matter wasn't
even very radical. At the time it was characterized in the press as
being Keynesian and "New Dealish," and certainly he incorporated
elements of his earlier experiences into all he said and did. By then,
too, Keyserling had acquired a working knowledge of Keynesian
thought—enough to be critical of much of it as not being based
upon solid empirical evidence and smacking too strongly of academia. Also, he had come to believe that much of the New Deal had
been ill-conceived, hastily organized, and simply wrongheaded.

All of this led him to two interrelated conclusions. The first was
that the prime goal for economists was to seek maximum growth
and use of available resources. The object of any Administration, he
wrote, was "the achievement of the highest levels of production and
presumably the highest standards of living that are within our
reach." In early 1947 he observed that the amount of national income lost due to inactivity during the Great Depression was about
equal to that expended during the war. This was the kind of comparison he would draw on many occasions during the next three-
and-a-half decades. While Galbraith criticised the frivolity of some
consumer goods, Keyserling spoke and wrote of the tragedy of unused workers and machines.

All measures aimed at increasing production should be used and
encouraged, and so Keyserling approved of low interest rates, monetary growth, tax cuts, and other incentives. Critics charged Keyserling with fighting yesterday's battles. Perhaps growth had been a
problem in the 1930s, they suggested, but this no longer was the
case. What did he have to contribute in the fight against inflation?
Conservative critics would observe that even Keynes, in his book
How to Win the War, suggested that the government should raise

taxes when inflationary pressures mounted. Keyserling disagreed. In his view, higher prices resulted from an imbalance between supply and demand. Thus, America's postwar inflation occurred when armies of consumers rushed to purchase relatively scarce goods. This would be a temporary phenomenon, he thought, and would end when industry caught up with demand. In 1946 and 1947 some economists called for continued controls, and others thought wartime taxes should be retained so as to stifle demand. Keyserling saw reasons to maintain some controls for a while longer but thought government stimulation of production was the best way to deal with rising prices. In any case, he said, inflation was not as much a national threat as was depression.

This is not to suggest that Keyserling was insensitive to the pains caused by inflation. The process resulted in hardships and served to reallocate wealth, often in unfair ways. But during inflationary periods employment remained high and factories operated on double shifts. To Keyserling, depressions meant the waste of human and material resources and so remained the greater problem.

In an article entitled "Must We Have Another Depression?" published in 1947, Keyserling analyzed the postwar inflation, which he predicted would soon end. The danger was that it might be succeeded by a sharp economic downturn. This was not because history repeats itself. "It has a more solid basis. While all economists do not agree as to all the causes of the last depression, a listing of the causal factors generally agreed upon indicates that many of these factors are again present now or will be present within a few years." He went on to state some of them:

> the tendency of our productive capacity to outrun our mass buying power, the chronic weakness of such bellwether industries as residential construction, the seeming reluctance of capital investment to expand as dynamically as once it did, the uncertain elements in foreign trade, the enormous disparities in the price and wage structure, and huge differentials in the enjoyment of national income by regions or by individuals.

Above all, he concluded, "the country as a whole has not yet adopted and put into action a fully rounded anti-depression program."

That America needed such a program was Keyserling's second conclusion. This was the unfinished work of F.D.R's New Deal; he thought it should become the centerpiece of Harry Truman's Fair Deal.

In this period Keyserling wrote more than a dozen articles in which he argued for economic planning. He noted that the classical economists of the nineteenth century had believed the economy came into balance naturally through the free interplay of the market. For example, high prices caused manufacturers to produce additional goods, and these forced prices downward. Similarly, low prices encouraged higher consumption, which meant that prices would rise in the face of added demands. This same automatic behavior distributed wealth in the form of wages, rents, and profits. Keyserling called it "the price-enterprise system," which was the essence of the private sector.

This system broke down in the 1930s. The early New Deal tried to rehabilitate it by encouraging businessmen to produce additional goods and provide minimum wages. "These efforts accomplished some substantial recovery—in spite of mistakes made by men who were necessarily trying something new and were working with imperfect tools that no one now would want to dig up again."

The New Deal turned to different remedies after the early programs failed or were declared unconstitutional. According to Keyserling, the reformers bypassed the price-enterprise system, and replaced it in large part with "compensatory spending" by government agencies. The new belief, Keynesian in inspiration, was that the public sector would take up the slack.

World War II erupted before this new approach could be afforded a fair test in peacetime. Keyserling noted that the economy did expand rapidly from 1939 to 1941 as a result of what amounted to compensatory spending, but he still believed "vigilant attention to price-wage-profit policies was essential to keep the economy stable." In any case, the proper relationhip between prices, wages, and profits could not be discovered "by using some past period as a model." In the postwar world, he believed, even the most devoted advocates of compensatory spending would come to understand that "the behavior of the price-enterprise system is central to the welfare of our economy."

Keyserling was no socialist. Nor was he a Keynesian in the sense that the school was described by academics. He didn't believe the American people would accept in a time of peace the kind of rigorous controls they had put up with during World War II. He had more faith in the private sector than did most of his conservative critics. What he had in mind was a central agency that would help direct the various segments of the economy, offer predictions, and recommend programs. It would set goals, ask questions, and provide expertise:

> The goals that we should set up have to be reasonably specific. Do we need additional airfields more or less than we need additional power development? Do we need new housing more urgently than we need a larger output of radio sets? How much steel do we need for our total industrial output at full employment? Do we need additional doctors and nurses more or less than we need additional salesmen?

The central agency would work with the President and Congress to answer these and related questions. But it would not intrude directly into the price-enterprise system.

> Our economy is so rich and flexible that we don't need to draw up minute classifications of production and employment. That can be left to the "operation of the market," in response to business forecasting and consumer preferences. But we do need some broad *goals for the economy* before we can evaluate the price, wage, and profit policies which determine *what* goods and services are produced and *who* gets them.

Keyserling had faith that through close contacts and in a spirit of cooperation reasonable men in government, business, and organized labor could agree upon prices, wages, and profits. All would realize that the alternative would be depression and that any new economic collapse would result in a sharp limitation of the price-enterprise system. "Neither those 'liberals' who betray nostalgia for the New Deal of the nineteen-thirties (which accomplished much but not nearly enough) nor those 'conservatives' who would reincarnate the economic philosophy of the nineteen-twenties (which worked after a fashion for a time, but was brutal and reckless) should be allowed to say the last word." In other words, Keyserling was seeking a new approach and one that was closer in spirit to the free market than most Keynesians of the time would have preferred.

Could it be made to work? Much depended upon cooperation between major interest groups which rarely in the past could come to terms over division of wealth and power. Apparently Keyserling believed the central planners would be able to accomplish this, but he didn't say how it could be done. Instead, he relied upon rhetoric to convince the skeptical.

> All those of good will who have accepted as the first tenets of their faith that political democracy and economic justice are insep-

arable—that economic progress and economic stability are compatible—should be able to move forward together, in the recognition that we have all registered both splendid achievements and disastrous mistakes in the past, and that we all need to do a better job in a future filled with such enormous problems and with such infinite promise.

Keyserling hoped the Council would become this kind of planning organization, that after cooperating with the President to establish goals and set priorities its members would fashion a program and work for its adoption. This involved testifying before congressional committees, lobbying where necessary, and in other ways behaving as a public advocate.

This was the crux of his disagreements with Nourse. Keyserling wrote that on most policy matters they were more or less united.

> The only serious difficulty and discord within the Truman CEA involved the issue of whether CEA should testify before Congress on occasion, more particularly before the Joint Economic Committee when it held hearings on the Economic Reports of the President. From the onset Nourse insisted that CEA should not, on the alleged ground that to do so would force him either to disagree at times with the President publicly or to defend Presidential policies which he deemed unsound.

Keyserling also implied that Nourse hoped to keep his distance from Truman and so remain in office after an expected Republican victory in the 1948 presidential election.

It was more complex than that. The two men did have serious differences on matter of policy. Nourse believed inflation was the nation's most serious economic problem, and he advocated higher taxes to cut back on demand. As previously indicated, Keyserling was more concerned with a possible depression, and he asked Truman to seek a tax cut that would stimulate the economy and provide additional goods and services that would hold prices in line. In the interim, Keyserling was willing to employ selective wage and price controls; Nourse opposed them vigorously. Keyserling wanted the Treasury to maintain control over the Federal Reserve Board so as to assure low interest rates. Nourse spoke out in favor of higher rates and also thought the Board should have a greater degree of freedom than was the case in the late 1940s.

And so it went. As for testifying before congressional committees, it is true that Nourse refused to do so, but that was as much a matter of personality and temperament as anything else. The Chairman delivered many prepared addresses, most of them quasi-academic in nature; this was his forte. He did not relish the idea of a give-and-take battle with congressmen as an advocate (rather than an expert) before committees. "The Council's advice is in terms of economics, not politics," he wrote a few years later. "The President has always had ample sources of *political* advice. In setting up the Council, Congress saw no need for adding another." Vice Chairman Keyserling felt otherwise, and in any case he had wide political experience. Often he filled in for Nourse in congressional hearings and was happy to do so. Not only had he great experience in such matters, but he cleary felt this was his proper arena.

Finally, there was the matter of the backgrounds of these two men. Nourse always considered himself an academic who happened to be in the public service. He deplored Keyserling's antics, especially appearances at political gatherings, and in his memoirs wrote critically of the fact that "Mr. Keyserling found no impropriety in appearing before political or even partisan groups as well as Congressional committees." Nourse said he "felt misgivings as to the consequences of his participation either in party pow-wows or Congressional inquiries." As for Keyserling, he remained as ever distrustful of academics in general, and to him Nourse was typical of the breed. "Dr. Nourse was simply unable to adjust himself to the nature and the problems of the Presidency. He could never understand that the President of the United States has too many things to do to engage in long bull sessions on economics of the kind that take place at The Brookings Institution."

Clearly Nourse's view that the Council could somehow remain above politics was naive. Moreover he and the President never really appreciated each other's talents and strong points. After leaving the White House, Nourse told a reporter that Truman "doesn't like to deal with scientists and economists," and characterized him as "an economic illiterate." This was after the President had purportedly told several people, "Well, the Doctor was a very nice old gentleman, but he wasn't very practical." Keyserling was practical. Truman understood this and saw in the Vice Chairman a kindred soul. Despite occasional differences, the two got along very well together.

At first, however, they had different priorities. Innately Truman was more conservative than Keyserling. He hoped for balanced budgets (and even surpluses) and believed inflation a more serious threat to the national well-being than depression. In early 1949, when it appeared a recession was brewing, Truman spoke of the need for a $4 billion tax increase to balance the budget and said most of it would come from businesses. He also wanted standby authority to impose wage and price controls. At a press conference, he told reporters that a balanced budget would be desirable even should the economy turn downward. Nourse agreed with this line of thinking. Keyserling opposed it but publicly denied the tax increase would harm the economy. Shortly thereafter he wrote that "sensational overplaying of a few soft spots in the economy and of some recent increases in unemployment should not be permitted to distort judgement or to produce a "fear psychology."

By May it was clear the economy was in decline; the Federal Reserve Board Index of Economic Production stood at 179, 16 points below where it had been in November. The unemployment rate was over 6 percent and rising. On the other hand, there were signs that inflationary pressures were easing, and Truman rejoiced at the news.

The White House came under fire. Liberal publications warned Truman to avoid the errors that destroyed the Hoover presidency. Auto chief Walter Reuther said "Nineteen hundred and twenty-nine can happen again in 1949." Senator Walter George of Georgia, the chairman of the Finance Committee and no liberal, came out against the tax increase, calling instead for a stimulative cut. Liberal Senator James Murray of Montana joined with conservative Representative Wright Patman of Texas to introduce a measure providing for government aid to depressed areas. Pressures on the White House were building. Clearly something had to be done to halt the decline.

It was then that Keyserling challenged Nourse directly. The Chairman continued to support the fight against higher prices and for a balanced budget. He told reporters the economy was in a "healthy state of disinflation" and had not "fallen out of bed." In contrast, Keyserling called for abandonment of the tax measure and Administration support for a kind of economically stimulative program such as that he had written about earlier, including higher Social Security payouts and public works.

Truman didn't need Keyserling to tell him that the recession had divided his political support and could shatter his hopes for a successful presidency. However, the economist did provide him with a rationale and a program. In early June the President conceded there had been a "moderate downward trend," which meant the tax in-

crease was as good as dead. In his midyear economic report, prepared
largely by Keyserling, he said, "We cannot expect to achieve a
budget surplus in a declining economy. There are economic and
social deficits that would be far more serious than a temporary
deficit in the Federal budget." Then he presented the entire panoply
of Keyserling programs—the Social Security increase, public works,
a higher minimum wage, and improved farm support levels. The
President also called for closer cooperation between government and
business. "We cannot have prosperity by getting adjusted to the
idea of depression—by cutting investment or employment or wages
or essential government services."

Thus, Truman signaled the victory of Keyserling over Nourse
and also healed the breech with liberals of his own party. Nourse
spoke out against continued budget deficits and inflationary programs, while Keyserling worked to convince legislators of the soundness of the Administration program. Asked his opinion of one of the
Chairman's speeches, the President snapped, "I am very certain that
Dr. Nourse didn't know what he was talking about. Although he is
an economist, he knows absolutely nothing about Government financing." Clearly the situation could not continue unresolved. That
summer Nourse submitted his resignation. Shortly thereafter it was
accepted, to become final on November 1. Truman was pleased.
"Now we can appoint Leon," he told several staffers. Keyserling indeed was named acting Chairman, but the formal appointment as
Chairman was put off for half a year.

The delay was caused by opposition from within the President's
inner circle of advisors, on Capitol Hill, and from academics. Treasury Secretary Snyder thought Keyserling a trifle radical; John
Steelman feared displacement from a position of influence. Even
some of Keyserling's friends weren't certain he could handle such
power or that they wanted him to become a "strong man." Republicans and several conservative Democrats considered him too much
of a politician for their tastes. It was common knowledge that several Ivy League professors opposed Keyserling on the ground that
he lacked professional status. "They came down from Massachusetts," wrote Keyserling later on, to tell Truman's associates of this.
They "didn't like the fact that I did not hold the Ph.D. degree in
economics." "There is utterly no basis in fact for this kind of objec-
tion," wrote Clark Clifford to Truman. "While 16 years of preoccu-
pation with national economic programs have prevented Mr. Keyserling from following the traditional course of the academic econ-

omist, his actual work (including writing)in the field of overall economic policy, stabilization, and full employment has been voluminous and constant."

In the end Keyserling won the appointment but not before receiving heavy blows to his easily bruised ego. "The long delay was embarrassing to me, and in my view unnecessary," he wrote almost three decades later.

Keyserling continued to press for expansion while awaiting the appointment. "Economic stability requires economic growth," he told Truman in early 1950. "Maximum production and maximum employment are not static goals; they mean more jobs and more business opportunities in each succeeding year. If we are to attain these objectives, we must make full use of all the resources of the American economy." Truman agreed. By late 1949 (when the unemployment rate was close to 8 percent) he had become an advocate of economic stimulation. "I never found it necessary to expound general philosophy or theory to him," wrote Keyserling, "and he probably would not have had much interest if I had attempted to do so." The ideas of Keyserling and the political requirements of the President coincided. The Chairman recalls that Truman "almost always accepted the basic economic policies which I recommended to him, or which I joined in recommending."

Truman and Keyserling had to test their brand of expansionary economics in a wartime environment. The recession ended as a result of strong consumer demand and increased military procurement. By spring the unemployment rate had fallen to 5.5 percent. At the same time the recession had ended the inflationary pressures. For a few months it seemed the economy was functioning smoothly, on an even keel, with both growth and stable prices. Then, on June 25, the Korean War started, and Keyserling found himself in the midst of a new debate and contest.

Defense Secretary Louis Johnson, Snyder, and Budget Director Frank Pace held that the need for increased military spending would cause a new round of inflation, and that to contain it the President should ask for authority to impose strict wage and price controls and higher taxes. Their ideas dovetailed with those of military leaders who looked upon the Korean conflict as the first stage in a third World War, one that would require the same kind of economic mobilization employed during World War II. While agreeing that a mild form of controls might be needed if the war continued, Keyserling thought that accelerated economic expansion

would suffice to hold down inflation. In his optimistic midyear
Report, he wrote: "Our economy has the human and material resources to do the job ahead—if we achieve the unity that will enable
us to do our best." Also, he continued to see inflation as a minor,
transitory problem that would melt in the face of increased production. Finally, Keyserling was convinced that the Korean War not
only would be contained and not expand but that it would end
shortly.

Although he discussed a possible tax increase the following
month, Truman generally accepted the Keyserling prescription and
view toward the war. He did sign a bill giving him the authority to
impose controls and accepted a new tax measure that increased
taxes and provided for a temporary excess profits levy but for the
most part trusted in the solvent of increased production. And it
seemed to be working. By October Keyserling's faith and program
appeared vindicated, and his prestige within the White House high.

In November the Chinese intervened in the war, pushing back
the American and allied forces. To some this appeared the anticipated start of the third World War; most doubted it, but clearly it
would be a different kind of struggle, one likely to continue on for
years. Moving with the times, Keyserling recommended greater cen-
tralization of government efforts, the imposition of allocations for
scarce materials, mild controls over selected industries, and greater
cooperation with business and labor leaders.

Truman went along with this program. The Office of Defense
Mobilization was organized with Charles E. Wilson of General Electric its Director. Prices and wages within the automobile industry
were rolled back, and informal conferences with businessmen and
union leaders were organized. As Keyserling had recommended,
there was no sense of urgency or even of emergency in any of this.
Above all he wanted to retain the confidence of the business and
union communities, to convince them they would have maximum
freedom of action, which in turn would result in leaps in production.
But it was a losing battle. Within less than a month price and wage
increases down the line had caused Truman to come out for controls.
With great reluctance Keyserling followed suit. He knew further
losses were to come.

What would later be called the military-industrial complex was
growing rapidly. In some surface manifestations it resembled the
kind of structure Keyserling had called for in the mid-1940s. There
would be close cooperation between government and business, long-

term planning, and assurances of growth. Research and development would be encouraged and employment enlarged. But Keyserling had advocated government leadership in a consumer-and-capital-goods-based economy, one that could turn out the kinds of products and services capable of raising standards of living. He had hoped for a marriage of the kind of productivity seen during World War II with the dreams of the New Dealers of the 1930s. All of his training and experience had inclined him toward this point of view. Later on he would deplore Truman's failure to end the war swiftly. While supporting the dismissal of General MacArthur, he wondered whether the application of some of his recommendations as to the conduct of the war wouldn't have been better than what turned out to be an inconclusive effort.

In any event, the Chinese intervention marked the end of the Fair Deal at home, just as the eruption of World War II had concluded the New Deal. At the Jefferson-Jackson Day Dinner in 1952 Truman announced he would not seek another term. By midsummer it was evident that Dwight Eisenhower would be the next President.

Keyserling was 44 years old, a veteran of two decades of government service and still a young man as bureaucrats, politicians, businessmen, and even academics go. During his tenure at the CEA he had become one of the better known members of the Administration. He had perhaps as many "contacts" in Washington as anyone else of the period. But he also had enemies, and his reputation for intellectual brillance was at times balanced by one for arrogance and abrasiveness. Truman's rejection of his growth philosophy in the last years of his Administration hurt Keyserling and pleased those who disliked the man.

Keyserling's retirement from the Council was attended by worse humiliations, controversies, and misunderstandings than those he had been dealt prior to his accession to the chairmanship. House conservatives managed to push through a measure providing for a 25 percent reduction in the Council's 1953 budget, and soon after there were rumors the CEA might be disbanded entirely. At the time these actions and rumors seemed a vote of no confidence in Keyserling and a result of the way he had conducted himself in office. In addition, Senator Joseph McCarthy accused him of being "soft on communism," and claimed Mrs. Keyserling had once been a member of the Communist Party. The couple denied the charges, and later on Mrs. Keyserling was completely cleared of them by a government agency, but at the time such a statement from Mc-

Carthy sufficed to destroy careers. The House measure's effects were mitigated by Senate action, but rumors had been planted and the damage done. Even now people who should know better are convinced that Keyserling left office under a cloud and that this prevented him from holding a government office later on.

Such was not the case. Keyserling had opportunities to join large corporations in important posts, but he preferred to remain in Washington. He opened a law office, did some economic consulting, and from his newly formed Conference on Economic Progress spewed forth a steady stream of pamphlets criticizing the policies of the Eisenhower Administration and calling for stimulation for a sluggish economy. As indicated he had no trouble placing articles in leading liberal journals. In other words, Keyserling did not become a "nonperson" and in fact was looked upon as a leading spokesman for the economic policies of the left wing of the Democratic opposition. He opposed efforts by the new Chairman of the Council, Arthur Burns, to fight inflation by holding down growth and continued to claim that the only way to keep prices in line was through expansion, requiring tax cuts and reforms, efforts to gain the confidence of businessmen, and public works when and where needed.

In early 1960 Keyserling was identified with the Trumanites, which meant he opposed the nomination of John Kennedy. Thus, he could not hope for any office once Kennedy was elected. His economic views were more liberal than those of the new President, and in any case Kennedy already had a set of advisors, headed by Walter Heller, Paul Samuelson, and John Galbraith—academics all. On occasion he would be called upon to mediate differences between the White House and Truman, but Keyserling was not invited to make contributions to Administration programs.

The Kennedy academics, headed by Heller, were closely identified in the public mind with the New Economics, which had its roots in Keynesian doctrine. To Keyserling the professors seemed more at home with philosophy and models than with problems of the real world. Also, he felt the newcomers had divorced themselves from history and refused to learn from experience—his experience, in particular. Keyserling was only in his fifties, but he was looked upon as a relic, a figure of the past, by the Kennedy people. Anyone would have resented this and Keyserling, more touchy than most, felt the snubs resulted from stupidity, lack of knowledge, and boorishness. The Kennedy and Johnson advisors appeared to have accepted his goals and ideas, however, but they were interpreted and

applied clumsily. And of course he was given no credit for his accomplishments. "The widespread claim . . . that it is *all* new and
all good has been carried too far," he wrote later on. "This excess of
enthusiasm which has characterized a good many academic economists both in and out of the public service, is relatively harmless
so long as it is regarded as no more than a vainglorious boast that
'there were no great men before Agamemnon.' "

Keyserling also rejected their notion that somehow economics
could become an objective science, and he disliked the apparent
cold bloodedness of this new generation. "Some of the leading academic economists have gone simply wild about their econometric
models, and this trend in itself is corrupting the main body of economic teaching, research, and honorific recognition, at least if one
thinks of economics as a public-interest tool." He concluded that

> The shortcomings of the "New Economics" really boils down to
> this: It has tended toward copybook-maxim application of general
> theories, without constructing a satisfying picture of the econ-
> omy in operation and the goals to be sought. These defects arise,
> in the final analysis, from failure to observe the real mandate of
> the Employment Act of 1946.

That legislation remained the touchstone for much of Keyserling's activities in the late 1960s and through the 1970s. The new
economists returned to academia in 1969 with the arrival of the
Nixon Administration, but Keyserling remained in Washington, to
once again take up the cause of economic expansion. After the disastrous 1973-1974 recession he became chairman of the Task Force
on the Economy of the Coalition for a Democratic Majority and
from this pulpit called for growth policies that would bring an end
to both the recession and inflation. The prescription was familiar:
tax relief for low and middle income Americans, public works, low
interest rates and easy money, and selective and mild wage and
price controls. In an essay entitled *Recession, Inflation, and How to
Overcome Both*, published in 1975, he recommended "an immediate
and long-range program, comprehensive in nature, and directed toward restoration of maximum employment, production, and purchasing power by the end of 1976, or shortly thereafter." This recommendation provided the foundation for the Humphrey-Hawkins
Bill, for which Keyserling was a major drafter, that became law in
1978. This measure, which sets as a national goal the elimination of
unemployment and inflation, was a climax to efforts he had engaged

in for close to half a century. Keyserling said as much. "In fact, the current Humphrey-Hawkins Bill is substantially an effort to revise and amplify what was started during the Truman Administration."

Young economists weaned on Keynesian or monetarist thought and nurtured on Friedman, Galbraith, or Samuelson, often seem surprised to learn that Keyserling is still vigorous and politically active. This this is so is not startling, for he never sought a niche in academia. But if he is a relic he refused to act the part. Keyserling remains an important and respected advisor to the Democratic Party's liberal wing. Over 70 years old now and somewhat of a curmudgeon, he can still make news and an impact. And he will not be ignored. Several years ago he made a rare foray into enemy territory by addressing a meeting of the American Economic Association, comprised largely of academics. He criticised the antihistorical nature of leading thinkers in the field. "Where the economics profession has led us is monstrous." He called upon the audience to "help overcome the dismal poverty of American economics, and to commence promoting the real purpose of the Employment Act of 1946. Let's get on the track." Keyserling concluded by saying, "I may have offended some of your sensibility, but I hope that I may have appealed to your saving common sense."

Richard Strout, the veteran columnist, was at the meeting. "They did not seem offended," he wrote. "They gave him a big hand, and it was notable that a lot of the younger ones clapped loudest."

3

ARTHUR BURNS

FOR A FEW WEEKS IN EARLY 1953 it seemed the Council of Economic
Advisors would expire for lack of funds. Keyserling and other Truman appointees were packing to leave, and, since appropriations for
staff and office help soon would run out, they too were preparing to
seek new employment.

Incoming President Eisenhower had little formal education in
economics or experience with its practitioners. An instinctive conservative in monetary and fiscal matters, he possessed an almost
visceral distrust of abstract thinkers, whom he tended to view as
liberals. He was a man of action, and while president of Columbia
University had learned to avoid those professors who confused
ideas with reality, theories with practicality.

The new President understood that the way he dealt with the
economy might determine the success or failure of his entire Administration. During the campaign he often had conferred with Dr.
Gabriel Hauge, an economist who had taught at Harvard and
Princeton and also had directed statistical work at the New York
Banking Department. Hauge had helped write several Eisenhower
speeches and in the process had initiated the education of the
candidate in areas of fiscal and monetary policies as well as business
cycles. He also had won Eisenhower's confidence and would go on to

serve as one of the Administration's in-house economists. Hauge and others urged the new President to save the CEA, and they won their point. He also recommended Arthur Burns for the chairmanship. Hauge would later say that "bringing Arthur down was one of my most significant contributions."

Sherman Adams, a crusty and tough practical politician who had served as governor of New Hampshire, was Eisenhower's chief assistant at the White House, the person who guarded entry into the Oval Office. Later on he wrote of his first encounter with Burns.

> If somebody had asked me to describe the mental image I had of the type of New Deal official we were in the process of moving out of Washington, this was it—a glassy stare through thick lenses, peering out from under a canopy of unruly hair parted in the middle, a large pipe with a curved stem; the very incarnation of all the externals that were such an anathema to Republican businessmen and politicians.

Arthur Burns had made significant contributions to economic knowledge and today is considered a leading theoretician in the study of business cycles. Presidents, congressmen, and senators, and his peers within the profession, have remarked on his abilities to present a mass of complex material in a clear and logical fashion. After a long session with Burns one leaves with a feeling of enhanced knowledge, respect for one's ability to absorb it, and an appreciation of the man who had made all of this possible.

But the most lasting impression of such encounters is likely to be more sensory than cerebral. There is that pungent aroma of pipe tobacco, the twangy, nasal voice with suggestions of W.C. Fields and John Barrymore, and the sharp wit spiced with a clear awareness of his intellect and superiority over all who listen. Watching Keyserling testify before a congressional committee put one in mind of a partisan scrapper eager to score points. A Burns appearance, on the other hand, resembles nothing more than a graduate seminar in a very good university, which somewhere along the line is transformed into a lecture. Emerging from such sessions, elderly legislators have confided that they had a subconscious fear that some of the material they didn't fully understand might be on the next exam.

There is "an aura of awe about Chairman Burns," said *New York Times* reporter Clyde Farnsworth. He wrote that after one such lecture Congressman Robert Giaimo of Connecticut tried to sum up. "If I infer correctly, what you are saying is that the unemployment problem is really one of women and young persons." Before answering Burns took a long drag on his pipe and then transfixed Giaimo with the kind of cold but indulgent stare that must have reminded him of undergraduate days at the University of Connecticut. After a pause, Burns drawled, "I said a good deal more than that." When the laughter subsided, Giaimo closed with "Thank you. I will stand on the inference."

In analyzing his chief, an associate once said that "He is a dominating personality. You sense it simply by the hush that falls over a room when he walks into it." And Burns knows precisely what he is doing on such occasions. More than any other economist—more even than John K. Galbraith—he is a master of theater, who appreciates as much as does any actor or politician that style often can be more important than substance.

Burns's style and appearance may be what Sherman Adams and other politicians think of as being academic, which is to say he looks somewhat austere, can wear tweeds easily, smokes those pipes (he has over a hundred of them), and, when the occasion calls for it, can mask his thoughts with complex rhetoric and jargon. He is as much at home with mathematical formulae as are all but the most obscure of the breed. But Burns is hardly the kind of other-worldly philosopher many businessmen and officials consider academics to be. Woodrow Wilson, who like Burns served both in academia and Washington, understood the situation, and he once told a friend that his experiences in Princeton had been a fine preparation for his future career. "I'll confide in you, as I have already confided to others—that, as compared with the college politician, the real article seems like an amateur."

Nor was Burns a liberal or a Keynesian—Adams and his kind tended to believe that the more initials a person had after his name, the more to the left politically he was likely to be. In fact, Burns not only is eclectic in approach but remains the supreme pragmatist and empiricist among major economists today. He retains an instinctive distrust of theories based upon deduction, especially those into which economists and other social scientists pour their carefully selected facts. Also, he is wary of emotional appeals to morality and impulsive leaps of faith. Instead, he prefers to gather an enormous amount of data and from this body draw limited conclusions applicable to special situations. When the conditions change, so will Burn's prescriptions and forecasts. In mid-career he wrote that a "subtle understanding of economic change comes from a knowledge of history and large affairs, not from statistics or their processing alone—to which our age has turned so eagerly in its quest for certainty."

Burns does not believe certainty is possible on a theoretical level and has never based recommendations primarily upon abstract theories. He is ever unsure of extending and expanding conclusions, of drawing specific lessons from history. He usually speaks with great confidence when called upon to do so, but Burns selects his words carefully, with a precision greater than that of most people in his discipline.

He has changed much over the years, in large part as a result of this willingness to study problems without many preconceived ideas. The man who entered the Oval Office as Sherman Adams looked on was a different economist from the one who stepped down as chairman of the Federal Reserve Board close to a quarter of a century later.

The supposedly austere Burns was quite a different kind of social scientist than was his impassioned predecessor at the CEA. Rarely in his career has Keyserling changed his mind on any matter of pressing concern; the faith and goals of the young economist who worked with Senator Wagner in 1933 were those of the framer of the Employment Act of 1946 and the lobbyist for the Humphrey-Hawkins bill of 1978. Keyserling always possessed a clear-cut philosophy, a vision of the future. One can easily predict what his position will be on a wide variety of issues, from the minimum wage to the amount of money to be expended on national defense. This is not the case with Burns. In contrast, he had developed a methodology for answering specific questions of a nonideological kind and then devoted a lifetime to refining it. Burns is concerned with verifiable facts that can be employed in resolving current issues, while Keyserling seeks justice. This moralistic approach has prevented Keyserling from adjusting to new circumstances and accepting compromises. Burns has managed both with grace. His lack of cant and willingness to reconsider positions affords his opponents only a moving target. Just when they think they have him cornered, he will come over to their side, in a way that makes him appear open-minded and generous.

Burns is a master politician, far more sophisticated in the uses of power and the art of swaying people than any other economist of his generation. This talent, more than the force of his ideas. accounts for his continuing influence and prestige. No other private citizen, with the possible exception of Henry Kissinger, is listened to with as much respect and as carefully as is he. Burns still has that commanding presence; people really do stop talking when he enters a room. "If God were an economist," said one of his nonadmirers ruefully, "he would look like Arthur Burns."

Many laymen assume Burns is of Scots origin and is a native Ivy Leaguer; his appearance and speech misled individuals far more astute than Sherman Adams. In fact he was born in 1904 in a part of the old Austro-Hungarian Empire that since has been annexed to the U.S.S.R. His parents, Nathan and Sarah Burnseig, were Jews who came to America in the last great wave of immigration prior to World War I. Nathan Burnseig was a housepainter, who earned a modest living by painting houses in Bayonne, New Jersey. Arthur attended the public schools there (he later told reporters that his name was shortened by a teacher who had trouble pronouncing Burnseig). Apparently the boy was a prodigy; he translated parts of the Talmud into German when only six years old, was recognized as a brilliant student, and in high school was the leader of the debating team. In 1921 he crossed the Hudson to enroll at Columbia College. Since his scholarship didn't cover books and living expenses, Burns worked at a wide variety of jobs—a waiter, salesman, and postal clerk. He also would paint houses and during the summers he became a sailor. A few articles of his on business subjects were accepted for publication by the New York *Herald Tribune*, and these brought not only added recognition but a few extra dollars.

Burns also had a large number of scholarly interests, running from architecture to dramatic criticism, but increasingly he was drawn to economics. As would be the case with Keyserling—at the same school a few years later—this was the result of exposure to a gifted social scientist who became a mentor and, later on, a colleague as well.

Wesley Clair Mitchell was one of the towering figures of American economics in 1921. A student of Thorstein Veblen at the University of Chicago, he had received his Ph.D. from there in 1899 and then gone on to teach at he University of California. By the time he arrived at Columbia in 1913, Mitchell was known for several important books in the area of financial history, and his *Business Cycles*, published soon after, established him as a leading theoretician in that field as well. He served as chief of the price section of the War

Industries Board during World War I, where he developed analytical techniques that would alter the course of economic thinking during the 1920s and 1930s. In 1918 Mitchell was elected president of the American Statistical Association. During the next two years he helped found both the New School for Social Research and the National Bureau of Economic Research, and he served as director of research for the latter organization while conducting classes at Columbia and the New School.

Mitchell was a talented teacher, an inspirational figure whose generosity and sensitivity attracted many students to his seminars and led them to careers in economics. He also served on several important government advisory boards, among which was the Committee on Social Trends in the Hoover Administration; Mitchell was one of the few professional economists who knew his way around Washington in the 1920s. But he never sought a career outside of academia and the National Bureau. It would not have been his style to do so.

Like Veblen, Mitchell was an institutionalist, which is to say he was concerned with all aspects of society, had a decided bias toward historical investigations, and believed that economics should be used in the cause of reform. He supported groups that worked for women's suffrage, civil rights, and improved settlement houses. But Mitchell was too gentle to engage in polemics, and he lacked the fire and humor that made Veblen such a major social critic. Besides, he thought human institutions too complex and fragile to be altered without great care. He urged would-be reformers to study issues without bias before undertaking programmatic changes. Economics, he said, should become a science, for only then could it be used effectively to improve society. "I want propositions that can be tested for conformity to fact," he told his wife. "I want such tests to be made. In short, I hope we shall develop a science of economics that has such a definite application to actual behavior that it will be a safe guide in efforts to improve economic organization." Thus, the National Bureau was formed "to encourage, in the broadest and most liberal manner, investigation, research and discovery, and the application of knowledge to the well-being of mankind; and in particular to conduct, or assist in the making of, exact and impartial investigations in the field of economic, social, and industrial science." For a start, the Bureau undertook a major study to determine the size and distribution of national income. Mitchell led a team in writing *Income in the United States*, the Bureau's first publication, and his

Business Cycles: The Problem and Its Setting, was its tenth release and for years its best seller.

Income in the United States resembles a census report more than an economics treatise. There are plentiful statistics, explanations of them, and few generalizations; this is the kind of work one refers to, but does not read from cover to cover. Mitchell understood this. He hoped to gather materials which taken together could provide ammunition for those interested in reforms, but he would not undertake that task himself. Later on he would compare American industry to an army comprising many companies, each with a leader who knows something of what is going on elsewhere, but none with a vision of the whole. Each businessman understood his own company and in addition had knowledge of the industry in which it operated, but none had the tools for or interest in an analysis of the economy as a whole. "The charge that 'capitalistic production is planless' therefore contains both an important element of truth and a large element of error." The task of the National Bureau, as Mitchell saw it, would be nothing less than to gather statistics and commission monographs that would enable a national leader—presumably the President—to fabricate an all-embracing program. As early as 1920 Mitchell wrote and spoke of the need for central planning and of the importance of economists in the formulation of such programs.

These were the ideas, approaches, and aspirations of Burns's mentor when the two men first met. The young scholar saw in Mitchell a man of fine character and charm whom he admired, and a social scientist whose methods and interests appealed to him. As for Burns, he clearly was one of the more promising students in Mitchell's seminars. He was elected to Phi Beta Kappa and in 1925 received both his B.A. and M.A. degrees. After a brief stint at Columbia's extention division he joined the Rutgers faculty and while there conducted seminars in economic statistics. Meanwhile Burns became involved with several projects at the National Bureau, published scholarly articles that gained him some status within the profession, and worked on his doctorate under Mitchell's supervision.

The Great Depression began and there was talk of social revolution. Tugwell and Keyserling were preparing to leave Columbia for Washington to participate in the creation of the New Deal. Meanwhile the National Bureau published monographs on a wide variety of subjects, from the purchase of medical care to the planning and control of public works, but none of them addressed the problems of the depression directly and in fact seemed unconcerned with present national difficulties.

Burns's dissertation, *Production Trends in the United States Since 1870*, was of this genre. Published in 1934 by the National Bureau, it contains no references to the depression of that year. In his preface, Mitchell noted that Burns "studies the widely varying rates at which many American industries have grown from decade to decade since the 1870s, and seeks to ascertain what general features have characterized this sample of increase in production."

As one might expect from a Ph.D. thesis prepared under the Mitchell aegis, *Production Trends* is based upon carefully gathered and verified empirical evidence from which have been drawn circumscribed conclusions and theories. It is a rather dull work, written by a specialist for other specialists, and although it was well reviewed and remains interesting for its methodology, the book might be ignored today were it not written by a person who was to become so eminent later on. Also, in it Burns present ideas and an approach he would refine in later books and articles, written at a time when he had emerged as one of the leaders of the non-Keynesians in America. Finally, in *Production Trends* can be seen a view of the economy Burns would bring to government in the 1950s.

The author observes that no industry has grown at a constant rate and that at one point or another all of them undergo shrinkages. Some will then decline steadily, while others experience stagnation or rebirth. Entrepreneurship is one of the causes for this. Wise and farsighted businessmen can alter the shape of an industry and for that matter so can foolish and myopic ones. More important, however, is Burns's version of the technological imperative. The greatest growth for a new industry will come in its early years, he writes, and in this period it may also cause great dislocation.

> The increasing replacement of farm work animals by automobiles and tractors has resulted in a rapid retardation in the production of horses and mules, has tended to retard the lumber industry, and has released millions of acres of crop land—which means that the increasing mechanization of agriculture has contributed to the retarded growth of certain of its branches, especially the production of oats and hay.

Similarly, the electrification of railroads led to a decline in coal production, improved methods of reclaiming raw materials affected mining operations, and the growth of labor-saving devices in industry meant that demands for labor declined.

Each industry had its own "trend cycle," determined as much by its inner dynamics as by exterior forces. Mitchell had said as much in *Business Cycles* seven years earlier, but Burns carried the idea forward, refining it through empirical investigation. He noted that the trend cycles usually are longer than the general business cycle, though of course each affects the others. Still, not all industries suffer during depressions or advance in periods of expansion.

That this is so is obvious to economists and laymen today. For example, one might expect a decline in a new car sales in bad times to be accompanied by advances in purchases of used cars or at least an increased use of public transportation. Consumers might turn from expensive fresh produce to canned foods; businessmen schedule fewer meetings but use their telephones more. The Great Depression did not adversely affect motion pictures and radio, since both industries were in strong growth phases. Cigarette sales actually increased—this industry usually does well in times of distress. But not even the most spectacular boom could have saved vaudeville and the horsecar. Later on, during the Eisenhower years, television set sales would be unaffected by three recessions, and of course other examples could be cited.

On the other hand, most mature industries tend to move with the general business cycle. Steel and housing, for example, cannot do well when most fabrication and construction businesses are in a slump. The prices of most commodities decline in periods of depression and rise in boom phases.

This was a familiar concept in 1934, but Burns received credit for having verified the existence of trend cycles by use of empirically derived statistics. Still, this work was reviewed as an outgrowth of Mitchell's earlier efforts and little else. Economists wanted to see how much further Burns would carry the ideas and whether he would be more daring in the field of theory than was his mentor. More important, would he address the problems posed by the Great Depression? In 1934 Mitchell was seen by the Keynesians as an apologist for the old order, a person whose ideas regarding some kind of self-regulating mechanism simply had not worked.

During the mid-1930s Burns ventured into this area, starting by developing several ideas which later on would distinguish him from Mitchell but which at the time were little noticed. Like Mitchell, he argued that one of the major tasks of business cycle theory was to anticipate coming events. He too believed that some intervention was necessary early in the downturn, so as to maintain confidence on the part of consumers and businessmen and to keep the economic machine going. Should this not be done, or should political leaders fail in their efforts to stimulate private spending and investment, the federal government would have to undertake the task on its own. Burns supported the National Recovery Administration, especially in its attempts to create a more optimistic atmosphere in industry. He praised the work of the Federal Reserve banks in helping to expand the currency and lower interest rates. Later on he thought the public works program not only was necessary but an important means of breathing life into the private sector. "This policy commends itself because it is a proposal for actual spending by the government, and because it directs the additional spending to the industries in which there is the greatest proportion of unused resources, namely the durable goods industries." But he went on to maintain that the Great Depression was a special case, that this business cycle differed importantly from all others and should not be considered a model for the future. Furthermore, Burns wrote, its worst excesses could have been avoided by prompt and relatively minor actions in the late 1920s.

In 1934 Burns returned to Columbia as a full professor, and it generally was understood he was Mitchell's heir-apparent at the National Bureau. Now the two men started work on what would turn out to be a major opus, *Measuring Business Cycles,* which was published two years later, with Burns the senior author since most of the work was done by him.

This book carried forth and expanded upon the concepts Mitchell had been developing in the area of business cycles for more than three decades. It opens with a carefully worded definition that first appeared in Mitchell's 1927 opus. "A cycle consists of expansions occurring at about the same time in economic activities, followed by similarly general recessions, contractions, and revivals which merge into the expansion phase of the next cycle." Then, as the title promises, the authors go on to show how cycles develop and how they might be measured. Burns and Mitchell constructed hundreds of time series to illustrate the movements, which they show are so highly complex as to defy easy generalization. Finally, they set forth a conclusion which is at the same time a logical extension of Mitchell's earlier volumes and a signal that a new phase in his work might begin. "This tendency of individual series to behave similarly in regard to one another in successive business cycles would not be found if the forces that produce business cycles had [only] slight regularity." Implicit in this statement is a belief that cycles resemble one another and that a knowledge of the behavior of past cycles would offer a guide to future ones. Mitchell had suggested as much in his pre-World War I writings, but at that time he refused to offer generalizations on the subject. "The uncertainty attending present forecasts of business conditions arises chiefly from the imperfections of our knowledge concerning these conditions in the immediate past and in the present," he wrote in *Business Cycles*. Now it appeared that together with Burns and others at the National Bureau he had sufficient data to take the next step. If economists could comprehend all of this, perhaps they could recommend measures that would prevent booms and busts and even eliminate or at least mitigate depressions.

Some of their work paralleled that of Keynes and his disciples. Years later Milton Friedman would claim that much of Keynesian thought had been prefigured by Mitchell in his 1913 version of *Business Cycles*. That he failed at that time to present a full-blown explanation of economic fluctuations was in large part due to temperament; Mitchell was ever reluctant to draw his material together, add a measure of imagination, and give birth to a major theory. In a critical review of his work—the title is "Measurement Without Theory"—T.C. Koopmans implied that Mitchell was more a statistician than an economist and that *Measuring Business Cycles* was long on description but short on ideas and conclusions. Thus, he could offer little in the way of remedies for the Great Depression and later economic dislocations.

But there was more to it than that. The Keynesians tended to deal with the economy in the aggregate. They would paint a picture with broad brushstrokes and then put forth programs to restore prosperity. Thus, their critics would later charge that their solution to all problems was to increase spending, incur deficits, and enlarge the powers of the federal government. In contrast, Mitchell and Burns would study the thousands of components of the economy and then put them together to form an approximate picture of the whole. Whereas a Keynesian tended to claim resolutions of problems could be simple, Burns noted that "business cycles are complex phenomena—far more so than has been commonly supposed."

> The sales of a large firm may be dominated by the tides in aggregate activity; the fortunes of a small firm are rather at the mercy of personal factors and conditions peculiar to the trade or locality. Some activities, like local transit or net gold movements between the United States and Great Britain, are apparently free from

cyclical fluctuations. Others, notably farming, undergo cyclical
movements, but they have little or no relation in time to business
cycles.

Burns was quick to add that "almost nine-tenths of Mitchell's
basic sample of approximately 800 time series fluctuate in sympathy
with the tides of aggregate activity." But even here their movements
are not uniform. Coal and iron production, for example, conform
more closely to the general business cycle than do outputs of textiles
and gasoline. "Employment conforms better than wage rates, bank
loans than investments, open-market interest rates than customer
rates, stock prices than bond price, etc." Like Mitchell, Burns was
at the same time fascinated and dismayed by the intricacies of the
problem. That there was such a thing as a business cycle seemed
evident, but what was it? Joseph Schumpeter, in commenting on
their work, suggested that it was ephemeral but nonetheless real, and
he offered this analogy in the hope of clarifying matters somewhat:

> The members of a family circle produce a certain moral atmos-
> phere which, in a sense, is the result of their individual behavior.
> But nevertheless this atmosphere, once created, is in itself an ob-
> jective fact that in turn influences the behavior of the members of
> the family: the members of the National Bureau family of time
> series jointly produce the cyclical situations, but they are all of
> them also being shaped by the existing cyclical situation.

A medical analogy might be closer to the point. As doctors, Mitchell and Burns would marvel at the complexities of the human body.
They would be slow in treating diseases and certainly in advocating
surgery and, when they did so, would proceed cautiously, hoping all
the while the body possessed the fortitude to heal itself. Such individuals make fine diagnosticians, but they often are uncertain as to what
remedies to prescribe.

In contrast, the American Keynesians were ever prepared to cut
away and offer recommendations on healing the body and spirit.
They were convinced their intervention would have positive results
and that if one dose of medication was good, two would be better.
Little wonder, then, that the Keynesians tended to dismiss Burns and
Mitchell as old-fashioned practitioners with little to offer in the field
of public policy, while the leaders of the National Bureau were most
adept at pointing out flaws in Keynesian constructs. From this it
would follow that activist Democratic administrations would seek
economic advice from the Keynesians, while conservative Republi-

cans would discover in Burns and others like him people whose ideas
regarding government intervention into the economy were similar to
theirs.

Mitchell was 72 years old when *Measuring Business Cycles* appeared. Soon after he fell ill and was unable to complete his work in
progress, *What Happens During Business Cycles*. This book appeared after his death in 1948, after heavy editing by Burns. Like
most of Mitchell's other scholarly productions, this was another brick
in the wall he had constructed for much of his life. It would not have
been a capstone, even had Mitchell lived, for he was incapable of
such a production. The subtitle indicates as much: it was *A Progress
Report*.

As expected, Burns became director of research at the National
Bureau, and the work there went on pretty much as it had during
Mitchell's tenure. In some respects Burns was a sharper critic than
his predecessor and a more formidable adversary in debate, but this
resulted from personality differences; in all others things, he was in
the Mitchell mold. "We wish him Godspeed," wrote Edwin Wilson
who knew both men. "'May he never become a slave to the fulfill-
ment of the business cycle project." In this, Wilson was suggesting
that Burns would do well to strike out on his own. Mitchell himself
had once written that "it is probable that the economists of each generation will see reason to recast the theory of business cycles which
they learned in their youth." But Burns, who by now was in his mid-
forties and whose essential view of his profession had been formed
and hardened, would offer no bold new hypothesis but rather elaborate upon, refine, and update the Mitchell legacy.

In studies published during the 1940s and early 1950s Burns took
note of the expansion of government powers and wrote that this
meant political leaders would require a more complete knowledge of
how the economy operated. He stressed the need for better and additional statistics. Burns accepted the mandate set down in the Employment Act of 1946. "The principal practical problem of our generation," he wrote in 1946, "is the maintenance of employment, and it
has now become—as it long should have been—the principal problem
of economic theory." He felt government might undertake programs
to alleviate suffering, in general by "leaning against the economy."
Thus, he favored stimulative measures in times of slack and restrictive ones when it appeared the economy was about to overheat. But
he would go no further than this and stated strongly that all actions
should be carefully considered before being applied. Perhaps

speeches by leading Administration figures and meetings with labor
and business leaders would be better than spending programs or the
manipulation of interest rates and the money supply in correcting
economic imbalances.

In a 1947 essay entitled "Stepping Stones towards the Future,"
Burns dismissed the notion that the profession of economics had
reached a point where it could solve major problems, and he wasn't
even certain the arts of prediction had been refined to the point
where they were reliable.

> These stepping stones towards the future will become firmer with
> time, but two serious difficulties are likely to remain in the fore-
> caster's path: first, the imperfect tendency of history to repeat it-
> self; second, the forecaster's own hopes and fears about the future,
> which tend to insinuate themselves into his predictions, no matter
> how elaborate their statistical or mathematical scaffolding.

The following year, in the annual report of the National Bureau, he
wrote of "progress that has been made in recent decades," but
opened with the observation that economic knowledge "is so obviously inadequate for coping with society's ills. . . . " Many of
Burns's reports and papers would contain such a disclaimer. As late
as May 1953, when already in Washington, he would open a National
Bureau report with the sentence: "The gift of prophecy has never
loomed large in the endowment of economists."

Burns was far from being a humble person. Like Keyserling and
other leading political economists, he was considered arrogant by
some of his colleagues. In his case this derived not only from a generous appraisal of his own intellect but also because Burns believed
he recognized nuances that eluded others. Because of this he was
reluctant to offer predictions. And if Burns, with all of his abilities
and information was in this situation, by what right did others set
forth their feeble projections?

Burns could lacerate and intimidate such people when he was of
a mind to do so—and more often than not he was. In writing in criticism of an essay by Alvin Hansen, in which that dean of American
Keynesians mildly rebuked Burns on a number of minor points and
set forth a theory of his own, he treated Hansen as though he were a
doltish graduate student:

> I look forward to the day when economists will not rest content
> until they have at least specified the observable conditions that

would contradict their theories, when the conformity of a theory to facts is respected no less than its logical consistency, and when carefully formulated theories are tested promptly and thoroughly in a score of research centers.

Burns went on to suggest that Hansen's problem might be found in his misreading of Keynes. "I do not see that Hansen's methodological comments have anything to do with the validity of Keynes' basic theory of underemployment equilibrium." Burns concluded by throwing down the gauntlet. Hansen not only had failed utterly to address the problem but "I do not believe that he would find the task especially easy."

Burns had emerged as one of the more formidable and forceful conservative critics of Keynesian economics in the post-World War II period. "Their weakness is that they lean heavily on a speculative analysis of uncertain value," he wrote. The only important reservation he had regarding the Employment Act was a fear that Keynesians would use it as a vehicle to gain power. "The imposing schemes for governmental action that are being bottomed on Keynes' equilibrium theory must be viewed with skepticism," he said at the time. In Burns's view, central planning would not work well if it were based on Keynes' faulty assumptions. The Keynesians "lack a clear analytical foundation for judging how a given fiscal policy will effect the size of the national income or the volume of employment." In 1946 he said that "Men who wish to serve democracy faithfully must recognize that the roots of business cycles go deep in our economic organization, that the ability of government to control depressions adequately is not yet assured, that our power of forecasting is limited, and that true foresight requires policies for coping with numerous contingencies."

Yet public policy would not wait upon refined or adequate techniques. Burns appreciated the fact that regardless of the state of economic knowledge, it would be utilized by government to control and try to master the business cycle. Better his brand of knowledge than that of the American Keynesians, he thought, and so he edged closer to the political arena.

By 1950 he was willing to say that the goals set forth by the Employment Act of 1946 had to be accepted and implemented. The "challenge facing business cycle theory and policy" in the future would be "to glimpse economic catastrophe when it is imminent" and do all possible to prevent it. "The crucial problem of our times is the prevention of severe depression," he wrote, and, given the political realities of the post-New Deal era, this implied a need for intervention in the economy.

More than the Keynesians or any other school, the National Bureau had concentrated on measuring the economy's performance and using the data to predict future developments. Among the more important "lead indicators" were the average work week of production workers, an index of net business formations and one for new private house building permits, net changes in inventories, the money supply, a stock market index, and contracts and orders for plant and equipment. When several of these turned down, the Bureau would warn that a recession might be on the way. It was as though an advancing army set off flares; if properly read, the defenders would know what to expect and how to react. Thus, at the beginning of a downturn there could be automatic tax relief for corporations and increases in unemployment benefits. Since no two recessions were exactly alike (something that could be demonstrated by comparing time series) each would require a different set of actions. Furthermore, the same indicators could be used to anticipate economic overheating—the onset of inflation. On such occasions Burns might prescribe tax increases and curbs on consumer credit, but he could not do so in advance. First he would have to analyze the indicators.

Burns saw the economic cycle as a river, with dangerous rapids and whirlpools along the way broken by stretches of becalmed waters. A skilled navigator knows how to read signs of coming dangers and is ever prepared to take remedial steps before finding himself in an intractable situation. If this were done—and if all segments of the economy understood that the government had gathered an arsenal of policies and was prepared to meet all emergencies —there would be created an atmosphere of confidence. Investment would expand, jobs would be available, and prosperity and growth would be achieved.

Burns had followed Keyserling's career in the CEA with interest and no little dismay. In his view the Chairman had used carefully selected information and incomplete statistics to support a jerry-built scaffolding of vast and windy generalizations; in other words, he was not a prudent man. Burns rejected the notion that the Council should lobby for political programs, and of course Keyserling felt otherwise. Furthermore, he considered Keyserling a poor economist at best, more a political reformer and ideologue than a social scientist. Burns had seen the CEA become a battleground in Congress and felt it "had fallen into pretty bad disrepute." At the same time he followed the 1952 presidential campaign, watching and listening to candidate Eisenhower. Burns knew Gabriel Hauge and recognized in Eisenhower's pledge to use countercyclical programs to fight recessions an echo of ideas he and Hauge had discussed and upon which they were in agreement.

Burns could hardly have been surprised when the offer was made to head the Council. While later claiming to have accepted with reluctance—"I was, after all, deeply involved in work at the National Bureau"—there never was serious doubt that he would accept. For years Mitchell and he had argued that the White House needed the services of a body similar to the National Bureau, which would provide the President and the Cabinet with detailed information upon which to base policies. Now he would create one. Burns knew that Eisenhower had little formal knowledge of economics, and, while this in itself might not be a problem, the fact that his closest advisors were rather primitive in their approaches to the subject might be dangerous. For example, Treasury Secretary George Humphrey was a strong advocate of tax cuts and budget balancing under practically all circumstances. He and others almost instinctively rejected notions they deemed "New Dealish" in origin, design, and intent. Burns had spent two decades preaching the virtues of pragmatic, inductive, and eclectic economics. In order to get his points across he would have to become a persuasive politician. The temptation to do so, to be close to the centers of power and demonstrate his talents, would have been difficult for this proud and self-confident man to resist.

Burns probably also considered an aspect of Mitchell's career. His mentor had been an advisor to Herbert Hoover in 1929 and at that time had seen the depression coming. Mitchell suggested countercyclical programs, and, while some of them had been accepted, others were deemed too radical or unusual by the White House of that period. In 1953 Burns thought he saw signs of a coming economic decline, one that might scar the Administration of the first Republican President since Hoover. At the CEA, and as a leading advisor to Eisenhower, he might be in a position to mitigate its effect and at the same time test theories refined at the National Bureau.

One of Burns's most delicate tasks would be to work with, around, and through Secretary Humphrey. Historians of the period sometimes write as though these two men were contesting for Eisenhower's fiscal and monetary soul. Certainly they had differing priorities and approaches, and this added to the impression that a contest was going on. Burns was troubled by signs of recession, and wanted to prepare for it. A highly successful steel executive before joining the Cabinet, Humphrey feared inflation more than he did recession, convinced as he was that it was eroding the nation's economic innards. As he saw it the Administration's primary task should be to balance the budget and cut spending, policies that would result in an economic slowdown but at the same time bring about price stability. Eisenhower thought highly of Humphrey. A story floating around Washington had it that on accepting the post, Humphrey had told Eisenhower, "I want you, if anyone asks you about money, to tell them to go and see George," and that the President agreed to do so.

If Eisenhower's ideology was in tune with that of the Secretary, he had more in common temperamentally with Burns. During the campaign he had told conservative audiences that he intended to balance the budget as soon as possible and cut back on spending programs but promised minorities and working class people that there would be vigorous federal intervention into the economy if recession or depression should threaten. His first State of the Union Address, delivered in January 1953, had phrases that were pure Burns. "It is axiomatic that our economy is a highly complex and sensitive mechanism," said Eisenhower. "Hasty and ill-considered action of any kind could seriously upset the subtle equation that encompasses debts, obligations, defense demands, deficits, taxes, and the general economic health of our Nation. Our goals can be clear, our start toward them can be immediate—but action must be slow."

The Eisenhower agenda, however, differed from that of the CEA Chairman. The President said he would cut federal spending that year and prevent the development of new inflationary pressures; Burns thought that if this were done, the movement toward recession would be accelerated and deepened. Furthermore, Eisenhower would afford top priority to a balanced budget; Burns saw a need for deficit spending if the recession became severe. Finally, the President would not consider a major tax cut until all of this was completed—and Burns thought quick tax relief one of the most efficient methods of preventing the recession from beginning.

During the next few months Burns tried to win Eisenhower's

confidence while working with allies to halt recessionary pressures. In particular he supported a tax cut passed during the Truman Administration that was due to go into effect under Eisenhower and even wanted to enlarge upon it in a way to encourage increased capital investment. George Humphrey also yearned for lower taxes, though for philosophical as much as economic reasons, and he became a perfect ally and front man. Allowing the Secretary to take the lead, Burns provided him with facts, statistics, and arguments to buttress his presentations at Cabinet meetings. In the end the President accepted the revisions, for which Humphrey received credit. Through 1953 and into 1954, debate on the proposed tax cuts continued in Congress, with Burns on hand to deliver expert opinion and support for them. Eisenhower observed his actions, met with Burns on a weekly basis, and saw how he came to dominate Humphrey. In the process, Burns moved closer to the President's inner circle.

Burns continued to stress the need for countercyclical weapons and in this spirit helped frame the Administration's housing program. This was one area in which Republicans had favored government intervention; no less a personage than Senator Robert Taft had cosponsored legislation to provide federal funds for new housing. Taft and Eisenhower both spoke out regarding the need for action to alleviate the shortage in dwellings. Burns saw in this a means whereby the President might stimulate a key segment of the economy in time of recession, or conversely, dampen inflationary pressures should they intensify. As had been the case with tax revision, he had allied himself with forces stronger than his own in order to acquire a new weapon with which to lean against the business cycle.

A similar political stiuation existed in regard to proposed expansion of unemployment insurance so as to cover additional workers and provide them with increased benefits. This had been talked about for several years and in 1953 was supported by a coalition of liberal and labor organizations. To this was added the backing of the Department of Labor's Bureau of Employment Security, which along with Burns was concerned about the possibilities of recession. Thus was formed a temporary coalition of reformers and Administration moderates, the former hoping to expand upon the legacy of the New and Fair Deals, the latter interested in yet another means of dealing with fluctuations in the business cycle.

In his first half-year in office, Burns demonstrated abilities at forming such alliances, while at the same time impressing Eisenhower with his knowledge and abilities. Hauge was an important ally in the White House, and Burns sought additional ones in other branches of the executive branch. Early in the Administration he obtained Eisenhower's approval to form an Advisory Board on Economic Growth and Stability (ABEGS), which would comprise representatives of several Cabinet offices as well as the Federal Reserve Board, the Budget Bureau, and the White House. As CEA Chairman, Burns would preside over ABEGS and present its recommendations to the President. In this way he became a de facto economic chief-of-staff and came to be seen as such by the White House.

Burns took care not to challenge Humphrey's power or to antagonize the man in any way. The two met often to discuss Administration policies, and Burns deferred to the Secretary whenever he could. As it happened, Humphrey's credibility as a financial expert was shaken within a few months after he assumed office. With great enthusiasm he set about tightening the money supply so as to prevent a burst of inflation when price controls were ended. In April the Treasury marketed over a billion dollars in long term bonds, a large offering for the time that dampened the market for corporate issues. At the same time his ally, Director of the Budget Joseph Dodge, announced reduced appropriations requests on the order of $4.5 billion. The Humphrey-Dodge program depressed the securities markets as the tight money condition appeared to push the economy closer to recession. Swift action by the Federal Reserve in expanding the money supply saved the situation. "Humphrey admitted himself that he had tightened credit a little too much," recalled Sherman Adams. "The crisis passed, but it left its mark as an error in Humphrey's fiscal calculation and raised some questions about the stability of the administration's money policies." It also helped boost Burns's stock, since he had warned all along that an overly energetic antiinflation program might push the nation into a recession. In terms of power, the Burns-Hauge axis had scored points, while that of the Humphrey-Dodge had a mark against it. This incident meant that when the recession came, the leadership role in fighting it would be played by ABEGS and not the Treasury.

A month after Humphrey turned the screws, the anticipated news regarding an impending recession came out of the National Bureau. Burns's former colleagues there announced that five out of its eight most important lead indicators had turned downward. Particularly discouraging was the clear evidence that business inventories were rising. Unless retail sales picked up soon, orders from factories

would be cut sharply, and this would ignite a recession. Burns noti-
fied his staff at the CEA that "attention should be focused upon
measures to be taken within, say, the next six months—when, by
whom, for what purpose, and with what probable effect." Shortly
thereafter he structured ABEGS for a role in "preparing the mind
for future acceptance of things that would have to be done to counter the recession."

No one who was aware of Burns's scholarly work or who had
listened to some of his lectures on the subject delivered in the late
1940s should have been surprised by his advice to Eisenhower and
the Cabinet in the summer of 1953. He advocated prompt but relatively mild countermoves at first, words of confidence and symbolic
gestures by the Administration to calm consumers and businessmen.
Next there could be an easing of credit restrictions and perhaps a
tax cut. Then, as a last resort, the Administration might sponsor
accelerated public works programs. All of these measures could be
found in the Keynesian bag. The key difference between them and
Burns lay in the matter of stress, priorities, and spirit. Burns would
intervene reluctantly in extreme situations; at the start of recessions
some Keynesians almost joyfully unleashed a panoply of programs.
That this difference existed was apparent in 1953, and it made the
Eisenhower Republicans appear *laissez-faire* in comparison with
their predecessors. In early September, as the unemployment rate
inched up, the *New York Times* exaggerated matters by observing
that "the Eisenhower Administration might be headed into the first
test of the adequacy of a hands-off approach to the national economy."

Later in the month Burns appeared before the Cabinet to deliver his regular report. Most of his lead indicators told him that a
recession was imminent. There were declines in the prices of farm
goods and common stocks. Business failures were on the increase
and housing starts were sagging. The inventory situation had
reached a serious stage. The proper medicine at this time, he said,
was tax reduction, a looser monetary policy, a more generous loan
policy, and words of confidence from the White House. Three days
earlier Secretary Humphrey had announced—with obvious personal
reluctance—that the Administration would not attempt to postpone
tax reductions due on January 1. Now he turned to Burns and said,
"We must not let this happen. You must tell us what to do."

Burns noted that the President's popularity was higher than
ever; three out of four Americans asked thought he was doing a

good job. Several Cabinet members suggested that Eisenhower go on television to tell the nation how stable the economy was. This he did not do, but at the October 8 press conference the President answered a question about the economy in the deliberately ambiguous way that had become his trademark on such occasions. "When it becomes clear that the Government has to step in, as far as I am concerned, the full power of Government, of Government credit, and of everything the Government has will move in to see that there is no widespread unemployment and we never again have a repetition of conditions that so many of you here remember when we had unemployment." The President would issue further calls for national self-confidence and would promise actions if and when they were needed, but in public at least he would do little else.

Following Burns's advice, Eisenhower asked the Cabinet to prepare contingency plans for economic stimulation. The Treasury remained out of the long-term money market, and this helped remove pressures on interest rates. The Federal Reserve cooperated by easing credit conditions, engaging in open market operations that increased the money supply, and in other ways indicating a willingness to work toward an easier monetary policy. The Defense, Post Office, and HEW departments prepared programs to be instituted should fiscal stimulation be needed.

The economic indicators continued to point the way toward recession in October and November. Despite record Christmas sales, the outlook worsened in December. By January almost all the indicators were down, showing a declining gross national product while unemployment was 4.7 percent and rising. Yet Eisenhower's popularity remained constant, with 71 percent of the public approving of the way he was handling his job. The President continued to talk of the need to "maintain a steady, unshakable attitude of public confidence in the capacity of the American economy for continued growth," and he rejected pleas that he institute a major public works program. On February 5 the Federal Reserve lowered the discount rate to 1¾ percent, an indication that monetary policies would continue to be the major weapon in the struggle. Twelve days later Eisenhower said he anticipated an upturn. "So far as using the powers of the Government are concerned, why, we are using them gradually." Of course, "if this thing would develop so that it looks like we are going into anything major, I wouldn't hesitate one second to use the very single thing this Government can bring to bear to stop any such catastrophe in this country." Critics charged that this was a rewrite of the old G.O.P. slogan, "Prosperity is just around the corner," last heard in the early years of the Great Depression. "Next to Eisenhower," wrote one critic, "Cal Coolidge and Herbert Hoover were positively eloquent."

Within the Cabinet, however, Eisenhower asked Burns to continue coordinating various public works programs, keeping them in readiness for when they might be needed. He designated July 1 as a tentative date for large-scale government action, and the President also prepared a request for supplemental appropriations should they be needed. Eisenhower asked Burns to appear at every Cabinet meeting henceforth.

Burns's role as the President's economic physician had been clearly established. The medicine he had prescribed had been taken, and now he was watching the temperature, trying to understand its meaning and reporting it to the President and the Cabinet. Eisenhower was still in full command, and Burns could have done little without Humphrey's full support. He had that support, along with the President's complete confidence. Thus, Burns had reached a summit; no previous economist had ever exerted so great an influence in the inner circle during peacetime.

In mid-March Burns told the Cabinet he discerned some early signs of recovery, leading Eisenhower to state at a press conference that "Your Government does not intend to go into any slambang emergency program unless it is necessary." At the next Cabinet meeting Burns presented a list of actions to be taken if recovery did not become apparent soon. These included liberalized mortgage requirements to stimulate housing, accelerated depreciation allowances to provide a push for capital spending, and other means to ease the money situation. In early April Eisenhower told Burns he was now ready to do all of these things and more, but the Chairman asked him to hold back for a while longer. The recession was developing in an unusual fashion. For almost nine months the aggregate statistics had declined, yet there was no significant falloff in such areas as plant expansion and commercial building contracts. To this Defense Secretary Charles Wilson added that there had been an upturn in automobile sales, an indication of growing consumer confidence.

The following week Burns reported that while the industrial situation remained weak, the financial area remained stronger than had been anticipated. This too was puzzling. Apparently investors and bankers had great confidence in Eisenhower's ability to lead the nation out of the recession. Soon one or another of these indicators would change direction—either the financial indicies would decline or industry would pick up—and Burns suspected the latter would take place.

Through April and May pressures for public works continued to build. At times Eisenhower seemed almost eager to take action, as Democrats advocated New Dealish programs and Republicans feared the stigma of depression would harm their chances in the congressional and state elections that year. But Burns continued to uncover evidence that the recession was nearing its turning point. In late May he told the Cabinet that for the third consecutive month increases in industrial orders and production had surpassed decreases. He thought the President might accelerate already existing programs involving the repair of federal office buildings and bridge construction but didn't believe more was required by way of fiscal stimulation. Eisenhower followed his lead; despite pressures from all sides he refused to trigger the large-scale public works programs then in readiness.

Burns told the Cabinet on June 4 that the length of the work week in April had increased over that of the previous month. This was taken as a sign that unemployment soon would decline. A week later his report was still more optimistic. Now Burns was almost certain the public works program could be shelved. Perhaps there could be additional stimulation for housing and highway construction, but little more than that would be required to have a smooth transition to an expanding economy. Eisenhower was delighted and paid the Chairman the supreme compliment. "Arthur, you'd have made a fine chief of staff during the war."

According to all reports, Burns appeared calm and cool throughout the ordeal. Others showed doubts, and some came close to panic; he never seemed to be less than a scientist presenting evidence in an almost dispassionate manner. Perhaps this was why he was so convincing; as one observer later noted, "He had an effective bedside manner." Still, Burns came out of this experience a changed person, though it was not apparent at the time. Making policy recommendations for future actions was quite different from gathering data about past depressions, and Burns had discovered he was pretty good at it. Also, he had spent the past two decades in debate with Keynesians, a contest in which he found himself often on the political right. For the past two years he had had to deal with Humphrey and other Administration conservatives, and in this context he was a centrist, if not a trifle left of center. He had come to realize that the differences between his views and those of the Keynesians were not as great as he previously had imagined. Finally, he had worked with some of the leading political figures in the nation and had learned of the strengths and flaws of that breed, as well as the limitations and extent of their power. In the White House he always served as advisor, as resident highbrow, and, while he was influential, it was a staff position that carried little direct power of its own. At the National Bureau he could order; in Washington he had to persuade. For a man of Burns's intellectual arrogance, it must have been difficult to do this with Cabinet members and others who, while admirable in many ways, were his intellectual inferiors. Before and after his CEA service Burns was never known as a man who suffered fools gladly, but he did so in this Washington tour.

On July 23 Burns announced that almost all his indicators told him the recession had come to an end. After the two world wars, the nation had suffered severe economic traumas. There had been only a relatively minor ripple after the Korean conflict and for this Burns received a share of the credit.

The Chairman wrote the Economic Report for 1955, which Eisenhower delivered in January. In it the President spoke of the antirecession program and claimed the government had "influenced the economy in two principal ways: first, through the automatic workings of the fiscal system; second by deliberately pursuing monetary, tax and expenditure policies that inspired widespread confidence on the part of the people. . . ." Could this effort have succeeded without the presence of a popular and almost universally trusted and believed chief executive? Would the Burns prescription have worked if a Truman or a Nixon were in the White House? What portion of the credit should be given to scientific economics and what to political charisma? Or might it have been that a different kind of economy had come into being in the postwar world, and that the prewar time series and cycle theories had to be scrapped or at least greatly revised? Throughout the crisis such questions must have been posed by members of the Council. Later on Burns noted that his predictions and advice had not been quite as good as Eisenhower had thought. Quite a few of his series had not behaved as he thought they would, and, contrary to expectations, the upturn in the autumn of 1954 was somewhat hesitant. This accounted for some Republican losses in the congressional elections that year. But Eisenhower had no trouble winning a second term. Having now seen a presidential canvas from the inside, Burns came to appreciate the art of politics more than he had earlier. Somewhere along the line he became less of an economic scientist and more a believer in effective political leadership during slumps.

Burns resigned from the Council shortly after the election and was succeeded as chairman by Raymond Saulnier, another CEA member who earlier had been a colleague at Columbia. Now Burns returned to his academic post and also resumed his office at the National Bureau. But he remained on call as an unofficial White House advisor, while defending Administration policies at scholarly meetings and debates. Burns already had become a celebrity of sorts and he clearly enjoyed this new status. Also, as one of the few prominent Republican economists, he often was asked to serve in advisory capacities. The National Bureau provided him with a podium from which to address other academics; his standing as a successful CEA chairman gave him a far wider audience.

In his papers on business cycles Burns continued to advocate the same kinds of remedies put forth at the Council and earlier. By so speaking and writing he became a leading critic of the New Economists, most of whom were younger men who favored large-scale tax cuts even in times of prosperity so as to maximize growth. These men also had little fear of deficit spending and unbalanced budgets. Burns frowned at such heresies and warned that this approach, if followed, would lead to runaway inflation. As before, he would employ countercyclical measures to flatten the business cycle. Speaking at Fordham University in 1957, Burns summarized an address, entitled "Policies for Coping with Inflation," with this:

> In other words, if the economy is operating close to its full capacity and the budget is already balanced, the government must discipline the natural impulse to use the larger revenues yielded by existing tax rates to finance new expenditures. In such circumstances it is desirable to strive for a sizeable surplus by severely limiting any increases in expenditures and, wherever possible, reducing them. Not only that, but if a surplus already exists, the objective under the assumed circumstances should be to increase it.

With words like this, Burns remained a leading spokesman for economic orthodoxy.

In 1961 Burns took a parttime post as a member of President Kennedy's Advisory Committee on Labor-Management Policy and as the only conservative economist there spoke out against what he deemed to be government actions that might erode business confidence. Since Kennedy's economic advisors were most concerned with matters of growth, Burns elected to meet them on that ground. He sounded the alarm against inflation when they advocated a major tax cut in 1962 and 1963; such a course of action, he warned, might result in unbalancing the economy in ways that could prove harmful for years to come. Burns countered with a recommendation for mild tax relief for high income individuals and corporations. This would cost little, and a confident business community would expand operations, in this way providing the kind of growth so desired by the New Economists. Ever eclectic and pragmatic, Burns sought ways of integrating his ideas and goals with those of the Kennedy and Johnson advisors. By 1964 he was advocating annual minor tax cuts as a means of stimulating the economy. He presented the idea in such a way as to win support from some Republican leaders. Moderate New Economists applauded this "conversion" and might have agreed when Burns claimed that "the average dollar spent by private citizens is more productive of wealth, and therefore more conducive to growth, than the average dollar spent by government." In this period President Johnson received a good deal of support from businessmen who considered Burns the leading American economist.

Though a partisan, Burns managed to remain on good terms with most of the Kennedy and Johnson economists. Like them he was an academic—he knew the folkways and vocabulary of the tribe. Equally important was his continued commitment to empirical economics and his distrust of theory and his willingness to adjust his ideas to realities. In 1967 Burns conceded that the Kennedy-Johnson fiscal policies had worked well. "The massive tax cut was its bold conception," he said of the Kennedy CEA, "and the enactment of such a measure at a time when the economy was advancing smoothly was a triumph of the 'new economics.'"

Some years later Richard Nixon would announce his conversion to Keynesianism. Whether or not this truly was the case is questionable. But in the 1960s Burns traveled a few miles along that path, and in this period he was Nixon's leading economic advisor.

In late 1967, when it appeared Nixon would seek the Republican presidential nomination, Burns prepared to leave the National Bureau. He was 63 years old, close to retirement anyway, and said he had important research to complete. It was evident, however, that

he was ready to return to public life. Shortly after Nixon's inauguration he announced that Burns would be named Counselor to the
President, a Cabinet-level post that had just been created. Other
economic soothsayers had only one season in the spotlight. Arthur
Burns, in some respects the most influential of them all, would have
two, as we shall see later.

4

JOHN KENNETH GALBRAITH

In the late summer of 1953, as Arthur Burns instructed President Eisenhower and the Cabinet on the fine points of business cycle theory, the stock market staged a rally. Burns thought he saw signs of a coming recession, and scores of securities analysts came to the same conclusion. They advised clients to sell. But they didn't and instead rushed in to buy shares. As a result the rally continued in the face of economic decline. In November the market crossed over its old 1929 high of Dow 381 and kept on going.

What was behind this advance? There was talk of speculative pools, manipulations, of the public's being taken for a ride, and of a coming crash.

The following month William Fulbright announced that he would lead the Senate Banking and Currency Committee in an investigation of the market's actions over the past year or so. "The situation looks very dangerous to me," he told reporters. "It is reminiscent of 1929."

The Committee gathered information and lined up witnesses in January and February. Stock Exchange officials and experts were scheduled to appear, along with a handful of investment bankers and old timers. After the hearings had concluded—on an indecisive and puzzled note—most agreed that its star had been John K. Galbraith, who even then was one of the nation's most famous economists.

Galbraith appeared before the Committee on March 8. In his prepared paper he noted that American capitalism was famed for its cycle of "boom and bust," and he warned of a sharp reversal that could come. Galbraith would not say the nation was headed toward a replay of the 1929 crash, but he did observe there had been an increase in speculation and went on to note that the increase in short sales and margin buying was "an unhealthy sign." "This market could go up due to the pursuit of capital gains . . . and there could be a collapse." Under questioning from Republican Senator Irving Ives of New York, Galbraith conceded that comparisons between 1929 and 1953 had been overdrawn, but he did see similarities between the current market and conditions in 1928. "A determined government, at any time in 1928, could have stopped the boom," and he urged the Committee to recommend measures to do that, the most important being the imposition of 100 percent margin requirements and the elimination of preferential rates for capital gains taxes.

As Galbraith testified, the market opened and prices collapsed. The Dow closed at 409, for a loss of over seven points. This led Fulbright to remark that "A lot of people will blame us . . . if the market falls out of bed." Winthrop Smith of Merrill Lynch disagreed. "Some days it sells up, some days it sells down. Sometimes we think we know why; some days we don't. This time I don't know why, but I doubt very much it was Professor Galbraith's testimony."

Generally speaking, however, Wall Street did blame Galbraith and Fulbright for the collapse, and so did the press the following day. For years afterwards Galbraith would prize one newspaper article that carried the headline, "Egghead Scrambles Market." And it didn't end there. Republican Senator Homer Capehart demanded he be recalled to testify on his past associations. The Senator had learned that Galbraith had been one of Adlai Stevenson's advisors and speech writers in the 1952 presidential campaign. "His known philosophy fits in with what I have felt was the purpose of these hearings: namely, to discredit the Eisenhower Administration and to cause people to lose faith in the economy." Capehart went on to say that one of Galbraith's articles contained sections favorable to communism. Later on Capehart would retract this suggestion, but in any case it did not appear to have harmed his target.

In fact, Galbraith was one of the few who came out of the inquiry well. Though already famous as an economist, political figure, and author, he had now achieved added recognition. Some Wall Streeters came to see him as their leading critic, a major adversary of finance capitalism, and Galbraith delighted in this. The Fulbright hearings also provided a good backdrop for his next book, *The Great Crash, 1929*, which was released a few months later and sold well in the financial district. The author later remarked that he was pleased with this and added that the paperback version did poorly in airports—where bookstores were reluctant to carry a work with that title.

Galbraith's ideas on the crash, as well as on a variety of other subjects, were well known to the literate reading public and to his peers, but they had little direct impact upon public policy. At no point would his views be openly embraced by any chief executive—ironically, Richard Nixon would come closest to them all in accepting his prescriptions. For many years Galbraith was at the center of things, the friend and advisor to political leaders. But he has never been able to convince those in power to accept and fight for his ideas or try to put them into practice. John Kennedy used his pen, but rejected Galbraithian economics and shortly before entering the White House dispatched his old friend a half a world away to India, where he represented his country, produced a couple of books and a score of articles—and cabled advice to Washington.

Part of the reason for this can be found in Galbraith's position in the theoretical spectrum. He is a self-proclaimed radical in that he calls for a major reorientation of economic thinking and drastic changes in public policy. While often bold in their hypotheses, mainstream economists as a rule are not utopians. Rather, they are prepared to work with the world as it exists. Almost all of them are wary of programmatic change; they follow the dictum often quoted by nineteenth-century economist Alfred Marshall: *Natura non facit saltum*, which translates as "Nature doesn't move in sudden jumps." Thus, Galbraith's suggestions that antitrust laws be repealed, that the weapons industry be nationalized, and that America accept wage and price controls as a permanent part of the system (recently he has called for a "comprehensive incomes and prices policy") have been rejected by most of his peers, Keynesians as well as Friedmanites. Furthermore, many of them both resent and appear to envy

Galbraith's ability with words; if nothing else, the man is one of the finest prose stylists of the time. Some may bristle when Galbraith claims that if an economist's work cannot be understood, it means he either lacks wit or hasn't thought out his positions clearly.

This is not to suggest that economists automatically reject out of hand all clear expository writing. Arthur Burns, Paul Samuelson, Milton Friedman, and many others are capable of turning out journalism readily comprehensible to intelligent laymen. But these men and other leaders in the profession also have written many arcane, scholarly treatises and monographs, dotted with complex equations and written in a language reserved for those initiated in the ways of the craft. They have formulated limited hypotheses, tested them in the approved fashion, and then drawn cautious conclusions. Galbraith has done none of this. Though some of his defenders note that one book, *A Theory of Price Control*, could be called scholarly, and that Galbraith does evidence a knowledge of mathematical economics, even this work is devoid of scholarly paraphernalia. It would appear that Galbraith is unwilling to undertake such projects.

More to the point, he couldn't write such a piece if he tried, for the man simply doesn't think along those lines. He is more wide-ranging than any other person in the field—Galbraith has authored travel books, fiction, and even a mock-sociological work under a pseudonym. And he is witty. In his memoir, *The Scotch*, written as he says "in odd moments," he notes that he had been responsible for some of Adlai Stevenson's "elevated sallies" in the 1952 and 1956 campaigns. "Often, with appropriate circumspection, other members of the campaign party would congratulate me on some particularly pointed thrust including ones with which I had nothing to do. I always found myself recalling the earlier warning. Humor is richly rewarding to the person who employs it. But it has no persuasive value at all.

Neither does it serve to elevate one's status in academia. This too doesn't seem to worry him, for Galbraith is at least as arrogant and as vain as Burns. Alone of the economists in this work he has published books that appeared on the best-seller lists. More of his volumes have been purchased and read for sheer enjoyment than have those of all the others combined. (Paul Samuelson's now-classic textbook, *Economics*, may have been purchased by more people —students for the most part—but as every professor knows, more texts are sold than are read, and in any case, as good a writer as Samuelson is, he cannot match Galbraith for wit and clarity.)

And this, too, did his reputation among academic economists little good. To them Galbraith is too much the celebrity—the kind of person historian Daniel Boorstin once described as being famous for being famous. He is at home with artists, show business personalities, and television talk show hosts. In fact he was the author and host of the British Broadcasting Corporation's "The Age of Uncertainty," which dealt with the history of economic ideas. Perhaps no other economist but he could have made such abstract ideas so palatable and even interesting to a general audience. In its American showing, each "show" was capped by a short talk in which one of Galbraith's critics attempted to refute his interpretations. Most of them put scores of holes in them, but once again Galbraith came out of it unscathed.

He never has aimed his words at such critics. Rather, he continues to seek a much wider audience, as can be seen from the title of one of his most recent books, a short volume written with Nicole Salinger entitled *Almost Everyone's Guide to Economics*, which is more a polemic and simplified introduction to Galbraithian economics than anything else and released shortly after his 70th birthday. In it he describes himself as a political economist rather than an economist pure and simple, and, given his penchant for seeking political solutions, this makes sense. As with most of his works, the sweep is vast, the vision interesting, unusual, and suggestive, and the conclusions buttressed by slender evidence and anecdotes. It is an entertainment more than a treatise, but anyone who can make modern economics entertaining surely possesses a fine gift. Galbraith concedes that few accept his ideas, especially those regarding the nature of the marketplace. "The traditionalists have certainly dug their heels in on this one—formed a circle with heads in and rumps out like the buffalo herds under attack in the West" is the way he puts it.

Will Galbraith ever again have a *direct* influence on a chief executive? Given his age, the focus of economics in recent years, as well as the self-imposed limitations derived from his own career and advocacies, the chances seem slim. Keyserling continues to advise liberal Democrats and speak out for New Dealish programs, and Arthur Burns can expect to be listened to in Washington for as long as he cares to talk on current issues. But Galbraith already has assumed the mantle of the grand old man of the unconventional wisdom. "Are you depressed?" asks Salinger as the close of the book, a question that affords the theatrical sage a chance at playing the farewell scene. "Only at not being young and seeing a chance to be fully involved in the change that lies ahead," he replies. "The battles will be wonderful, the distress of the comfortable extreme." In his view, "it will be or can be a lovely time for the profession"—and for him as well, since the call to power may yet come.

Galbraith was born in 1908 in Iona Station, a farming community not far from the northern shore of Lake Erie in Ontario, Canada. His father, William, was a farmer and in addition was active in local politics and helped found several businesses. As the son put it, William was "a man of standing" in the region, a leading Liberal and a devout antimonarchist. Apparently the two got along well with one another; William Galbraith is the only person in the pages of *The Scotch* who is more than a caricature or there to illustrate an anecdote.

Young Galbraith attended local schools and then went on to the Ontario Agricultural College at Guelph, a branch of the University of Toronto, where he majored in agricultural economics and from which he graduated in 1931. By then he was 23 years old, an age when most people's ideas, values, and ambitions already are fairly well established. Yet to that point Galbraith had had no prolonged exposure to urban living or urbane people. Of his teachers at Guelph he was affected only by O. J. Stevenson and E. C. McLean, who helped develop their student's prose style, not his economics. "They were men who deeply loved their craft," he later wrote, "and who were willing to spend endless hours with a student, however obscure his talent." Later he would say that his ideas were influenced by Keynes, Marx, and especially by Thorstein Veblen, the eccentric and brilliant institutionalist, but he knew these people through their writings, and, judging from his own, it would appear he read selectively.

Galbraith had no true mentor, no person he emulated. More than most scholars, he was a self-made man, an original in design if not in content.

Prior to graduation Galbraith received an offer of a research assistantship in agricultural economics at the University of California at Berkeley. He accepted, enrolled for graduate study there, and two years later became an instructor in his specialty at the Davis extension. Meanwhile he studied under Ewald Grether, M. M. Knight, Paul Taylor, and Robert Brady, none of whom had much of a reputation in the field. Some of them did introduce him to Veblen's writings, however, and one book, *The Theory of Business*

Enterprise, had a profound impact upon the young scholar. "I can still remember my excitement when I first read the book in the thirties while a student at Berkeley," he recalled four decades later.

Galbraith was introduced to Keynesianism by Leo Rogin, a somewhat more distinguished scholar than the others, who had "a sense of urgency that made his seminars seem to graduate students the most important thing then happening in the world." But Berkeley and Davis were far from the center of American intellectual ferment, and were what in those days could be considered respectable but decidedly second-rate institutions. Yet Galbraith later wrote, "Never before had I been so happy."

In the spring of 1933, as he put the finishing touches on his Ph.D. dissertation—"California County Expenditures, 1934"—Galbraith applied for and then received an offer of an instructorship at Harvard that paid $2,400 a year, which was $600 more than he was receiving in California. The call to Harvard, the nation's most prestigious university and the center for American Keynesianism, was something most scholars in his circumstance would have prized, but, as Galbraith tells it, he had no desire to leave California and meant to use the offer as a lever to pry additional money out of his dean. This move backfired. Galbraith was congratulated and invited to go east. So he did. As he later wrote, "The great love of my life was over."

That summer Galbraith worked as an associate economist in the Agricultural Adjustment Administration. "Economists were in short supply," he wrote, and so the Harvard-bound scholar got his first taste of working with the Washington bureaucracy. As he tells it, he was lost in the crowd. The AAA was one of the yeastier parts of the New Deal apparatus, employing such men as Adlai Stevenson, George Ball, and Jerome Frank, all of whom became important national figures later on. It also contained a large communist cell, one whose members included Alger Hiss, Lee Pressman, and Nathaniel Weyl. As for Galbraith, he was part of no inner circle. "I never at the time achieved the distinction that allowed me to know any of them."

For a while Galbraith taught agricultural economics and a few other courses at Harvard, while serving as tutor at Winthrop House, where he came into contact first with Joseph Kennedy, Jr., and then his younger brother, Jack. At the same time he staked out a position in an area of research.

Alvin Hansen and Seymour Harris were senior professors at

Harvard, and they led many young instructors in the path of Keynesian analysis. Joseph Schumpter, one of the most original thinkers
in the field, was also there, and in the midst of the Great Depression his gloomy prognosis for capitalism also won converts and followers. If Galbraith was influenced by them, or even came into close
contact with these men, his work did not show it. Rather, he became
interested in ideas put forth by another Harvard economist, Edward
Chamberlin, who in 1932 published his *Theory of Price Competition*.
New Dealers Adolph Berle and Gardiner Means released their *The
Modern Corporation and Private Property* the same year, and this
too appears to have influenced Galbraith, as did a book by English
economist Joan Robinson, *The Economics of Imperfect Competition*,
which was published the following year. Drawing upon these works
and adding his own interests, Galbraith published several articles in
scholarly journals in which he outlined his view of the economy.

Chamberlin and Robinson noted that many large and financially
secure companies with monopoly or oligopoly positions had suffered
less than might have been expected from the depression and in fact
had been able to divorce themselves, in part at least, from the workings of the law of supply and demand. Picking up on this and re-
peating some of their points, Galbraith wrote that by virtue of their
power and abilities at stimulating demand through advertising, major firms could lure consumers to their products and services. In addition they could maintain prices in the face of declining demand,
drawing upon reserves until consumers came to them. In contrast,
the farmers, lacking such influence, were at the mercy of the marketplace. In bad times, then, they suffered from declining prices for
their products, while having to purchase manufactured items at close
to their old prices.

Though he did not put it this way at the time, Galbraith was
suggesting there were two distinct parts of the economy. One, which
he later termed the "market sector," comprised many small firms
that vied with one another and relied upon the kind of self-regulating mechanism described by classical economists. By virtue of competition they were obliged to offer the best product at the lowest
price. Inefficient firms either reformed, were absorbed, or left the
field, while superior ones came out on top. This was contrasted with
the more powerful "planning sector," in which competition either
was nonexistent or imperfect, and firms avoided self-regulation and
functioned under a different set of rules. They manipulated consumers, rigged prices, and controlled supplies. This was done not in the

name of maximizing profits, but of creating a stable environment. Highly complex economic organisms have to be assured of reliable sources of raw materials and predictable demand for finished goods. Large firms could and did plan far ahead. Fluctuations, uncertain demand, competition in which costs and losses could be enormous were to be avoided. Galbraith agreed with Berle and Means that the first sector was dominated by small capitalists, businessmen, and farmers, and the second by managers and bureaucrats. In the mid-1930s, however, he was not prepared to offer suggestions on how to deal with this situation.

Galbraith married Catherine Atwater in 1937 and set off for a year at Cambridge as a social science research fellow. Keynes was there part of the time, though ill, and the revolution in economic thinking he inspired was in full swing. Given his interests and personality, Galbraith could not help but become part of the movement, but he continued to be interested more in the ideas of Chamberlin, Robinson, and Berle and Means. In part this was due to his lifelong distaste for abstract theory, and a good deal of Keynesianism was headed in this direction. More important, however, was that Galbraith was coming to believe that the ailments of society were too deep for the kinds of medicine offered by Keynes and his followers. Little in their canon would treat monopoly and oligopoly power, for example, or restore a measure of competition to an increasingly important segment of the economy. Galbraith appreciated the pressing need for economic recovery in a nation with double-digit unemployment, but he thought far-reaching reforms were also needed. In particular, political power would be required to act as a corrective to economic concentration.

This idea was presented in a short book Galbraith wrote with reform-minded industrialist Henry S. Dennison. Released in 1938, *Modern Competition and Business Policy* presented Galbraith's view of the two sectors in a clear fashion and stated that there was need for vigorous federal regulation of oligopolies. First of all, a commission should be organized to study the situation, establish facts, and present recommendations to a Board of Review. This body would work with large corporations and industry groups to draw up codes of conduct, which then would become the basis for legislation. To bring large firms under greater control, the authors would oblige them to obtain national incorporation. They had little use for the antitrust approach then being employed by the Justice Department. By their very nature some industries—such as utilities—appeared destined to be dominated by large corporations, and oligopolies were not necessarily evil. But they had obtained too much power, were divorced from economic constraints, and so should be regulated or at least curbed by the enlarged authority of the federal government.

There was little that was new in any of this. In addition to drawing upon the works of leading oligopoly theorists, the authors had been preceded by the New Nationalism crusade of Theodore Roosevelt in 1912 and F.D.R.'s experience with the National Recovery Administration in the early years of the New Deal, both of which had been predicated on pretty much the same ideas found in *Modern Competition and Business Policy*. The Temporary National Economic Committee already had received its mandate to engage in the kind of study Dennison and Galbraith recommended, and in 1938, it appeared that body would come to the same set of conclusions presented in the book. This was a derivative work, then, and in addition lacked the kind of sparkling prose one later associated with Galbraith.

The same might be said of a second book, *Toward Full Employment*, which carried the names of Dennison and Ralph Flanders but was drafted or ghosted by Galbraith. This was a rehash of Keynesianism. "It was only slightly more readable and even less read than Keynes," wrote Galbraith later on. Neither work was taken too seriously, and only served to indicate that he had formed some kind of understanding with liberal New England businessmen. They had hired him and other Harvard faculty members to offer them a crash course in contemporary economics, an experience Galbraith thoroughly enjoyed.

Ambitious academic economists weren't supposed to engage in this kind of activity or write these kinds of tracts, but Galbraith didn't seem to give the matter much thought. Already he had discovered that academic life was somewhat dull; he was not cut out for that kind of career or reputation. Galbraith preferred the company of men of affairs and action to that of most of his scholarly, theory-oriented colleagues. Furthermore, he enjoyed explaining economics to men like Flanders and Dennison rather than to undergraduates, and he spent more time writing than with his students. Lacking important connections and friends at Harvard who might have helped him along, he left there in 1939 to accept an assistant professorship at Princeton, and he used this post as a launching pad for a Washington-based career.

World War II soon began, and the New Deal was being dismantled in preparation for an American role in the conflict. While leading bureaucrats were being shuffled into new posts, Galbraith managed to obtain an assignment at the old stand. Together with G. G. Johnson, Jr. (a recent Harvard Ph.D.), he produced *The Economic Effects of Federal Public Works Expenditures, 1933-1938* for the National Planning Board. In this work Galbraith and Johnson recommended extensive long-term projects so as to combine "idle men and idle resources for useful public construction." This monograph was addressed to an economy in depression but was released at a time when war-related enterprises and massive government spending were bringing the nation out of the economic depths. It was a well-reasoned and—for a government document——engaging effort and under the circumstances badly outdated. But it did provide Galbraith with his ticket to Washington. In 1940, while completing it, he became an advisor to the National Defense Advisory Commission, and the following year he left Princeton to become an official in the Office of Price Administration and Civilian Supply.

Few jobs in Washington could have suited Galbraith better. Throughout the 1930s he had believed that the pricing mechanism in a large sector of the economy did not respond well to the law of supply and demand and that in effect prices were fixed by large corporations. Now the fixing would be done by government instead of by businessmen. In *A Theory of Price Control*, which is more a memoir of his wartime experience than anything else, Galbraith wrote that his office "controlled the prices of all steel mill products with far less man power and trouble than was required for a far smaller dollar volume of steel scrap." The reason was simple enough: the former industry was oligopolistic, the latter competitive. "I am tempted to frame a theorem that is all too evident in this discussion," he added. "It is relatively easy to fix prices that are already fixed." And it was true that throughout the war, the OPA had more difficulties dealing with small businessmen and companies than with the industrial tycoons and major corporations.

Galbraith resigned from the OPA in early 1943, the victim of political crosscurrents within the agency. He then tried to enlist in the Army but was rejected as being too tall. After a short tour at the Lend-Lease Commission, he left Washington for a position on the editorial board of *Fortune* magazine, where he worked on and off for the next five years. Later on Galbraith would credit this experience with having taught him to write, and while this wasn't the case, enough of "Timese" rubbed off on him to alter his style. Always a clear writer, he now permitted himself to illustrate points with witty examples, and in each of the Galbraith articles in *Fortune* there could be found at least two or three memorable phrases. In other words, he was becoming more a journalist than an academic. He also wrote scholarly articles for professional journals, however, and these served to maintain his credentials among former colleagues. Galbraith was 37 years old at the end of the war and already had the making of successful careers in academia, journalism, and government.

For a while he seemed unable to make up his mind on which path to follow. Galbraith left *Fortune* in 1945 to take a position as one of the directors of the Strategic Bombing Survey and then went on to head the Office of Economic Security Policy, which oversaw programs in occupied countries. He returned to *Fortune* in 1947 and almost immediately sent out feelers to Harvard, whose faculty he rejoined the following year. It was a sensible move. A light teaching load would enable him to do all the writing he had in mind at the time and participate in politics as well. Also, the Harvard connection would be a proper rebuff to some who during the next three decades would try to dismiss him as a lightweight pamphleteer.

A Theory of Price Control, which was released in 1952, was published by Harvard University Press, and received little notice outside of the profession; it would appear that this was Galbraith's bow to academia. That same year Houghton Mifflin released his *American Capitalism: The Concept of Countervailing Power*, which was directed at a wider audience—the kind of people who might have read his *Fortune* articles. "I think the reader will find this a good-humored book," he stated in the preface. "Yet this is an essay in social criticism. The task of criticism is criticism." In fact, the two books were on the same subject: the problems caused by large economic entities in a society in which the old verities no longer applied, and what might be done about it. Galbraith had addressed this issue in the 1930s and would continue to do so throughout his career. What expansion is to Keyserling and business cycles to Burns, the behavior of large corporations in the marketplace are to Galbraith: the source of his concern and the *leit motiv* for his writings.

American Capitalism is not a particularly well-organized book. In places Galbraith rambles, and he is too easily sidetracked into bits of economic theory and interesting but not particularly relevant anecdotes about the folkways of capitalism. But the heart of the work, a chapter entitled "The Theory of Countervailing Power," is forceful and clear. The theory is an outgrowth of ideas Galbraith set down in earlier articles and in *Modern Competition and Business Policy* but stated in a far more explicit fashion. It is in itself geometrically simple. "Private economic power is held in check by the countervailing power of those who are subject to it. The long trend toward concentration of industrial enterprise in the hands of a relatively few firms has brought into existence not only strong sellers, as economists have supposed, but also strong buyers as they have failed to see." For example, the growth of powerful labor unions was spurred by the creation of major corporations that had the ability to dictate terms to individual workers; large retail chains appeared as a counterweight to the development of concentration in the consumer goods industries; farmers formed marketing cooperatives to balance the powers of food processors and other organized purchasers of their goods. As for government, that grew for several reasons—as a force against the other sectors and, in reform eras, to assist the weaker party in its struggles against the stronger ones.

As a corollary to this theory, Galbraith added that the antitrust solution to this situation usually was misguided. More often than not the concentration of economic power resulted from technological developments, the nature of the marketplace, and economies of scale—the automobile and steel industries, to name just two, are hardly places for small enterprises. "To suppose that there are grounds for antitrust prosecution wherever three, four or a half dozen firms dominate a market is to suppose that the very fabric of American life is illegal."

Galbraith presents an economy that is almost Newtonian in balance. He says next to nothing about innovation, growth, or even depression. But he does have a good deal of comment on inflation. "Employers who are faced with demand for higher wages can pay them and pass the added cost along in prices with impunity. They do. The higher wages become, in turn, the source of the higher income which helps sustain demand at new prices."

Inflation can set the system on its end and quickly erode the balance and distort supply and demand. In *A Theory of Price Control* Galbraith states that "Inflation, more than depression, I regard as the clear and present danger of our times and one that is potentially more destructive of the values and amenities of democratic life," and he restates his belief in *American Capitalism*: "In any case there is no doubt that inflationary tensions are capable of producing a major revision in the character and constitution of American capitalism."

How can inflation be kept in check? Earlier Galbraith had said that large entities have the power to withstand pressures to cut prices, and he repeats this in these two books. Given his wartime experiences at the OPA, one might have expected him to advocate wage and price controls. In treating the same problem, Keyserling told Truman that increased production would dissolve inflationary pressures. In *American Capitalism,* however, Galbraith opted instead for a conventional Keynesian remedy. "Increased taxes and decreased government spending could reduce demand below the amount that is necessary to carry off the current supply of goods. There is also a possibility that, by restricting bank credit, business expenditures for inventories, plant and equipment and consumers' expenditures for durable goods can also be reduced." Will this suffice? Galbraith presents a good case for his remedy in *A Theory of Price Control,* but he notes that "wage and price controls are probably necessary in a state of limited mobilization," and then only in a limited way. "They ought, however, to be employed under conditions of an approximate equilibrium of demand and supply. They are an adjunct of the monetary and fiscal measures which maintain this equilibrium."

As expected, *A Theory of Price Control* was generally ignored while *American Capitalism* made the best-seller lists, even though both books shared many of the same ideas. "I made up my mind that I would never again place myself at the mercy of the technical economists who had the enormous power to ignore what I had written," said Galbraith in recalling the experience years later. "I set out to involve a larger community." So he did. *American Capitalism* received many favorable reviews in newspapers and magazines; its author was on his way to celebrity. But those reviews that appeared in professional journals were more critical of the work. Galbraith had not formulated his hypothesis in a scholarly way; nor had he marshaled the kind of evidence needed to substantiate his claims. He was credited with originality and boldness and debited for rashness and a tendency to overreach. Furthermore, there was little in the way of rigor in the book—not a single mathematical equation, for example—and this troubled the "technical economists." Instead, they found statements like this: "The contention I am here making is a formidable one. It comes to this: Competition which, at least since the time of Adam Smith, has been viewed as the autonomous regulator of economic activity and as the only available regulatory mechanism apart from the state, has, in fact, been superceded." Academic economists simply did not make such sweeping statements—at least not in print. Rather, they tended toward the more guarded prose of an Arthur Burns. Little wonder, then, that Galbraith came in for heavy fire when he appeared at the annual meeting of the American Economic Association in late 1953, and on that occasion he did modify some of his positions, which can be seen in the revised edition of the book that appeared three years later.

Other modifications resulted from the development of Galbraith's thinking and his increasing political activism, as well as his perception of changes in American society in the middle years of the 1950s. He served as one of Adlai Stevenson's speech writers in the 1952 and 1956 campaigns and provided advice, expertise, ideas, and recommendations for a variety of liberal Democratic politicians. As has been mentioned, *The Great Crash, 1929* was released in 1954. Essentially a noncontroversial historical work which nonetheless did contain a warning that it might happen again, it sold well and in paperback form quickly became required reading in many undergraduate classes in American history and economics. Out of a series of lectures he fashioned another book, *Economics and the Art of Controversy,* which came out the following year. In this barely noticed work, published by Rutgers University Press, Galbraith stated that most of the old economic issues of the New and Fair Deals no longer interested people or even were subjects of hot debate. Labor's right to organize, government's duty to intervene in the economy and even plan for economic objectives were conceded by almost all Americans. At one time a demagogue like Huey Long might make a national career on economic issues; Senator McCarthy had little interest in the subject. Quoting some unnamed philosopher, Galbraith said "Our present need is for some new platitudes." Though he wouldn't say what those should be, he was fairly certain they were on their way.

Galbraith produced his contribution to the debate, *The Affluent Society,* in 1958. In the preface he indicates that he had been working on it for over two years, but in that period he also lectured and produced a handful of articles and reviews in which some of the ideas in the book were tested. No author could have asked for more in the way the stage was set prior to publication: *The Affluent Society* got to the bookstores shortly after the Soviets launched the first sputnik, while Americans asked themselves why they had been bested in the

first round of the space race—in Galbraith they found the beginning
of an answer. "No action was ever so admirably timed," wrote the
author in his preface to the second edition. "Had I been younger
and less formed in my political views, I would have been carried
away by my gratitude and found a final resting place beneath the
Kremlin Wall. I knew my book was home. A vastly less productive
society had brought off a breathtaking and also, who could tell, very
alarming achievement." Galbraith concluded that "Surely they were
using their more meager resources more purposefully."

It might be argued that *The Affluent Society* has been the most
influential book on American society since the end of World War II.
Certainly it is Galbraith's most popular work, the one for which the
reading public knows him best. This is not to say that it is more
original or has a more lasting significance than the others, but that
no other work by an American economist has had such an impact or
stirred so much debate.

Within a few weeks of its appearance most major newspapers
and all the news magazines published stories about the book, its
message, and the author. According to them, Galbraith was saying
that America was a nation of self-centered hedonists lured into purchasing goods they really didn't need by skillful advertisers and
manufacturers eager to control markets and that this was happening
while public services deteriorated. Galbraith's remedy, they said,
would be to pay less attention to automobiles and more to public
transportation, to have better schools and fewer television sets, improved parks rather than private swimming pools. If he had his way,
so the articles went, the role of government would be expanded, and
the public sector would receive a larger share of the gross national
product. Since Galbraith devoted little space to economic growth,
this would presumably come at the expense of the private sector—in
the form of higher taxes and less consumption.

Much of this was distorted or oversimplified or not what Galbraith had written; *The Affluent Society* was a best seller, but many
people who purchased or discussed the book hadn't read it. In some
cases Galbraith was not at fault. For example, he was criticized for
ignoring the persistence of poverty. In fact he did devote the better
part of two chapters to the subject and indicated his belief that the
public sector had a responsibility to deal with the issue, which he
thought might best be handled by a new system of unemployment
insurance and transfer payments. In an article in the *New Republic*
entitled "Eggheads and Politics," Keyserling charged that Galbraith

underestimated the seriousness of the problem and that his solutions were inadequate. In the book he suggested that one family out of thirteen could be classified as being poor. Keyserling noted that one-fifth of the nation was below the poverty line and another fifth was living a deprived existence, and he called for massive increases in production rather than income redistribution to end the situation. Perhaps he didn't appreciate the extent of poverty, thought Keyserling, because Galbraith had a cloistered life in academia.

That such arguments would dominate discussion of the book was to have been expected at a time when the nation was undergoing a reexamination of its values, but it served to detract from what many economists saw as the central theme of the work. One can perceive in *The Affluent Society* a logical progression in Galbraith's thoughts and catch a glimpse of where he was heading. In *Modern Competition and Business Policy* he sketched an economy in which one sector was dominated by giant corporations, and he called for vigorous government policies to control them. Then, in *American Capitalism,* he presented an economy in balance by virtue of countervailing powers, and he demonstrated how large entities could bypass supply and demand factors, how competition was eliminated as a control on their activities, and the ways managers and bureaucrats thought. Now, in *The Affluent Society*, he rejected the notion of consumer sovereignty. Galbraith states that the nature of industrial enterprises requires them to be able to plan ahead, to produce goods for which the demand is assured. They do what they can to satisfy felt needs but also are engaged in manufacturing them when necessary through advertising and salesmanship. "Wants thus come to depend upon output," he writes, with the result being that Americans continually are being stimulated to crave things they really don't need—and wouldn't want were it not for the nature of the system. This implies that the gross national product has to be analyzed by qualitative as well as quantitative means—the tail fins on a superpowered automobile are not as necessary for well-being as is bread. "In technical terms it can no longer be assumed that welfare is greater at an all-round higher level of production than at a lower one. It may be the same. The higher level of production has, merely, a higher level of want creation necessitating a higher level of want satisfaction." The assertion here is that if individuals were not prompted to crave more goods, to become large-scale consumers of the latest fad items, much of the economy could be diverted to take care of those public areas—schools, parks, and the like—that were being neglected. "One cannot defend production of satisfying wants if that production creates the wants." Thus, Galbraith's conception of a balance of powers in the economy as presented in *American Capitalism* was altered into one in which the large-scale producers dictated what would be produced and who would consume it. There was a clear necessity, then, for the powers of government to be called into play to correct the situation.

American Capitalism had been released in the last year of the Truman Administration; *The Affluent Society* appeared in the middle of Eisenhower's second term. The country was in a new recession, with the unemployment rate at over 7 percent, but the inflation rate in 1958 was close to 2 percent—considered uncomfortable if not threatening in that period. Galbraith by now had dispaired of fiscal and monetary policy as effective means of controlling inflation. "My views on the inflation problem have changed (and I trust developed) over the years." Now he opted for the alternative of a form of wage and price controls. These would not be across the board, as was the case during World War II. "It need not cover all industries. No problem exists where there are no unions and where employers obviously have no discretionary power over prices." It is not inappropriate that the public should intervene," wrote Galbraith, "when it is the public that pays."

Once again Galbraith offered bold hypotheses and statements, memorable phrases, and delightful anecdotes in place of the usual apparatus of scholarly verification. Many academic reviewers pointed this out in their journals and in addition noted that most of his ideas were derivative; Galbraith relied heavily (and never denied it) upon Veblen, Keynes, and others. These criticisms stung, although he usually managed to give better than he got, both in debate and in print. And as had been the case with *American Capitalism*, none of this mattered much insofar as the impact the book had on the general public was concerned. With the success and celebrity of *The Affluent Society*, Galbraith achieved an enhanced status as public philosopher, phrase-maker, and all-around wise man on the lecture and television circuit. Around this time too one comes upon references to him by initials—JKG—something usually afforded only presidents, and then not all of them.

During the late Eisenhower years Galbraith taught, lectured widely, and published articles on a variety of subjects in popular magazines. He also began work on a new book, one that would elaborate and expand upon ideas presented in *The Affluent Society*.

All of this was put aside in 1960, when he joined the Kennedy entourage as speechwriter, advisor, and academic talent scout. For a while it appeared Galbraith was headed for a top spot in the Treasury or the chairmanship of the Council of Economic Advisors, but he probably wasn't considered seriously for either posts. Feeling a need to placate the financial community, Kennedy selected Douglas Dillon, a moderate Republican, for Treasury Secretary. Galbraith recommended Paul Samuelson to head the CEA, but Samuelson wasn't interested in a Washington career, and so the post went to Walter Heller instead. As for Galbraith, he told Kennedy of his desire to take the new President's old place in the Senate, but Kennedy wanted him to go to India as his ambassador, and with some reluctance he accepted.

Galbraith spent three months in Washington prior to taking up his post in New Delhi. In his memoir of the Kennedy years, *Ambassador's Journal,* he implies that he did comparatively little in this period outside of trying to get confirmed by the Senate. From India he would send Kennedy advice on economic matters as well as on foreign affairs—among other things, he urged the President to stay out of Vietnam. "Kennedy liked some of Galbraith's economic ideas," said Samuelson, "and he thought a lot of them were awful." Almost from the start Galbraith was at odds with Heller and other somewhat orthodox Keynesians who were trying to talk Kennedy into supporting a tax cut to stimulate the economy. Galbraith argued that taxes should be maintained and that stimulation should come from enlarged spending in the public sector, just the kind of approach one would expect from the author of *The Affluent Society.* Heller later told a writer that "Ken's long shadow kept falling across the scene at the White House—arguing for expenditure increases. Sure, in our hearts we all wanted them. But in our heads, we knew we couldn't get them."

Given the nature of the times and Kennedy's own innate conservatism in such matters—as well as the kind of economists he had around him in Washington—Galbraith's ideas hadn't much chance of being implemented. "Kennedy liked Galbraith," said Samuelson. "People like me were just advisors. People like Ken were friends." But friendship didn't include espousal of what was deemed radical economics and this variety of social experimentation.

In July of 1963 Galbraith left his ambassadorial post to return to Harvard. Some accounts said that he went to Cambridge so as to maintain his tenure, but more likely there wasn't much of a future for him in Washington. Had he gone there he might have become a presidential speech writer and assistant, but this was not for him; as he had written in his journal regarding the plight of Arthur Schlesinger, "No sane man should take a staff position as distinct from some line responsibility in Washington. One should get his power, not from the man above but from the job below. One should be not one of the people the President wants to see but one that he must see." Given this attitude, he was far better off at Harvard, where he would have his own base of operations and from which he could mount intellectual forays.

In any case, the question became moot a few months later, when Kennedy was assassinated. While many of President Johnson's Great Society programs were closer in spirit to Galbraith's views than were those of the New Frontier, the two men had little else in common. Besides, Galbraith opposed the Johnson policies toward Vietnam, which eventually would lead him to take an activist role within the Democratic Party and the Americans for Democratic Action to deny him a second term. Furthermore, he wanted to complete the book he had started in 1960.

This work, *The New Industrial State*, was released in 1967. In his foreword Galbraith writes that it benefited from his "diplomatic interlude," in that he "might have published the more primitive version" had he done so in the early years of the decade. Galbraith goes on to say that it "had its origins alongside *The Affluent Society*. It stands in relation to that book as a house to a window. This is the structure; the earlier book allowed the first glimpse inside."

Once again he had published a derivative work, one that many critics claimed merely updated Veblen's *The Engineers and the Price System* and *The Managerial Revolution* by James Burnham. G. C. Allen, a British economist, summed up much of the feeling when he wrote that "he puts forth as if they were novel and heretical various propositions about industrial society which have been accepted as commonplaces by many economists for several decades." Others would criticize him for using outdated and inadequate material or even for lacking a clear knowledge of the structure and workings of the American business system. "It is unlikely that the economic system can usefully be described either as General Motors writ larger or as the family farm writ everywhere," said Robert Solow of M. I. T. in a particularly devastating review in *The Public Interest* entitled "The New Industrial State, or Son of Affluence." Even in the newspapers and more popular magazines the reception was not as enthusiastic as that which had greeted *The Affluent Society,* perhaps because on this occasion the timing was not as fortuitous nor the central theme as bold and arresting.

The centerpiece of the book can be found in Galbraith's analysis of the development of capitalism, which is somewhat patterned after that found in the opening section of *The Communist Manifesto.* In the eighteenth century, he writes, the landlords were key elements in the economy. Then, with the coming of industrialization, money came to rule and later on, by the process of unionization, labor achieved a measure of power. Just as Marx had done, Galbraith praises the entrepreneurs. "Apart from access to capital, his principal qualifications were imagination, capacity for decision and courage in risking money including, not infrequently, his own." But his day is over. "He is a diminishing figure in the industrial system," writes Galbraith, for that system requires a different kind of talent. Increasingly, knowledge and those who know how to organize it will be required of industrial leaders. "None of these qualifications are especially important for organizing intelligence or effective in competing with it," he writes in his obituary for the businessman. "Power has, in fact, passed to what anyone in search of novelty might be justified in calling a new factor of production," which Galbraith calls the technostructure.

He is not precise in defining it.

> This is a collective and imperfectly defined entity, in the large corporation it embraces chairman, president, those vice presidents with important staff or departmental responsibilities, occupants of other major staff positions and, perhaps, division or department heads . . . It includes, however, only a small proportion of those who, as participants, contribute information to group decisions.

These are leaders of a different kind from Veblen's technocrats, and in fact almost anyone with decision-making powers in a large corporation might be deemed part of the technostructure.

These individuals are not motivated primarily by greed, which is to say they do not wish to maximize earnings to enrich themselves: "The members of the technostructure do not get the profits they maximize," for these do not accrue to them, "but rather remain within the corporation or are distributed to shareholders in the form of dividends." Thus, there is a separation of power and the rewards of power.

Yet the technostructure does attempt to contribute to the growth
of the corporation, for only through growth can they divorce themselves from bankers and others whose funds are needed to keep the
firm going and from shareholder demands for higher dividends and
capital gains. In Galbraith's view, autonomy is their goal, and profits
contribute to making this possible.

The giant corporations developed as they did as a result of technological advances, and as time went on these became more complex and costly. Once it had been possible to conceive an idea for a
product, draw up plans, obtain a plant, and put the items on the
market in a matter of months, and for a relatively small cost. This is
still being done in the enterprise sector of the market, but Galbraith
says that this portion of the economy is declining in importance. For
a giant corporation to do this would require years of planning and
the commitment of enormous amounts of money. Thus, the corporations have to be certain their products will be absorbed by consumers, and, as he had in *The Affluent Society*, Galbraith once again dis-
misses the idea of consumer sovereignty.

Now Galbraith draws these two ideas together. The giant corporation needs compliant consumers, and the best, largest, and most
available of these are governments. "At each point the government
has goals with which the technostructure can identify itself. Or, plau-
sibly, these goals reflect adaption of public goals to the goals of the
technostructure." Six years after Eisenhower's warnings about the
power of the military-industrial complex, Galbraith stated that the
technostructure and the government bureaucrats enjoyed a symbio-
tic relationship. Government contracts are secure and enable the
corporations to marshal energies effectively and make long-range
plans, and government needs the products only the technostructure
can provide. Thus, Galbraith offers a rationale for the continuation
of the Cold War.

The argument concludes with an appeal for change and a means
whereby it might be accomplished. Due to the highly complex nature of modern technology, the technostructure has a continuing
need for educated and trained individuals, for knowledge workers,
and these are turned out by institutions of higher learning. This too
was a familiar idea, one discussed by educators since the end of
World War II. At Galbraith's old home, the University of California,
Clark Kerr had put into practice the concept of multiversity, an
entity that would help guide governments and large corporations.
The Kennedy Administration had been peppered with "multiversi-

tarians," and indeed Galbraith was one of them. Now he called upon his colleagues to divert the technostructure from its goals of foisting unwanted or unnecessary goods upon consumers and government and turn to the pressing needs of society as a whole—those he had sketched in *The Affluent Society.* Characteristically, he does not offer suggestions as to how this will or can be done. Nor does he appear to understand how unrealistic a proposal it is, given not only the position of academics in American life, but the wide diversity of their political and social goals.

Galbraith concludes this book with the hope that "Men will not be entrapped by the belief that apart from the goals of the industrial system—apart from the production of goods and income by progressively more advanced technological methods—there is nothing important in life," and of course he hopes others will accept the path he sees before them. "If other goals are strongly asserted, the industrial system will fall into its place as a detached and autonomous arm of the state, but responsive to the larger purposes of the society."

Some reviewers considered *The New Industrial State* the capstone of what increasingly was called "Galbraithian economics," as distinct from the Keynesian, monetarist, Marxist, and other varieties. In *American Capitalism* he had presented the system more or less in balance as a result of countervailing powers; in *The Affluent Society* Galbraith offered an interpretation of the decline of the market system, the nature of pricing and demand, and the role of the planning system in ruling the economy, and in the end he suggested government redress the balance; finally in *The New Industrial State* he came up with proposals for reforms in a wide variety of areas. Through the three books ran the theme that inflation was built into the system and would have to be dealt with if it was to flourish. Increasingly he became convinced that wage and price controls for the planning sector were the only solution.

There seemed little more that needed saying. But Galbraith was only 59 years old when the last of these books appeared, and he had a national audience. Given the nature of the times it was not surprising that he expanded his activities more than at any previous time in his career.

Within a period of less than three years—from 1967 to 1969— Galbraith published a slender volume on How to *Get Out of Vietnam,* a novel about the State Department *(The Triumph),* and a co-authored effort on *Indian Painting.* His pamphlet on *How to Control the Military* was a rehash of portions of *The New Industrial*

State in which he called for nationalization of the military-industrial complex, and *Ambassador's Journal,* perhaps the best memoir of the Kennedy era and Galbraith's most personal book since *The Scotch.*

Through all of these works, and many articles, speeches, and television appearances, ran the common theme of opposition to the Vietnam War, which Galbraith later said dominated his thinking in this period. As a leader of the Americans for Democratic Action he supported the insurgent candidacy of Eugene McCarthy in 1968 and worked for the alteration of the Democratic Party. But in addition to all of this he managed to produce several articles for academic journals and meetings, and he began work on another book, *Economics and the Public Purpose.*

Had McCarthy won the nomination and gone on to become President, Galbraith might have returned to Washington, perhaps as Treasury Secretary. At it was he went into political opposition, not only to the incumbent Republicans, but to the mainstream of his own party. But he had unexpected rewards to go along with the disappointments. In 1971, as inflationary pressures increased, Galbraith appeared before the Joint Economic Committee to urge wage and price controls, a remedy President Nixon had sworn he never would accept. CEA Chairman Paul McCracken blasted Galbraith in a letter to the *Washington Post* dated July 28. This was a spirited defense of free enterprise and the price system and a slashing attack on its enemies. "Being a novelist and wit, Galbraith can dismiss the problems of carrying out the policy he proposes. Being government officials, we cannot. Being a Democratic partisan, he can proclaim that we are now in an economic crisis. Being the successors to a Democratic Administration, we feel relief at having averted the crisis which the policies of our predecessors were heading." But on August 15 the President announced his New Economic Policy, including wage and price controls, with McCracken in charge of some of its details. That day Treasury Secretary John Connally was asked whether the "American economy is out of kilter because big unions and big corporations have acquired the power to impose wage-price packages on the rest of the economy." To this Galbraithian question Connally offered an equally Galbraithian reply: "I think there is much to be said for that. Yes, I think at some point in the not-too-distant future we're going to have to take a look at the capacity of big business and big labor to abuse power in this country."

The second reward came from academia. At the time of the

Nixonian wage-price freeze Galbraith had been nominated to serve as president of the American Economic Association. He was confirmed in office in December, with no visible opposition of any consequence.

For a while it appeared Galbraith would settle down to a role as gadfly and seer. In 1972 he appeared in tandem with an old friend, William Buckley, in the role of commentator at the national political conventions. He made intellectual contributions to Democratic candidate George McGovern's programs, which were roundly criticized as being far too radical for the national temperament, and so they were, given the results of the election that year. With the advent of the second Nixon Administration Galbraith's public career seemed about to go into eclipse. But there were yet other articles and books to be written. He published several essays on the role of women in the economy and others on the nature and future of capitalism. These were a prelude to the release in 1973 of *Economics and the Public Purpose*, which he implied should be considered his crowning effort.

This book did not receive the kind of critical attention or acclaim given *The Affluent Society*, nor did it achieve the sales of *The New Industrial State*. But in many ways it was a more complete work than either of them, more logical and unified in its conclusions.

As had become his custom, Galbraith uses the first part of this new book to recapitulate arguments presented in earlier volumes. Once again the reader is introduced to the technostructure, the separation of ownership and management, the planning and market sectors of the economy, and the errors of neoclassical economists. There is a new touch in a section on the role of women in the economy, but this really is irrelevant to the main body of the work.

In his previously published books Galbraith carefully distinguished between the planning and market sectors, exploring the strengths and benefits afforded by the former and constrasting these with the weaknesses of the latter. The kinds of planning and economic control he preferred either were not needed by or would be harmful to the market sector, and he lacked a clear-cut means of distinguishing between the two. Now he urged small businessmen to unite so as to achieve greater collective strength, and he would ask the same of professionals and others capable of doing the same. Were this accomplished, we would once again have a kind of geometric harmony not unlike that presented in *American Capitalism*. And this would set the stage for a far-reaching reform effort.

Galbraith would eliminate stockholder capitalism. Owners of shares in large corporations would exchange them for debt obligations and complete ownership would pass to government. "In principle there would be no effect on management from such a change. The stockholder disappears, but the stockholder was previously powerless." He offers as a model the Tennessee Valley Authority in the United States and Renault in France, "which are indistinguishabe in their operations from so-called private ownership."

Private enterprise capitalism thus disposed of, everything falls into place nicely. He would nationalize—or perhaps a better way of putting it would be to say that he would bring under national control—such weak parts of the economy as public transportation, medical care, and housing. "These industries cannot function in the market system. They do not develop in the planning system." And yet they are indispensable. Echoing a message contained in *The Affluent Society*, Galbraith says, "With economic development the contrast between the houses in which the masses of people live, the medical and hospital services they can afford and the conveyances into which they are jammed and the other and more frivolous components of their living standard—automobiles, televison, cosmetics, intoxicants—becomes first striking and then obscene."

The military-industrial complex also would be nationalized. This change, he says, would be "one of form rather than substance," since "for the large, specialized weapons firms the cloak of private enterprise is already perilously, and even indecently thin.'

Finally, Galbraith would institute comprehensive national economic planning, and he does not shrink from calling it by its conventional, familiar name. "For unduly weak industries and unduly strong ones—as a remedy for gross underdevelopment and as a control on gross overdevelopment—the word socialism is one we can no longer suppress," and for a simple reason. "The socialism already exists."

Under Galbraith's version of socialism there would be higher minimum wages, income redistribution from the wealthy to the poor, environmental controls, and wage and price controls so as to contain inflation. All of this, too, was conventional with Galbraith and familiar. But toward the end of the book he throws out an idea, with no analysis, to indicate that more will be heard from him in the future. "National planning systems, operating internationally, also require a measure of international planning." Does he mean to suggest support for an integration of national economies? This is not clear, but with the publication of this book Galbraith passed beyond the range of economics into that of utopia building. For most practitioners of his profession, economics, like politics, is the art of the possible. Today's Galbraith tends to talk more like a prophet and visionary than he does an economist.

Other works followed. Galbraith wrote a light account of his visit to China in 1972 and a popular treatise on *Money: Whence It Came, Where It Went*. He derived a history of economic thought from his television series (*The Age of Uncertainty*), and there were the usual stream of articles, media appearances, and interviews. In 1979 he presented yet another collection of essays and reviews, *Annals of an Abiding Liberal*. Soon it became evident that there would be no major addition to or expansion of *Economics and the Public Purpose*. Insofar as politics was concerned, he was reduced to the role of commentator, analyst, and outsider; there would be no place for Galbraith in the Carter Administration, no further dreams of electoral office. Also, he retired from Harvard, and so departed from academia. Thus, of the three careers he had pursued simultaneously—politics, teaching, and writing—only the last remained, and he didn't seem to have anything new to add to the canon.

Almost Everyone's Guide to Economics came out in 1978, and while other economists would have been delighted by the attention paid it and the sales, neither were up to the old Galbraith standards. This is a simple work, easily comprehended by almost any bright high school student. Nicole Salinger's questions were almost naive, and at times she acted as a straight man for a Galbraith quip. Much attention in this book is played to the problems of inflation, and Galbraith's solution is a Comprehensive Incomes and Price Policy, or CIPP for short. In effect, this is permanent wage and price controls, a policy Galbraith had been advocating for years. And in a nation plagued by inflation, it may be we will have it yet. But if and when it comes, it may do so without Galbraith.

Shortly before this book appeared Frederick J. Praston released a study entitled *Perspectives on Galbraith*. In it Robert Solow was asked about his place in the history of economic thought. "I think Ken will be remembered as an historian and a philosopher," he replied, "but I don't think he will be primarily remembered as an economist. Economics is becoming more and more a technical subject like dentistry. Ken is not going to strike the future as a great dentist."

This is fair enough. Whether or not it will turn out as Solow

indicates depends to a large extent on where the nation will be
headed over the next two or three decades. If Galbraith's solutions
to inflation and his prescriptions for planning are accepted by future
governments, he may look like a prophet to historians writing a century from now. Yet Solow—an important figure in current academic
thinking—is correct, for even now many of his colleagues still think
of Galbraith as little more than a gifted amateur. But he will retain
a large audience for as long as he cares to speak and write. He also
might reflect that no one is writing or thinking of putting together
a popular book for general readers entitled *Perspectives on Solow.*

5

PAUL SAMUELSON

NINE MONTHS AFTER JOHN KENNEDY delivered his memorable Inaugural Address, one of his more important economic advisors, Paul Samuelson, gave his own as the new president of the American Economic Association. Early in the talk he noted that his scholarship had been in a wide variety of areas.

> Many of them involve questions like welfare economics and factor-price equalization; turnpike theorems and osculating envelopes; nonsubstitutability relations between Minkowski-Ricardo-Leontief-Metzler matrices of Mosak-Hicks type; or balanced budget multipliers under conditions of balanced uncertainty in locally impacted topological spaces and molar equivalances.

Having delivered himself of this list, he added, "My friends warn me that such topics are suitable merely for captive audiences in search of a degree—and even then not after dark." Instead, Samuelson's topic that evening would be one on which he had written many illuminating essays: "Economists and the History of Ideas." He then proceeded to list and comment upon the individuals he considered the most important and influential economists of all time. These included the familiar names—Adam Smith, David Ricardo, John Stuart Mill, Karl Marx, Alfred Marshall—with a bow at the end in the direction of John Maynard Keynes. But he opened with a few words on the way reputations are made, in which he paid a form of homage to "one of our members who is far away tonight toiling on a distant shore." He was referring to Galbraith, who already had taken up his office in New Delhi.

Nowadays, he remarked, you don't obtain prestigious chairs of economics "by virtue of your social eloquence; indeed, until academic tenure has come, you are best advised not to write for *Harper's* or the *Manchester Guardian* (to say nothing of the *National Review* or the *New Republic*) lest you be indicted for superficiality." It has gotten to the point, thought Samuelson, where "Good writing itself can be suspect," and so Galbraith has suffered for that sin. In particular, he referred to the way some economists denigrated *The Affluent Society*. Most works by economists either are read only by their fellow professionals or reach a barely larger audience: *The Affluent Society* was not for these but for all literate people. "When we economists think how often in recent years people have been asking us, 'What do you think of *The Affluent Society?*'—and how embarrassing the question has been to so many of us busy beavers—we can appreciate that this work stands as good a chance as any of being read and remembered twenty years from now."

Such generosity on the part of one world-famous economist for another is not unusual. These people know one another fairly well; their paths cross in Washington, professional meetings, and the lecture circuit. Despite ideological differences they comprise a close-knit and exclusive fraternity, held together by respect for intellect and accomplishment if not for politics. More than any of them, perhaps, Samuelson can afford to be generous, for he occupies a position in modern economics that is unique. As indicated in his presidential address, his scholarly work covers a wide field. *The Collected Scientific Papers of Paul A. Samuelson*, a three-volume work that takes in the period from 1937 to 1971, contains 335 items, and fills close to 2,700 pages. This does not include testimony before congressional committees and many speeches and articles in popular magazines. Nor does it contain columns from *Newsweek* magazine, which reach a wider audience than do Galbraith's books.

And of course there is his famous text, *Economics: An Introductory Analysis*, the first edition of which appeared in 1948, to be followed by a new one every three years thereafter. A careful reading of the consecutive editions would be the best way to trace the development of mainstream neo-Keynesian thought since the end of

World War II, a situation duly noted by many radical and conservative economists. Each new edition is reviewed in the journals as though it were a contribution to economic knowledge. For years Marxist economists have looked upon Samuelson as the leading proponent of reform capitalist views, and he remains their chief target. Conventional economists may attack Galbraith in their journals; who but Samuelson would become the subject of a two-volume effort by Marxist Marc Linder, called *Anti-Samuelson?* Nothing more is needed than the simple title; every economist knows what to expect—an exegesis of what some say has been the most influential text ever written.

This is so not only because a large majority of students in freshman economics courses have been required to obtain a copy of the book but rather because the professors teach from it. The words the class hears will be those of Dr. Jones, but chances are the ideas expounded will be pure or adulterated Samuelson. Galbraith has instructed the postwar, literate reading public in his variety of economics. Samuelson has performed that duty for members of his profession; he has interpreted modern Keynesian ideas for his peers.

At the time Samuelson was awarded the Nobel Prize in 1970, most people thought it had been for reason of the text, but in fact the honor came as a result of the hundreds of papers contained in the less-familiar *Scientific Papers.* His Memorial Lecture in Stockholm, entitled: "Maximum Principles in Analytical Economics," was a vintage effort. There was something in it for nearly everyone. The text is clear, the mathematics elegant (but for lay persons probably incomprehensible), with forays into economic history, references to his previous works, and touches of humor.

Toward the end of his talk, Samuelson complained of not being able in a single lecture even to scratch the surface of the issue, and with that he veered off in another direction, noting that "one of my abiding concerns over the years has been in the field of welfare economics." Why this switch? Perhaps it was because Samuelson wanted to end his talk with a story and a message, neither of which had anything to do with the title. The story concerns H. J. Davenport, a friend of Thorstein Veblen and an economist of some note in his day. Davenport once said, "There is not reason why theoretical economics should be a monopoly of the reactionaries." "All my life I have tried to take this warning to heart," said Samuelson, "and I dare call it to your favorable attention."

But Davenport's stricture, which may have been true for turn-of-the-century America, is badly outdated. In the American context at least, people he would call "reactionaries" haven't been able to obtain much of a hearing, either in academia or before the general public, for close to half a century, and they even lack a first-rate text with which to challenge Samuelson in freshman courses. And while Milton Friedman remains a giant of the political and economic right, Samuelson dominates center stage and a portion of the left as well. In this regard, he has no real rival.

Samuelson was born in Gary, Indiana, in 1915. His father, who owned a small drugstore there, was a moderate socialist and a middle class businessman, which was not a contradiction in that period. When Paul was eight years old the family moved to Chicago and another drug store. Samuelson says he has fond memories of growing up in the Midwest during the 1920s and 1930s. Though he often alludes to the problems of being one of the few Jews in the places he lived, he clearly was in the midst of a circle of loving relatives, and he had little fear of deprivation. He also speaks of a mathematics teacher at Hyde Park High, Beulah Shoesmith, who influenced many of her students to go on to achieve eminence and who apparently had that kind of impact upon him.

As a young man Samuelson wasn't sure what he wanted to do with his life. He was interested in all of the social sciences as well as most of the sciences, and he could have gone off in any of a dozen directions. But his choice of a college presented no problem; he would attend the University of Chicago, which was within walking distance of his home.

The New Deal was about to begin. America was headed into a period of intense liberal reformism, one in which the tenets of free enterprise capitalism would come under heavy and continued attack. And at the height of this movement, Samuelson would study at the school which, then as now, was the citadel of laissez-faire economic thought.

What Harvard was becoming for Keynesianism, Chicago already was for neoclassical economics. Frank Knight, a leading figure in the attack on Keynes, was a star of the economics department and in his prime. Jacob Viner, the conservative economic historian, made his contribution too, as did Henry Simon, who rehabilitated monetary theory and used it as a weapon against Alvin Hansen and his Harvard colleagues. These men were training the next generation of neoclassicists—Milton Friedman was at Chicago when Samuelson arrived, and so was George Stigler, whose dry wit would later make him one of the few economists capable of matching Galbraith in irony and metaphor.

Samuelson came to the University with a deficiency in economics, and so he was enrolled in an introductory course taught by Aaron Director, perhaps the most libertarian member of the faculty —who later became Milton Friedman's brother-in-law and beside whom the more famous economist seemed almost a socialist. Director and others at Chicago challenged Samuelson's innate reformism at a time when it seemed the American economic system was cracking up and change was in the air. Samuelson enjoyed the clashes but did not become a believer. Rather, as the Hoover Administration appeared to founder, he drifted further into a Keynesian orbit. Thus, he was something of an intellectual loner as an undergraduate—and he seemed to enjoy this too.

Through most of this period he was undecided as to his major and toyed with the idea of a career in sociology, biology, or anthropology. Given a stimulating teacher, Samuelson would become a temporary convert to the discipline, if not to an ideology. This would continue until he came across the next interesting person or subject, when the process would be repeated. Apparently Samuelson continued to do well in whatever he undertook, and he remained cocky and self-confident, no small accomplishment in the depths of the Great Depression.

Toward the end of his stay at Chicago, Samuelson decided to became an economist. He received his B.A. in 1935, and in that year was also awarded one of the eight Social Science Research Council fellowships in that subject. Characteristically, he decided to continue his studies at Harvard, where he would receive an entirely different perspective on the subject. Now he came under the influence of Alvin Hansen and took courses with Joseph Schumpeter and Wassily Leontief, three of the nation's most important scholars. Galbraith was a young instructor in this period, and also on the campus were many other men who later on would make their marks in the profession—Henry Wallich, Robert Triffin, and James Tobin are among the best known and most influential. This was, perhaps, one of the most exciting periods in the history of academic economics, when an open and often impolite struggle was waging between the neoclassicists and the Keynesians. Samuelson was one of the few people who had put in significant time at both command posts.

In 1936, Samuelson's second year at Harvard, Keynes published his *General Theory of Employment, Interest and Money,* one of the half-dozen most important books of the past century. Hansen was prepared to interpret it for American audiences, and Samuelson was equipped to appreciate the work. "I have always considered it a priceless advantage to have been born an economist prior to 1936 and to have received a thorough grounding in classical economics," wrote Samuelson ten years later. "It is quite impossible for modern students to realize the full effect of what has been advisedly called 'The Keynesian Revolution' on those of us brought up in the orthodox tradition." It couldn't have gone off better if planned.

As Samuelson recalled, *"The General Theory* caught most economists under the age of thirty-five with the unexpected virulence of a disease first attacking and decimating an isolated tribe of South Sea islanders. Economists beyond fifty turned out to be quite immune to the ailment. With time, most economists in-between began to run the fever, often without knowing or admitting their condition." Samuelson was 21 years old in 1936.

The following year he produced his first scholarly articles, "A Note on Measurement of Utility," which appeared in *The Review of Economic Studies,* and "Some Aspects of the Pure Theory of Capital" for *The Quarterly Review of Economics.* An additional five articles appeared the following year, all in prestigious journals and all studded with equations. Samuelson was writing for the profession, and in a way that would win him respect from his elders.

In an article entitled "Interactions Between the Multiplier Analysis and the Principle of Acceleration," Samuelson made what his peers considered an important contribution to Keynesian thought. In addition, he presented an idea from which would later develop a key doctrine of mainstream economics in the Kennedy years. "A constant level of governmental expenditure will result in an ever-increasing national income, eventually approaching a compound interest rate of growth," he believed. "A single impulse of net investment will likewise send the system up to infinity at a compound interest rate of growth." Thus, while a capitalistic economy may undergo cyclical fluctuations such as those described by Wesley Mitchell, these could be controlled and even—given proper methods—eliminated. Samuelson presented a model for this in his article but no empirical evidence. He did not apologize for this. "Contrary to the impression commonly held, mathematical methods, properly employed, far from making economy theory more abstract, actually serve as a powerful liberating device enabling the entertainment and analysis of ever more realistic and complicated hypotheses."

Arthur Burns and others at the National Bureau frowned upon such practice. How could one generalize about the impact of investment upon the business cycle without gathering together the kind of data required to support the conclusion? Burns had done this for his set of comparatively modest theories in *Measuring Business Cycles;* Samuelson had attempted to dispose of a significant aspect of the nature of growth in advanced capitalist societies in a matter of four pages. This was more than an argument between pre-Keynesian and Keynesian brands of economics. It was an important indication of the differences in approaches between historically minded institutionalists like Burns and the coming generation of econometricians, one of whose leaders Samuelson appeared to have become.

Samuelson was awarded his Ph.D. in 1941, by which time he had published close to a score of scholarly articles, some of which were elaborations upon basic Keynesianism and which taken together marked him as a fast-rising economist of that school. His dissertation, somewhat immodestly entitled *Foundations of Economic Analysis* in its published form, received the David A. Wells Prize, awarded annually to Harvard's outstanding economics thesis. Although it was not published until after the war, the work's methodology and approach were known earlier within the profession and would be expounded upon in Samuelson's many articles of the period. *Foundations* is the rock upon which the author's academic reputation was erected.

As the title indicates, this book is an attempt to present a basic, unified view of the methodology of analysis. It does not contain a radical, arresting, or novel message, such as that found in *The Affluent Society,* for example. Although the work is still in print and has been translated into many languages, it is close to being incomprehensible to the lay reader. There is no central theory in this work. Samuelson did present an analysis of the way consumers make choices, called revealed preference, which is more a critique of the uses of index numbers than anything else. Also, he elaborated upon some of Hansen's ideas regarding Keynesian constructs, which was more of interest to readers of *Econometrica* and *The Annals of Mathematical Statistics* than to those of *Harper's* or the *New York Times Magazine.*

The true significance of *Foundations* can be found more in Samuelson's language than his ideas. Where the neoclassicists employed words and sentences to convey ideas, he would utilize numbers and equations. Samuelson was hardly unique in this; the 1930s and early

1940s was a period during which mathematical economics was on the rise, and one might barely get through the *General Theory* without a knowledge of calculus. Furthermore, it was not even new; Léon Walras, a French economist of the late nineteenth and early twentieth century, had presented economic ideas mathematically, most notably in *Elements of Pure Economics,* and this work, more than the *General Theory,* provided much of the inspiration for *Foundations.* (In his presidential address, Samuelson would say, "Today there can be little doubt that most of the literary and mathematical economic theory appearing in our professional journals is more an offspring of Walras than of anyone else.")

Samuelson preferred mathematical to verbal statements, not because such formulations were value-free—in fact he takes pains to deny this is the case. Rather, he was seeking the kind of precision numbers made possible. "The laborious literary working over of essentially simple mathematical concepts such as is characteristic of much of modern economic theory is not only unrewarding from the standpoint of advancing the science, but involves as well mental gymnastics of a peculiarly depraved type," he says in his preface; but toward what goal?—to find regularities in theory, which presumably would lead to the creation of an economic model, with the next step being the setting forth of policy and prediction. What Arthur Burns hoped to find in his compendium of time series, Samuelson expected to uncover in economic theory. Either man might have written these words that appear at the beginning of *Foundations:* "It is proposed here to investigate these common features in the hope of demonstrating how it is possible to deduce general principles which can serve to unify large sectors of present day economic theory." But what follows in Samuelson is a mathematical demonstration of Keynesian constructs; in contrast, Burns would have tried to show correlations and advance or lag sequences between various industries over time.

That *Foundations* was a major contribution to American Keynesian thought was generally acknowledged, and the award of the Wells Prize seemed to mark Samuelson as Hansen's logical successor at Harvard. But he faced obstacles there difficult if not impossible to overcome. In the early 1940s Harvard, like many other colleges and universities, practiced a barely disguised form of anti-Semitism when it came to making appointments. Some Jewish academics who knew and accepted most of the rules of the game and were adept in the ways of campus politics were able to overcome this; usually such individuals also had powerful sponsors and somewhat inept opponents as well. But Samuelson was cocky and had long irritated his chairman, Harold Hitchings Burbank. He was too promising to pass over entirely, and so was given an instructorship—this being a slap in the face considering his publications and the degree of fame he already had achieved. Still, Samuelson wanted to remain in the area, so he took the post. Then the Massachusetts Institute of Technology approached him with an offer of an assistant professorship, which was accepted. "It will take half a century for the department to recover from that anti-Semitism," said Harvard economist Otto Eckstein in 1979. "Harvard lost the most outstanding economist of the generation."

During World War II Samuelson served as consultant for the National Resources Planning Board and, later on, the War Production Board. In 1945 he went to the Fletcher School of Law and Diplomacy to offer a course in international economic relations. But for the most part he remained at M.I.T., teaching his classes and helping develop computer techniques for tracking airplanes at the school's Radiation Laboratory.

Samuelson continued to produce scholarly articles in this period, and in these he attempted to describe in mathematical language the workings of the economy. But one of the most important tasks of economics is to offer predictions and make policy statements, and he was not prepared then to extract these from his theoretical works. At the same time, however, Samuelson could not resist the temptation to engage in debates. In articles in popular magazines and political journals he set down his thoughts on where the country was headed and what should be done. In place of his usual mathematical constructs was clear and even vivid prose; there is no evidence of model making or theory here but instead historical development and exposition. This other side of Samuelson—the journalist—would become increasingly important after the war.

The message in most of these articles was that there would be a major depression when the fighting ended and that the government would have to use Keynesian methods to bring about a recovery. The logic was inescapable. With the closing down of procurement programs and the disbandment of the Army and Navy would come large scale unemployment and underutilization of plant capacity. It would be the 1930s all over again. With the exception of Keyserling and a handful of others, a majority of economists saw trouble ahead, and Samuelson was one of that number. There might be a short boom when controls were ended, he thought, but this surely would be followed by a collapse such as that experienced in 1919–1920. In a 1943 essay entitled "Full Employment After the War," Samuelson recommended vigorous government intervention:

> The final conclusion to be drawn from our experience at the end of the last war is inescapable. Were the war to end suddenly within the next 6 months, were we again planlessly to wind up our war effort in the greatest haste, to demobilize our armed forces, to liquidate price controls, to shift from astronomical deficits to even the large deficits of the thirties—then there would be ushered in the greatest period of unemployment and industrial dislocation which any economy has ever faced.

He repeated this message several times in the next year and a half. In a two-part article in the *New Republic* that came out in autumn 1944, Samuelson warned that the end of the fighting would be followed by a replay of the 1930s' depression.

He couldn't have been more wrong, and for several years thereafter Samuelson hedged his predictions, though in the 1950s and 1960s he gradually threw off his caution. These were the two aspects to the man. When dealing in generalities, Samuelson was as positive and as certain of results as any doctrinaire social scientist. He was more circumspect when interpreting specific problems. There were just too many variables to consider, he would write, to claim that the implementation of a program would have a definite quantifiable impact upon employment, inflation, or growth. In 1956, in an article entitled "Economic Forecasting and National Planning," he warned that those economists who publish forecasts are doomed to be misunderstood or misinterpreted. Professionals understand and appreciate the complexities and subtleties of the economy and the limits of prediction. "But the clients of forecasters, in Congress and out, tend to be confused by anything but a single figure, and few have learned how to use such probability spreads in private or political decision-making."

Samuelson conceded that advances in economic knowledge and analytical techniques made it possible to offer more accurate predictions in the late 1950s than had been possible a generation earlier. Still, forecasts were based upon assumptions regarding the development of the economy, prices, foreign affairs, political leadership, alterations in taste, and many other factors. "I think we're converging toward a kind of irreducible Brownian motion," he said around this time, "or you could give it a highfalutin name like the Heisenberg indeterminacy principle, because God Almighty hasn't made up His mind as to what business investment is going to be next year, so how can we read tea leaves and find out what it is?" He continued to hold to this opinion twenty years later, when he told an interviewer that he saw "no sign of anything, under present methodology, converging toward great accuracy."

Samuelson was a public figure by then, a scholar whose advice was sought and often accepted. This presented him with a dilemma. Insofar as his social goals were concerned, Samuelson might be described as a New Deal-Fair Deal Democrat with egalitarian inclinations. As a professional, however, he was a leading advocate of mathematical economics, not only because it was precise but also because such an approach was value-free and thus more scientific. One part of him called for political action to eliminate major problems, the other informed him that certainty was not possible, that economists lacked the ability to unravel most complex issues and offer diagnosis, much less prescription. Samuelson might be bold in setting forth a set of social goals or in creating theoretical constructs —"pure theories" in the professional vernacular—but when it came to offering programs and coupling them with specific predictions, he became temperate and even cautious.

Generally speaking, the larger the issue Samuelson has to address, the more expansive he will be in analysis and recommendation. On such occasions the reformer in him speaks, and this side of him can best be seen in his journalism and some of his speeches and political presentations. Samuelson the scientist emerges in his recommendations regarding specific rather than aggregate issues, in debates with other economists, and of course in his scholarship. More than any other major economist, he covers the entire field, not only in content but in form as well. That such a situation would develop might have been anticipated a quarter of a century ago, given Samuelson's interests and ideology.

In some respects, Samuelson's professional approach is a mirror image of Galbraith's (though their social goals are often quite similar). Galbraith is most comfortable when making vast generalizations on a qualitative basis; Samuelson prefers to investigate specific, limited problems and then set down conclusions in the form of equations. The former economist is an institutionalist concerned with macroproblems, while the latter thinks of himself as an analyst dealing for the most part with microeconomics. There are Galbraithians with clearly defined tenets and objectives; although he is admired by his peers, Samuelson has never put down a specific agenda for programmatic change or considered seriously setting down his vision of the future as Galbraith did in *Economics and the Public Purpose*. Galbraith sought a major political role in the 1960s and failed to achieve his ambitions; in that decade Samuelson was offered more power and influence than he was prepared to accept. Galbraith spent a professional lifetime setting forth a doctrine on containing inflation, while Samuelson became the leading apostle of growth in the Kennedy-Johnson years. Neither man has enunciated important ideas in the preserve of the other.

These two also are at opposite poles within the profession, for they stand for different roles economists might play in our culture. Galbraith presents a model for those who hope to achieve celebrity and influence the thinking of the general public; more than anyone else, he has made the subject intelligible to laypeople. As for Samuelson, he is one of a long line of scholars who have shown students the ways to achieve professional success, the esteem of their peers, and a distinguished if limited public role.

Samuelson climbed the academic ladder with ease. In 1947, the same year *Foundations* was published, he was promoted to full professor and also won the first John Bates Clark Award for the most distinguished work by an economist under the age of 40—he was 37 at the time. Samuelson had his pick of advanced courses but insisted upon teaching a section of introductory economics. Out of this came his classic text, which, as has been indicated, appeared the following year and within a decade captured half the market.

To say that *Economics: An Introductory Analysis* caused a revolution in the way the subject was taught would be going too far, but it clearly was written from a different perspective than most of the texts it replaced. No single work dominated the field in 1948, but almost all the important ones were institutional in approach, which is to say the material was organized and presented a historical and narrative fashion.

Elementary Economics by Fred Fairchild, Edgar Furniss, and Norman Buck, all of whom were on the Yale faculty, was fairly typical of the pre-1948 texts. This book first appeared in 1924, had gone through several editions, and provided a model of sorts for its imitators. "The plan of this book has dictated the continuous combination of theoretical analysis with historical narrative and discussion of practical problems," wrote the authors in one of their prefaces.

"Theory must be illustrated and justified by showing its relation to practical affairs." Furthermore, "We have sought to spare the student the confusion that comes from taking for granted knowledge which he cannot fairly be assumed to possess, and the treatment is correspondingly elementary." By this was meant that few new terms were introduced, and these were explained carefully. *Elementary Economics* contained only a handful of graphs and charts and, even in the late 1940s, no complex equations. The authors had chapters on the industrial revolution, the principles of banking, foreign exchange, government regulation of the railroads, and the farm problem. Today this kind of text might be used in a course in economic history offered by an historian; prior to Samuelson, this was the way freshman were introduced to economics.

They did not have to fight their way through abstract theories. Fairchild, Furniss, and Buck included no references to Keynes or Marshall. There was nothing on Adam Smith or David Ricardo. Marx was introduced as a historical figure, not as an analytical economist. Students interested in matters such as these, as well as in pure theory, might find them covered in advanced courses at only the better schools and sometimes not even there. Building upon the Fairchild, Furniss, and Buck foundation, an economics department might offer such intermediate courses as money and banking, foreign trade, agricultural economics, and labor economics. In the mid-1940s, an economics student at a decent college need not have known calculus or even the meaning of the term econometrics.

The early editions of Samuelson contained elements of this approach. There were chapters on the nature of a mixed capitalist enterprise system, business organization, the Federal Reserve System, and international trade. But in addition he introduced his readers to the theory of comparative advantage, monetary theory, equilibrium theory, and the like. As for ideological bent, Samuelson claimed he had written in the broad vein of neoclassicism, which in the third edition he defined as "a synthesis of the valid core of modern income determination with the classical economic principles. Its basic tenet is this: Solving the vital problems of monetary and fiscal policy by the tools of income analysis will *validate* and bring back into relevance the classical verities." Thus, he hoped this work would be looked upon as centrist insofar as doctrine was concerned. Still, he incorporated into it Keynesianism and New Deal thought and showed how some of the new ideas were not incompatible with the old.

The instructors and professors who had used Fairchild, Furniss, and Buck would have been able to teach from the first three or four editions of *Economics* without much difficulty. Over the years, however, additional theoretical and mathematical materials were introduced, while some of the institutional chapters either were eliminated or combined. The book remained quite readable, but, true to his natural bent, Samuelson attempted to wean students from words and toward numbers. There are sections in the tenth edition (1976), such as those dealing with price and income determination, that would have given students of the 1930s a great deal of difficulty, while an appendix on the "Rudiments of Marxist Economics" might have been beyond the grasp of some instructors left over from that period.

Samuelson would add new chapters and drop old ones in successive editions as the issues facing the nation were altered. For example, in the late 1950s and early 1960s he covered such ground as the economics of war and defense and growth in underdeveloped areas of the world, while in the middle 1970s he included material on sexual discrimination, ecology and growth, and, significantly, full employment and price stability. In each edition was a chapter on the history of theory, subtitled "Evolution of Economic Doctrine" in the latest one, that concludes with a brief introduction to the ideas of the New Left, for which Samuelson has little regard. At the end of the chapter, in "Questions for Discussion," he asks, "Now that you've studied economics, how have your economic views changed?" The discipline would have been seen through a Samuelsonian prism, of course, and this would have affected the answers significantly.

During the 1950s Samuelson appeared before congressional committees to offer his ideas regarding current problems, and he also conferred with important Democratic leaders, in the process becoming one of the party's in-house experts. He was critical of the Eisenhower Administration's policies for fighting inflation, which he believed required unnecessary sacrifices of economic growth for what amounted to relatively small gains in price stability. Samuelson believed inflation to be troublesome but hardly deadly, and in any case could be avoided by the proper use of fiscal and monetary policies, to which were added reforms in the tax code to encourage capital formation and redistribute income. There was little new in this; Keyserling had said as much a decade earlier. Nevertheless, Samuelson helped lead the way in the creation of the new econom-

ics of the 1960s. His development of the doctrine and later concession that it was flawed provided one of the more graphic examples of the failure of neo-Keynesianism to meet the problems of
the following decade.

During testimony before a congressional committee in 1956, Samuelson sketched his current thinking on important issues and as an
aside offered suggestions on how economists might be utilized by
government and what he would recommend if called upon to do so.
He reiterated his belief that "economic science is not only neutral
as to the question of the desired rate of capital accumulation—it is
also neutral as to the ability of the economy to realize any decided-
on rate of capital formation." Samuelson implied that the economists who served in the White House might function best as technicians—the Nourse approach. They could respond to specific inquiries regarding the impacts of spending and tax programs upon
wages and inflation, unemployment, and other variables. Each economist would have different ideas on the subject, but those who
achieved seats of power should be circumspect in making recommendations, for they risked relinquishing their scientific credentials
in order to become apologists. He conceded that few would be able
to resist the temptation. In any case, Presidents knew enough to
select men who mirrored their own ideas. Six years later, after tast-
ing power, Samuelson would say that "the leaders of this world may
seem to be led around through the nose by their economic advisors.
But who is pulling and who is pushing? And note this: he who picks
his own doctor from an array of competing doctors is in a real sense
his own doctor. The Prince often gets to hear what he wants to
hear."

Samuelson thought Eisenhower had done just this in bringing
Burns into his inner circle, but he also believed the economic advice he received was inadequate and wrong-headed, based on the
false assumption that a nation had to sacrifice growth in order to
achieve stability. This was the core of his prescriptive economics in
the late 1950s. (In the course of a debate with Burns a decade later,
Samuelson would call the fiscally stringent policies of the second
Eisenhower Administration—after Burns had left Washington—an
"investment in sadism" which made little sense given the current
state of economic knowledge.)

Was any other program possible? Samuelson appeared certain
that one existed. "With proper fiscal and monetary policies, our economy can have full employment and whatever rate of capital forma-

tion and growth it wants," he told the Joint Economic Committee. Furthermore, "a community can have full employment, can at the same time have a rate of capital formation it wants, and can accomplish all of this compatibly with the degree of income-redistribution it ethically desires."

Statements such as this one reflect the high optimism of the period as well as Samuelson's penchant for sweeping generalizations when speaking on nonspecific topics before a nonprofessional audience. He did not indicate how such a happy condition could be obtained, and the committee members did not think to ask him to do so. Doubtless Samuelson's extravagance on this occasion was an attention grabber. Nevertheless it did reflect his state of mind. Implicit in the statement was his growing belief that government intervention of this kind could bring about permanent prosperity and growth. This placed him at odds with the Eisenhower economists who were content to recommend measures to prevent excesses and abuses but otherwise would do little, and not tinker with the complex organism Arthur Burns often described in his lectures and papers. In other words, they believed Washington had no clear obligation to stimulate business or make certain the economy ran near its full capacity.

Samuelson had come to feel otherwise. To him unused capacity was wasteful, to be avoided if possible. And it was possible. Given the state of economic knowledge, economists could make the capitalist machine operate more efficiently. From this might be drawn a logical conclusion: government had an obligation not only to prevent a new depression or hold back inflation but also to assure as great a measure of growth as feasible and that this would imply an almost continual intervention in the economy—what later would be called "fine tuning." Furthermore, Samuelson was indicating that capitalism could be reformed—that socialists and Galbraithians were incorrect in considering it a moribund system.

This was Samuelson's major theme in the 1960s and afterwards. In this period he took positions on a wide variety of issues that placed his squarely in the activist wing of the Democratic Party. Yet he remained eclectic in matters of economic doctrine, as he had earlier. Unlike Galbraith, there was no kernel of a single, critical idea present in his writings that developed and matured over the years. Nor was there a complete merging of his social activism and impartial professionalism, though on occasion in the 1960s he appeared about to cross the boundaries. It is this division that enables

Samuelson to remain an economic scientist. Of all the soothsayers discussed in this work, he alone has rejected the role of political economist.

Samuelson likes to test his ideas in debates with other economists, sometimes on public podiums, more often in the journals, and it is here his style can best be appreciated. For example, in a paper entitled "The Pure Theory of Public Expenditure" that appeared in a 1954 issue of *The Review of Economics and Statistics,* he set down a proposition that was every bit as all-encompassing as any he would present before nonprofessional groups. "Given sufficient knowledge the optimal decisions can always be found by scanning over all the attainable states of the world and selecting the one which according to the postulated ethical welfare function is best. The solution 'exists'; the problem is now to 'find' it." Called to task for this simplistic notion and for other, similar statements, Samuelson responded by publishing "Diagrammatic Exposition of a Theory of Public Expenditure" in the same journal a year-and-a-half later. Under similar circumstances Galbraith might have relied upon wit and sarcasm to demolish foes, Keyserling would have gone on the attack, while Burns might have ignored it all. But true to his approach in such matters, Samuelson reconsidered his words, moderated some of them, and managed to gracefully alter his views. In particular, he backed down from earlier recommendations that government programs might be fashioned after a survey was made of contemporary practices. "One might even venture the tentative suspicion that any function of government not possessing any trace of the defined public good . . . ought to be carefully scrutinized to see whether it is truly a legitimate function of government."

Statements such as these, which might have come from a Friedmanite, caused some to complain that Samuelson presented a moving target, that he never remained in one place long enough for critics to mount an attack upon his position—in fact, that he lacked positions and at base was little more than a theorist of methodology. This was overstated, for with all of his calls for value-free science, Samuelson possessed a clear-cut political philosophy and set of social goals. Unlike Galbraith and Friedman, however, he usually seemed aware of the limitations that clashing beliefs imposed upon practice, and the frailties of scientific economics when confronted by political realities.

Given his growing prestige, interest in public policy, and, most of all, his outgoing personality, Samuelson was drawn to the fringes of politics. No matter which Democrat emerged to lead the party in the 1960s, he eventually would have had to seek advice from Samuelson and his kind. As it happened, his most important political encounter occurred as much as a result of geography as of shared beliefs.

As a representative and later senator from Massachusetts, John Kennedy was deemed a conservative on many economic and social issues, or, at the very most, a moderate. From the first, he had presidential ambitions, and, as Franklin Roosevelt had done in the early 1930s, he assembled a group of academics from his state to assist in the creation of programs and policies. Most came out of Harvard—Law School Professor Archibald Cox was one of the main organizers and talent scouts, while Seymour Harris, still the nation's most prominent Keynesian, was also there. Galbraith was close to Kennedy at this time, more out of friendship and a desire to continue in the education of the man he had known as a student than from any agreement with the politician's rather conventional ideas. In 1958, as Kennedy positioned himself for the presidential nomination, others were brought into what was called the "academic advisory committee," and Samuelson was in this group. Soon it became evident that his approach was more compatible with Kennedy's political eclecticism than was that of Galbraith and the others. As the election approached, his intellectual influence increased.

This is not to suggest that Kennedy was knowledgeable in economics or a Keynesian. During the primaries he was considerably more conservative than Hubert Humphrey, and in the election campaign he took some positions to the right of Richard Nixon. Shortly before Election Day, he said: "First, we are pledged to maintain a balanced budget except in times of national emergency or severe recession. Furthermore, we will seek to maintain a budget surplus in times of prosperity as a brake on inflationary forces." Such a view was somewhat at variance with his pledge to "get the country moving again" and his willingness to increase military spending so as to "close the missile gap."

Perhaps this rhetoric was part of the electioneering process, but it certainly did not make Kennedy look like an innovator. Throughout the campaign he was criticized by old New Dealers and Fair Dealers as a conservative, a person who would reject the heritage of Franklin Roosevelt and Harry Truman once in office. Leon Keyserling said as much on several occasions, as did Rex Tugwell.

The Kennedy people disregarded their Democratic counterparts of the FDR-HST period; even Eleanor Roosevelt was looked upon more as a symbol of the past than a resource for the future. By October it was evident that a Kennedy victory would bring a new group of people to power in the White House, with ideas and programs different from those of past Democratic administrations, and it also was manifest that the candidate himself hoped to be seen as a fiscal conservative so as to mollify the business community.

Shortly after the election, Samuelson was named to head a task force on the economy. In early January 1961, the President-elect's office released a document that was put together by this group and written by Samuelson. Entitled "Prospects and Policies for the 1961 American Economy," it was supposed to become part of the incoming Administration's policy agenda. There was little in it that any conventional Democratic economist of the 1940s or 1950s could have argued with, and certainly was in no way novel or radical. Those who hoped to find in it Samuelson's prescription for growth without inflation or unemployment were disappointed.

This was so because Samuelson continued to be a practitioner of the possible. By this time he and other Keynesians had become convinced that the skillful use of tax cuts and tax revision would stimulate business, aid recovery, produce increased tax revenues, and so balance the budget and maintain a strong dollar while unemployment declined. But he also knew that Kennedy would never consider such an approach, not only because it was unusual but also because he was calling upon the nation to make sacrifices, and a tax cut in the face of this would appear absurd. Having worked with the candidate for several months, Samuelson knew that he would prefer a set of recommendations that would result in balanced budgets, the kind that might appeal to a major portion of the Eisenhower constituency poised to label him as a wild spender intent on leading the nation into ever-expanding deficits. This kind of program hardly could be expected from the variety of economists Kennedy had gathered around him during the campaign and certainly not from Samuelson.

Later on some would claim that his economists were busily instructing the incoming President in the essentials of the new economics during the interregnum and that the lessons did not take hold for several months. While it was true that Kennedy was more conservative and conventional in his economic ideas in 1961 than he would be two years later, he probably was influenced more by political considerations than economic ideology in this period. As

Walter Lippman observed, "Kennedy's domestic policies don't reflect those of his economic advisors. They are sound, modern men, and the only reason he isn't going along with them is that he's got other matters to worry about. He can't take on a full fight with Eisenhower over budget policy, when he needs his support on other matters."

Appreciating this situation, Samuelson concentrated on short-term programs to restore prosperity. These were centered around new spending programs in such areas as defense, foreign aid, education, urban renewal, and other areas. As for reforms in the tax code, these too should be considered but only if recovery did not take place after a few months. "A temporary reduction in tax rates can be a powerful weapon against recession," he wrote. "At this time it would be urgently important to make sure that any tax cut was clearly a temporary one." Given the uncertain nature of international affairs, "and with new public programs coming up in the years ahead, sound finance may require maintenance of our present tax structure and any weakening of it in order to fight a recession might be tragic."

In so stating, Samuelson pleased Galbraithians who wanted high federal revenues to spend on works in the public sector and conservative Republicans who were disturbed by the idea of a tax cut at a time when budget deficits were large. Ironically, these two groups, opposite in most other matters, applauded this section of the Report, while those economists who considered themselves followers of Samuelson were disappointed. To them, the right kind of tax revision would stimulate production and consumption, cut back on unemployment, and enable the economy to function at capacity. Some of them may have been mollified by this statement:

> Specifically, if the American economy is to show healthy growth during this period and to average out at satisfactory levels of employment, we must learn not to be misled by statements that this or that is now at an all-time peak; in an economy like ours, with more than a million people coming into the labor force each year and with continuing economic change, the most shocking frittering away of our economic opportunities is fully compatible with statistical reports that employment and national product are "setting new records each year."

Still, the Report was more a document of the old economics than of the new.

Samuelson turned down an offer to become chairman of the Council of Economic Advisors, which was not surprising. He had no important differences with the Administration but preferred to speak independently from his M. I. T. pulpit and in magazine articles. Besides, he was unwilling to sacrifice intellectual independence for a semblance of political power. Unlike Galbraith and Keyserling, he had no mission in life that required the spotlight in Washington. But he remained on call for special assignments, and during the next few years he did bring his prestige to bear in favor of several programs.

Starting in the spring of 1961, Samuelson argued forcefully for a major tax revision to stimulate the economy. Soon he was calling the recovery program—based in large part on his Report—"a placebo program for recovery," designed more to win political support than maximize production and employment. In an article entitled "Economic Policies for 1962" published in February of that year, he conceded that "the resulting program of expansion has been something less than all that could be desired by academic perfectionists," adding that this was "the caste to which I happen to belong."

Samuelson blamed the situation on the Kennedy Administration's overriding desire to appear fiscally prudent. He rejected the notion that balanced budgets had a priority over growth and spoke out in favor of lower interest rates, increased spending, and tax revision. "Fiscal and monetary policy should tighten only when substantial misbehavior on the price, wage, and international fronts has developed and cannot be well met by more specific remedies." Meanwhile CEA Chairman Walter Heller conducted the fight for the kinds of program Samuelson supported and on occasion called him down from M. I. T. for support in the struggle.

Heller emerged as the leading spokesman for the new economics during the Kennedy years; Samuelson was content to remain on the sidelines as a commentator, supporter, and critic. As such he provided ammunition for the tax revision recommended by Heller in 1962 and 1963, and he even helped sharpen some of the wording for the final draft that was sent to Congress. Samuelson testified in favor of the measure but did so as one of many distinguished economists, and not as an advisor to the President. If he had any regrets in regard to his role and lack of an official forum, he did not show it. His scholarly output continued strong, and the *Newsweek* podium was an influential one. He didn't seem to need more than that.

In this period Samuelson showed greater confidence in the

ability of economists to make predictions and guide policy. "When I say that as an economist I am not very good at making economic forecasts, that sounds like modesty. But actually, it represents the height of arrogance. For I know that as bad as we economists are, we are better than anything else in heaven and earth in forecasting aggregate business trends."

The success of the 1964 tax revision had a good deal to do with this change in attitude. Samuelson and Heller had claimed it would prolong the recovery that had begun in 1961, and so it had. But at the same time, said Samuelson, "hard problems" faced the new economists. Three of these were familiar enough. "How can a mixed economy, dominated by private initiative but subject to public control and stimulus, raise its average rate of growth from, say, 3½ percent to 4½ or 5 percent?" he asked. Also, how could the balance of international payments be rectified, and how might chronic unemployment be licked? But the fourth problem was of a kind usually found on lists put out by conservatives. Samuelson was troubled by the renewal of inflationary pressures. Conceding it had been a problem during most of the century, he took note of "the apparent recent tendency for prices and wages to rise even when America is still intolerably far from reasonably full employment and capacity production." Could it be that steady prices were not compatible with a low level of unemployment? "I am fearful," he said, "that the institutions of our American economy are such that any time we approach reasonably close to full employment, we thereby face the threat of an inflationary price-creep."

Samuelson remained concerned with the economy's somewhat sluggish performance, but, from the mid-1960s on, his attention was increasingly drawn to the problems posed by cost-push inflation. The connection between these two issues had been discussed by a British economist, A. W. Phillips, in a paper entitled "The Relationship Between Unemployment and the Rate of Change of Money Wage Rates in the United Kingdom, 1861-1957," which appeared in *Economica* in 1958. In it was first presented "The Phillips Curve," by which the author demonstrated that there was a trade-off between rises in money wages and unemployment. In essence, he said that the greater the increase in wages, the higher would be the unemployment rate. Samuelson read the paper and was greatly impressed by its argument, seeing in the curve a vehicle that united the problems of inflation and unemployment and an analytical construct by which they might be resolved. "His findings are remarkable," he wrote in 1960, "even if one disagrees with his interpretations." Seven years later, in the debate with Arthur Burns, Samuelson went further: "One must not exaggerate the exactitude of the Phillips curve but nevertheless it is one of the most important concepts of our time."

Samuelson was too far-ranging an economist to devote his career to the amplification of the Phillips Curve, but he used it as a foundation for his future discussions regarding growth and inflation, and these clearly were the main issues facing many economists in the 1960s and 1970s.

"Experience suggests that in the short run there is a trade-off between the intensity of unemployment of men and capital and the intensity of price increase." This was Samuelson's version of the curve as presented in his debate with Burns. The problem facing modern economists, he suggested, was in finding ways to "move the curve" so that increases in the growth rate resulted in smaller advances in the inflationary spiral than might otherwise have been expected.

A trade-off was required. Was that extra increment in growth worth a further rise in the price level? In his textbook Samuelson noted that this was a moral, social, and political question as much as one involving economics, and he asked students to consider the following question: "Can mere science in political economy provide the same answer in the degree to which we should compromise between the evils of unemployment and of inflation for (a) Congresswoman Shirley Chisholm, who represents slum dwellers in Brooklyn, and (b) the Congressman for the elderly in Florida?" Ms. Chisholm would opt for growth and jobs, suggests Samuelson, while the Floridian would sacrifice these for stable prices required by retired people in his district.

Increasingly Samuelson had to face up to choices and alternatives like this one, which did not admit of the exclusion of moral values and could not be resolved by resorting to abstract formulas. A similar situation existed in relation to the Vietnam War in 1965. With the economy functioning at the top of its capacity, Samuelson told President Johnson that it would not be possible to conduct the war, continue Great Society programs, and also have price stability and that a tax increase would be needed to keep the economy under control. Galbraith was speaking out against the war, but Samuelson analyzed the situation from an economic point of view, keeping his politics out of his presentation. As it happened, Johnson chose to

ignore this analysis and continued to do so for another year, while
Samuelson and the CEA hammered away at the theme. They did so
as economists, for, after all, that was their area of expertise.

Was it possible to maintain the discipline apart from issues of
morality? Certainly Samuelson would agree that all economic decisions had a moral aspect, but, more than most of his colleagues in
the 1960s and 1970s, he continued to make the attempt at keeping
science and politics separate. Others would take positions on the
war, ecological concerns, energy programs, and race, basing these
upon the need for justice and a "sane society." Samuelson made no
secret of his feelings on these and other issues, but always he would
calculate costs and present alternatives. One side of him was wedded to the social goals of the Galbraithians, the other to the methodological approach and scientism usually associated with Burns.
Samuelson is a tolerant person in a period when public debate has
become shrill on a wide variety of issues. It will not be a comfortable position to hold in the early 1980s.

Samuelson's dilemma can be seen most clearly in his approach
to the problems of inflation. As prices rose more swiftly in the mid-
1970s, he recommended the more imaginative use of fiscal and
monetary policies. He spoke and wrote less about the need for
growth and more of the ethical problems involved in making policy
choices. Value judgments were required, at least as much as was
economic expertise, and this remained an area in which he trod
most gingerly. Galbraith had no such difficulty, as he recommended
permanent wage and price controls and income redistribution.
Neither did Friedman, who called upon the market mechanism to
provide solutions. Samuelson rejected the Galbraithian model as too
restrictive of freedoms, while he deemed the Friedmanites inhu-
mane in many ways.

Samuelson could recommend no clear solution to the problem of
how inflation could be held down without recession or a major alteration in the nature of American capitalism. Those hoping to find one
in his columns, testimony, or scholarly papers were disappointed.
Still considered the best exemplar of of modern neo-Keynesian economics, Samuelson could do little more than present the alternatives, analyze them, offer critiques, and then end by saying the matter cannot be resolved by economic analysis alone. Keynes sounded
a battle cry in the 1930s. Galbraith and Friedman do the same today. But there is none from Samuelson. He knows the right questions and can summon the raw material from which to fabricate

the answers. But he cannot resolve this major dilemma, which leads some analysts to conclude that Keynesianism has reached a dead end. Those students who go through the latest edition of *Economics* understand this. In his conclusion for the section on employment and price stability, Samuelson wrote:

> What is the moral? Start being cruel? Refuse to recognize that each new reform has, along with its benefits, some costs? Neither of these alternatives is really open to one. The moral, I would think, is to persevere in trying to find structural reforms that will retain and augment humanitarianism while at the same time hoping to encourage the system to behave more like the market-clearing mechanism that experience shows is conducive to both efficiency and stability.
>
> The task of political economy is never done.

6

WALTER HELLER

In the autumn of 1960 the nation was in the midst of both a recession and a presidential campaign, phenomena that usually make demands upon leading economists. From his perch at the National Bureau, Arthur Burns warned Richard Nixon that there would be no upturn in the economy prior to Election Day; the candidate understood that this issue might destroy his chances for the White House. Paul Samuelson had become the acknowledged economist-in-residence at Kennedy headquarters, while John Galbraith provided the Democratic nominee with intellectual stimulation and speech ideas. Leon Keyserling was dismayed by Kennedy's apparent conservatism. The two men had little in common, and so Keyserling had nothing to do with the campaign. Instead, he criticized the nominee's stance on a wide variety of issues, as though positioning himself to take a role in the reshaping of Democratic Party politics in the event of a Republican victory.

Walter Heller had no role either in fighting the recession or helping the candidate. Instead he was on the sidelines, engaged in running the economics department at the University of Minnesota where he had been, on-and-off, for the past fourteen years.

Although his name was known within the profession, Heller was by no means one of its superstars. He had written some interesting

118

articles and testified before congressional committees, usually on finance and tax matters, which were his specialties. On several occasions he had worked for the government and for the past five years had been an economic advisor to Minnesota's Governor Orville Freeman and a part time consultant to the state's Department of Taxation. Heller was 45 years old in 1960 and was tall, lean, and handsome in a grey, academic way. A moderate by temperament and a Keynesian by inclination, he was a mainstream economist in the Samuelson tradition. Heller had produced no novel thesis or major opus, and at his age it seemed unlikely he had one in him. There had been no urgent call to Harvard, Stanford, or some other top-ranked graduate school. In any case, he was fairly content with who he was and where he was. Heller had roots in the upper Midwest, was a respected and popular teacher at Minnesota, a resident expert at the state capital, and a recognized figure at professional conventions. In other words, he was a colonel in the Keynesian army and in 1960 hadn't much of a chance of reaching the rank of general.

Kennedy came to Minneapolis in October to attend a political dinner in his honor and meet with local Democrats. Although he had been invited, Heller had just about decided to remain at home that night. His wife was ill and he was tired. "We don't mix in politics anyway," he told reporters later on. But after dinner he dressed and drove down to the Leamington Hotel on the chance he might be able to see Kennedy and urge upon him some programs to stimulate the economy.

Had he not run into Senator Hubert Humphrey in the corridor Heller might not have been able to get past the guards. Humphrey recognized Heller from his appearances before Senate committees and escorted him into the candidate's suite. As it happened Kennedy was discussing the economy while changing his shirt. After Humphrey introduced Heller, Kennedy switched his attention to him. "How can you move a $500 billion economy with a $5 billion budget deficit?" he asked. "How come the German economy prospered at a 5 percent interest rate, while you fellows want easy money?" These were precisely the kinds of questions Heller had been prepared to discuss. The two men talked about them, and Kennedy asked other questions. "He just stood there scratching his chest while we talked and everybody else fell away," Heller recalled.

Throughout the campaign Kennedy had spoken of the need to "get the country moving again," and Heller was able to suggest methods by which this might be accomplished. None of his ideas

were novel or unusual; Kennedy probably had heard them from
Samuelson and other economists. But Heller's explanations were
precise, clear, and to the point. Kennedy was impressed by his manner and approach to problems, as well as his ability to field questions swiftly.

Their discussion lasted only a few minutes, for Kennedy had
other appointments. Heller drove home and that night composed
a memorandum on the subject of economic growth, which he sent
to Kennedy. Perhaps he fantasized about a call to Washington, but
later on he said that he did not expect one to be issued.

As has been indicated, Kennedy hoped that Samuelson would
become his chairman of the Council of Economic Advisors, but,
when it became clear he would not accept the post, Kennedy asked
his experts for recommendations. Samuelson spoke well of Heller,
as did others. Governor Freeman and Senator Humphrey sponsored
him. In addition, Kennedy wanted to diversify his Administration
geographically; Heller's presence would still criticisms about the
influence of Harvard-M.I.T. economists on the New Frontier. In
early December Kennedy asked Heller to come to Washington for
talks, and at that time he offered him the chairmanship. After thinking about it for a week Heller accepted.

In announcing the appointment Kennedy told reporters that he
intended Heller to have an important role in government, that he
expected him to deal "not only with the state of the economy but
with our goals for economic progress." In other words, he was to
be a policy maker and not merely a technician. At the time, however, it was assumed that Heller would be principally involved
with bringing ideas and recommendations from Samuelson to Kennedy. Few expected much from him, at least not in a government
that included Galbraith and other academics who had worked
closely with the candidate during the campaign. Lacking the Harvard connection and not part of the "Irish Mafia," he could not hope
for membership in the inner circle. Nor could Heller expect to be
deferred to because of his reputation. He was no stranger to Washington, but his connections there were minor when set beside those
of his predecessors. Nourse, Keyserling, and Burns had made important theoretical or legislative contributions prior to assuming the
chairmanship, while Saulnier had served on the Council for more
than a year and a half before being elevated to the post. But then
Galbraith was sent to India, and Samuelson remained at M.I.T. By
Inauguration Day it appeared Heller might become an important

policy maker after all, and articles on his personality, background, and beliefs appeared in the local and national press. Most of these indicated that he was a rather quiet person, not likely to press his ideas on anyone in the White House, and that should he try to do so, he surely would be overwhelmed by the forceful and dynamic young men with whom the incoming President had surrounded himself. Heller made the cover of *Time* in March, an indication he had achieved a degree of celebrity status, but in its story the magazine stated that he had obtained the chairmanship by chance—he was at the right place at the right time.

Perhaps this was so. Yet Kennedy, too, was fortunate, for in Heller he had found not only a forceful spokesman but a person adept in translating the ideas of the new economics into terms understandable to the layman. Later on, after leaving Washington, Heller would claim to have educated Kennedy in modern economic theory: "Experience of recent years has demonstrated that education—of the President, by the President, and for the President—is an inescapable part of an economic adviser's function. Access not just to the person but to the mind of the President is crucial," he added, and Heller had both. Reminiscing about his experiences five years later, he wrote that "the Council's access to the President is potential, not guaranteed. Unless personalities click; unless the economic advisor is both right and relevant; unless he gets off his high horse without falling obsequiously to the ground—his usefulness will be limited and his state of proximity to the President will gradually wither away." Far from withering, Heller's influence in the White House grew swiftly and steadily during the Kennedy years. Clearly things clicked between the President and the Chairman, though their backgrounds and personalities were dissimilar.

Heller's career had been conventional insofar as college professors were concerned. He was born in Buffalo, New York, in 1915, the son of German immigrants. Two years later his father, an engineer, took the family to Washington state, and when Walter was 6 they moved to Milwaukee, where he attended the public schools. A good student in a family that prized learning, Heller entered Oberlin College in 1931, at a time when unemployment was in the double digits and economic discussions were paramount. As with Galbraith and Samuelson, he was drawn to that subject. "The depression attracted some of the best young minds to economics," he later recalled. "Those of us who were growing up then saw the economy flat on its back. To explain why, and to try to do something about it, seemed a high calling." As an undergraduate, Heller pointed himself toward a career that combined academic life with public service, a fairly common ambition for young people in that period. Reading Hansen and other American Keynesians and watching the development of the New Deal, he became convinced that an aggressive, interventionist approach to economic maladies was needed. This, too, was normal for the times.

Heller received his degree from Oberlin in 1935 (the same year Samuelson completed his studies at Chicago) and enrolled for advanced work at the University of Wisconsin. At the time, Harold Groves, a charismatic professor and expert in the area of public finance and taxation, was the most eminent member of the department. It was Groves who led Heller into the study of the impact of taxation upon aspects of the economy, a subject in which he specialized later on. "It seemed to me the critical area, the jugular area, of government economic policy," he said. Groves also reinforced Heller's already liberal Keynesian outlook and helped him obtain a Social Science Research Council grant that enabled him to take a one-year tour of the nation so as to study state taxation methods, the subject of his Ph.D. thesis.

Granted his doctorate in 1941 and rejected by the military because of poor eyesight, Heller obtained a position as senior economic analyst in the division of tax research at the Treasury, where he helped create an income tax withholding system. In so doing Heller had to translate complicated economic theories into practical plans that were intelligible to politicians and bureaucrats, and apparently he excelled at this. He was named assistant to the director of the division in 1946, the year he left government service for an associate professorship at the University of Minnesota School of Business. After less than a year there, he received an offer to serve as chief of finance for the American military government in Germany and in this capacity played an important role in devising tax and banking programs that later played an essential part in that country's "economic miracle."

His work in Germany boosted Heller's reputation in Washington, and for the next dozen years he alternated between teaching stints at Minnesota and government assignments. In the process he became a recognized authority on an important but fairly narrow subject—the effects of taxation upon economic growth—but more so as a technician than a theorist. He was fashioning a most respectable career within the profession by honing his skills in this area. When congressional committees considered tax laws, they knew Heller was the man to call upon for advice and expertise.

Heller returned to Minnesota after a year in Germany but was called to Washington during the Korean War to create a tax program to finance the conflict. Then he was off to Germany again to assist its new government in the area of fiscal policy. In the 1950s he advised underdeveloped countries on economic development, drew up tax programs and reforms in Minnesota for Governor Freeman, and in early 1960 he fashioned a graduated income tax system for the Kingdom of Jordan.

Heller's insights into the relationship between taxes, economic growth, and social reforms were hardly novel. All economists understood that tax cuts stimulated the economy, in that citizens and businesses were provided with additional funds with which to make purchases and expand production. This was known long before Keynes wrote his *General Theory*; in 1690 an obscure English economist, Nicholas Barbon, had written that increased consumption would result in greater production and major benefits for workers and businessmen, and he advocated tax cuts toward that end. Nor was the idea particularly "liberal." In fact, stimulative tax reductions were associated more with conservative Republican administrations than with those of activist Democrats.

In the 1920s Presidents Warren Harding and Calvin Coolidge believed that tax reductions not only were justified but morally correct in times of budget surpluses. Some of the excess would be used to pay off a portion of the national debt, and the rest would be returned to the taxpayers in the form of lower rates. This philosophy produced four tax cuts in the 1920s, and each of them proved economically stimulative. Even though the rates were lower, the gross national product expanded so rapidly that total tax revenues actually rose. Given stable levels of expenditures, then, it would appear that tax reductions were compatible with both balanced budgets and economic growth. It seemed almost too good to be true: lower taxes would provide increased revenues, help maintain full employment, and all of this without additional inflationary pressures.

Herbert Hoover understood that a timely tax cut might bring the nation out of an economic slump. In his budget message of December 1929, he analyzed the darkening scene and asked for the fifth tax reduction since 1921. "Experience has shown that each reduction in taxes has resulted in revenue in excess of the mathematically computed return under the reduced rates," he said. "Undoubtedly

an increase in the prosperity of business brought forth by tax reduction is partly responsible for this experience. Such reduction
gives the taxpayer correspondingly more for his own use and thus
increases the capital available for general business." But the President prefaced this statement with an observation that the estimated
budget surplus for fiscal 1930 was $225 million, and for the follow-
ing year, $122 million. Were this not so, Hoover probably would not
have made this recommendation. The prime responsibility of government, so the contemporary wisdom held, was to safeguard the
integrity of the currency, and a tax cut that would enlarge the
deficit would destroy confidence in the dollar.

This was a key difference between the old economics of Herbert
Hoover and the new economics of Walter Heller. Hoover would cut
taxes as a matter of justice and perhaps to stimulate the economy
when the budget was balanced and a slump threatened; Heller
wanted to employ tax reductions when there was a gap between
the actual and potential performance of the economy and would do
so even if this required a substantial increase in the deficit. Along
with most other new economists, Heller was relatively unconcerned
about inflation, considering a minor uptick in the rate a small price
to pay for sizable increases in the gross national product. In any
case, said Heller (echoing Hoover, Coolidge, and Harding), the tax
take from an increased GNP would help bring the budget into balance. In fact, there might be a surplus, which might be used to pay
for desirable liberal social welfare programs.

The American economy expanded at a rate of less than 3 percent
per year in the 1950s, the result in part of tight money policies designed to fight inflation. During the 1960 campaign, Kennedy had
noted that the German and Japanese economies had expanded at a
5 percent rate in the same period, while the U.S.S.R.'s postwar
growth had been on the order of 6 percent. Kennedy thought a 4½
percent rate achievable, obtaining that figure from Samuelson.

Heller agreed. In a speech he delivered in early October—before
having met Kennedy—he said that 4½ percent growth might be obtained "through good fortune and good management." The difference between a decade of 4½ percent and 3 percent growth would
be $110 billion, which could be used to alleviate poverty and help
modernize the American industrial machine. The way to achieve
this incremental growth, thought Heller, would be through the imaginative use of tax cuts. He had argued for them during the 1950s

as the best way to close "the performance gap"—the difference between actual and potential GNP. Heller did not deny that this would result in temporary deficits. In testimony before the Joint Economic Committee in 1955, he had said that "we are now in a period when deficits are constructive. As others have pointed out to the committee, our rate of production is running some $20 billion short of our potential, maybe more. Therefore, Federal deficits are more likely to evoke a higher production response than a high price response." Expanding upon this, Heller suggested that the demands for goods and services created by a tax cut would eat into unemployment and enable producers to use excess industrial capacity and so would not be inflationary. On other occasions he said that tax cuts would make little sense if the economy was running at full blast, when in fact a tax increase might prove salutory.

It was not that simple, however. Heller often complained that he lacked reliable statistics from which to draw precise forecasts and that this hindered his work. How could an economist claim that a particular tax reform would have a specified effect on the GNP, employment, and inflation in the absence of plausible projections? "No conclusive evidence is available to prove that forecasting techniques are now a thoroughly reliable basis for discretionary stabilization policy," he wrote in 1957, and Heller continued to believe this when he assumed office four years later. As CEA Chairman he would have to provide Kennedy with such forecasts and in addition recommend specific policies and programs. Now that he had administrative responsibilities, Heller had to act as though predictability indeed was possible, and so he did. Soon he came to believe his own projections and accept his own statistics. Within a year he spoke as though certain that "fine tuning of the economy" was possible.

Samuelson and Heller agreed that a tax cut was needed to bring the nation out of the 1960 recession, but, as has been indicated in the previous chapter, this was politically impossible for 1961. Then too, Heller had to battle with John K. Galbraith for the new President's economic soul. Galbraith, of course, opposed the notion of a tax cut, arguing that the government needed additional revenues to spend in the public sector. If anything, he said, taxes should be increased for this purpose. Also, Heller stressed growth and was relatively unconcerned regarding the possibilities of inflation, while Galbraith spoke out in favor of income redistribution, had little to offer regarding methods of stimulating the economy by fiscal means, and was continually on guard against inflation. In their contest, Galbraith had some impressive assets, while Kennedy hardly knew Heller in January of 1961.

Still, the President was more responsive to Heller's approach than to Galbraith's. The Chairman seemed a "pragmatic" economist, at a time when "tough-minded realism" was in great vogue. That he was a political liberal was evident, in the way he talked of the need for increased housing and jobs for minorities, in his support of egalitarian measures, as well as in his sponsorship by such certified progressives as Humphrey and Freeman. But his approach and specific recommendations appealed to many conservatives, too. Who in the National Association of Manufacturers could oppose the idea of corporate tax cuts to stimulate investment? What member of a chamber of commerce would argue against personal tax cuts that would result in greater consumption and sales? Furthermore, Heller was able to demonstrate to Kennedy's satisfaction how it was possible to have both growth and increased public expenditures. The unemployment rate in early 1961 was close to 7 percent, and the President had made clear commitments to increased military expenditures and a wide variety of social programs, all of which would cost a great deal. While the spending would stimulate the economy, it also would increase the deficit, and Kennedy feared it would prove inflationary as well. Heller showed him how this need not be, and Kennedy urged him to use the White House as a podium to educate the American people in the new economics.

Heller began this work in March. In a bravura performance before the Joint Economic Committee, he sketched the outlines of his philosophy and tempted the legislators with a picture of an ever-expanding economy. At that time he said the performance gap was about 8 percent, which meant that if the economy could be made to operate at full capacity, the increase in GNP that year would be approximately $40 billion and that this would enlarge the tax revenues considerably. In fact, given the current expenditures estimates, Heller thought the Treasury would have a surplus of $11 billion. "The revenues of a fully operating economy would finance the Federal programs needed to accelerate the growth of productive capacity and meet national priorities at home and abroad, while leaving room for substantial retirements of Federal debt from budget surplus."

Tax reductions and reforms would trigger all of this but also create a pleasant problem, that of "fiscal drag." As Heller saw it, the expanding tax revenues would produce a budget surplus before full employment was achieved. The existence of this surplus would impede continued expansion unless it was put back into the monetary stream. The Galbraithians had a way to do this: public spending. As for Heller, he would recommend another tax cut. Thus, one reduction in taxes would lead to another, and the process would continue throughout the decade. It was the kind of vision few politicians could resist—if only they could be made to believe it possible. The inculcation of this belief was Heller's major task as CEA Chairman, which is why he stressed his role in educating Kennedy and why the President urged him to speak out on the issues.

Heller appreciated the nature of the political climate in early 1961. Like Samuelson, he recognized that public spending programs would appeal to many New Deal-Fair Deal Democrats, while conservatives in both parties would be wary of a large-scale tax cut. Privately he said that the impact of new programs would not be felt for many months, and he remained a consistent opponent of their use as a counterrecessionary weapon. (In a 1976 essay he noted that "the public works program launched in 1963 to speed recovery was still not completed . . . in the 1966-69 period . . . it is fair warning not to expect very much stabilization help from the public works sector.") In contrast, tax cuts would have an almost immediate effect on demand and then production. The best way to bring the recession to an end would be a "quickie tax cut," but he lacked support for such a device. Instead, Heller told the Committee that "the road to full recovery is a long one," and he talked of the need for additional spending programs. "The expansionary effects of government programs will be welcome even if they occur well after the recession has been reversed."

Heller's reluctance to expand the role of government in the economy and espousal of conservative means for liberal ends won him many supporters in both camps. That he had a knack for compromise, a talent for politics, and a way of expressing himself that pleased disparate individuals is undeniable. "It is often said that the study of economics makes people conservative," he wrote in his memoir of the Kennedy years. "It is hard to study the modern economics of relative prices, resource allocation, and distribution without developing a healthy respect for the market mechanism." Statements such as this one made him sound almost Friedmanesque. "But I do not carry respect to the point of reverence," he quickly added. "We now take for granted that the government must step in to pro-

vide the essential stability at high levels of employment and growth
that the market mechanism, left alone, cannot deliver."

In mid-1961 it seemed the recovery from the 1960 recession
woud not be as strong as had been expected. The unemployment
rate in July was 7 percent—up a fraction from the previous month—
and both the automobile and housing industries were sluggish.
There were two obvious methods of stimulating the economy: massive spending programs and a large tax cut. During the past few
months Congress had rejected many of Kennedy's programs, usually
on grounds that they were ill-conceived and would unbalance the
budget, thus opening the way for inflation. Those legislators who
had voted down increases in social welfare spending might have a
difficult time explaining to constituents their refusal to lower taxes.
Politically speaking, then, tax cutting was the most acceptable
method of accelerating the growth rate and lowering unemployment. Heller had lobbied for a tax cut, but the President's espousal
of one would be due at least as much to political necessities as to
economic lore.

The longer the economy stagnated, the greater would be the
chance for presidential initiatives on the tax front. Sorenson, Heller,
and everyone else at the White House understood this. Toward the
end of the year it appeared a revival was possible without new tax
legislation. "But as recovery waxed during 1961, his interest in economic matters temporarily waned," complained Heller. Once, while
lunching at the White House mess with his colleagues at the CEA,
Heller was approached by Sorenson, who called out, "There they
are, contemplating the dangers of an upturn."

Still, Kennedy talked often of the "heavy" tax system that summer and autumn. In October he complained that it "brings in
tremendous receipts at full employment—we don't want it to result
in waste of resources and manpower." But he also reiterated his
intention to balance the budget. From his statements of the period
it is clear Kennedy still believed tax cuts could be justified if they
were needed to bring the economy out of recession. Heller had yet
to win him over to a conviction that they could be employed to
achieve optimal growth when the economy was strong.

Heller's reputation as a political economist is based on the tax
reduction measure Kennedy accepted in the summer of 1962 and
was signed into law by Lyndon Johnson in February 1964. As Heller
put it, "This, the big income tax cut of 1964 ($14 billion at 1965, $11
billion at 1963, income levels) is rightfully regarded as the most

overt and dramatic expression of the new approach in economic policy." At the time, he and Samuelson rejoiced at this signal victory. Heller begins his memoir of the period with a celebration of the change. "Economics has come of age in the 1960s," he concluded, as a result of policies initiated by Kennedy and brought to their fruition by Johnson.

Heller is proud of having been the conduit through which the new economics came to the White House and of his role in educating two Presidents in the merits of tax cuts to stimulate the economy. But like so many experts in all fields, he tends to interpret the actions of politicians through prisms fashioned in his particular discipline. Kennedy had only one course in economics while a Harvard undergraduate, and at no point prior to 1960 had he demonstrated much interest in the subject. As President he faced a series of problems in many areas. Funds were needed for programs to assist the poor and minority groups; Democratic legislators and governors pressured him to support spending programs for their constituents; there were a series of crises in foreign affairs, running from the Bay of Pigs fiasco of 1961 through the Berlin crisis of 1962 to the Southeast Asia military buildup of 1963. Kennedy had to deliver on promises to win the space race and catch up militarily with the U.S.S.R. In addition to all of this, he was obliged to defend the dollar, whose international position had weakened somewhat by the time he came to office.

As has been indicated, Kennedy's economic orientation was traditional. At one point he said the two things he feared most were atomic war and an unbalanced budget. When the Berlin crisis erupted, his instincts told him to ask for a tax increase to help pay for the needed military buildup and also to impress upon the American people the seriousness of the situation. Heller, Samuelson, and others were able to talk him out of the tax boosts, but the President insisted on pledging to balance the budget for fiscal 1963. Later on Sorenson could claim that Kennedy had done this to avoid charges of being fiscally irresponsible, and he implied that the President understood and appreciated the need for a tax cut even then— that Heller's message had been absorbed and accepted. "Nevertheless his political judgement told him that a period of gradual reeducation would be required before the country and Congress, accustomed to nearly sixteen years of White House homilies on the wickedness of government deficits, would approve of an administration deliberately unbalancing the budget."

Heller had primary responsibility in preparing the 1963 *Budget Message*, a document that reflects his pragmatic approach to his job. "The Federal Government is expected to operate in 1963 with some surplus," he wrote. "To plan a deficit under such circumstances would be to increase the risk of inflationary pressures damaging alike to our domestic economy and to our international balance of payments." But having paid tribute to orthodoxy, he proceeded to offer an aside to the new economists. "On the other hand, we are still far short of full capacity use of plant and manpower. To plan a large surplus would risk choking off economic recovery and contributing to a premature downturn." Early in the *Report* is the promise of tax reform "aimed at simplification of our tax structure," but subsequently one finds a clear statement of Heller economics. "Faster economic growth in the United States requires, above all, an expansion of demand, to take up existing slack and to match future increases in capacity. Unless demand is adequate to buy potential output, accelerating the growth of potential is neither an urgent problem nor a promising possibility." Will this slack be taken up by new federal spending programs (the Galbraith approach) or by an increase in consumer demands made possible by a tax cut (Heller's proposal)? "A pragmatic decision will almost certainly involve both," he hedged. "The choice of a balance between public and private expenditures is an important choice for society. . . . And it should be made by weighing the urgency of alternate use of resources, rather than by appeal to simple solutions on one side or another."

After a year in office Heller was winning his battle with the Galbraithians, but the President remained unconvinced that the new economics was sound. Kennedy understood that Heller's approach would give him a far greater degree of flexibility than did the old orthodoxy. He remained uncertain as to which way the economy was headed and had to keep his options open. In addition, he required policies which, once implemented, would have an immediate impact upon the economy. This meant he couldn't lock himself into pledges for a balanced budget or rely upon spending programs of uncertain merit. He was more interested in recovery than reform. Thus, the President would (in Heller's words) "paper over" a deficit, and provide only token leadership for those who wanted massive increases in social welfare spending.

The unemployment rate for January 1962 went below 6 percent, and the following month Kennedy celebrated by talking of balanced budgets and softening his position on tax cuts. "Therefore, for the present time there is not a chance of tax reduction," he said during a press conference. "The key will be whether we can have continued prosperity." The recovery was sluggish, however, and in March and April Kennedy indicated that he might have to change his mind regarding taxes. Then came the steel confrontation, followed by the sharpest decline in stock prices since the 1930s. A near-panic situation developed, as business leaders talked of the possibilities of a major depression. Action clearly was needed, and the chief weapon in his arsenal was Walter Heller's tax program.

The signal that Kennedy was prepared to act came in a commencement address delivered at Yale in June. The result of a collaboration between Arthur Schlesinger, Galbraith, Heller, and others, it is generally conceded to have been one of Kennedy's best efforts. In it he spoke of the myths then current that prevent the "essential confrontation with reality." Chief among these was "the problem of our fiscal policy."

> The myth persists that federal deficits create inflation and budget surpluses prevent it. Yet, sizable budget surpluses after the war did not prevent inflation, and persistent deficits for the past several years have not upset our basic price stability. . . . Debts, public and private, are neither good nor bad, in and of themselves. Borrowing can lead to over-extension and collapse—but it can also lead to expansion and strength. There is no single, simple slogan in this field we can trust.

Heller was delighted with the reception afforded this speech. Many businessmen and business publications thought well of it, and, as a bonus, Treasury Secretary Douglas Dillon, considered a guardian of fiscal responsibility, said that he was pleased to hear talk of the stimulative effects of tax cuts. "As his economic advisors, we were confident that this speech marked a new era in American economic policy," wrote Heller, and shortly thereafter Kennedy sent his tax reform package to Congress for consideration.

Yet Kennedy was not certain as to the exact dimensions of the tax cut. In autumn 1962, wrote Sorenson, "the President remained unenthusiastic, if not skeptical, about tax reduction," and in mid-December he was plagued by doubts as to whether or not the potential gains were worth the possible political risks. Heller's notes of a meeting with Kennedy on December 14 read, "As of the moment, the President is shaken on the question of the tax cut . . . I have never seen the President so anguished and uncertain about the correctness of his course on a domestic matter in the two years that I have served with him." The reasons for this, said Heller, were counterpressures from Galbraith who together with several Cabinet members pressed for spending programs, as well as complaints from congressional Democrats—liberals and conservatives—who thought a tax cut at that time unnecessary.

A few weeks prior to this meeting, several newspapers had carried stories of a split in the Democratic camp. On one side were "conservatives" headed by Heller and Dillon, while on the other were keepers of the New Deal-Fair Deal flame, which included Galbraith and an increasingly critical and vocal Leon Keyserling. Heller had helped draft a speech that Kennedy was to deliver to the Economic Club of New York the following day, and part of the President's anguish resulted from the knowledge that it might create new dissension in his own ranks. Furthermore, the press had billed it as an indication of where Kennedy was headed, as well as a preview of his approach to the 1964 election. But it would also be a pitch to the business community. "If I can convince them," Kennedy said, "I can convince anybody."

In his speech the President spoke of the need to keep spending in check, but the heart of it was concerned with the tax cut. Rates were too high and revenues too low, he said, and "the soundest way to raise the revenues in the long run is to cut the rates now." The choice was not between surpluses and deficits: "It is between two kinds of deficits: a chronic deficit of inertia . . . or a temporary deficit of transition, resulting from a tax cut to boost the economy, increase tax revenues, and achieve—and I believe this can be done—a budget surplus."

The speech, a skillful blending of new economic ideas with conservative catchwords and goals, was a huge success. "It sounded like Hoover," wrote Sorenson, "but it was actually Heller." An enthusiastic Kennedy called his Chairman to say, "I gave them straight Keynes and Heller, and they loved it." But the message was attacked from both the political left and right. Galbraith called it "the most Republican speech since McKinley." In a letter to House Minority Leader Charles Halleck, Eisenhower characterized the Kennedy approach as "fiscal recklessness."

From that point until his death less than a year later, Kennedy pressed forward for his tax reform package. Heller, Dillon, and their staffs put together a three-stage reduction in personal income taxes and important cuts in the corporate rates and capital gains treatments, the latter geared to stimulate investment. Heller defended this approach as being well within the Democratic reform tradition, but much of his support came from Republicans. Arthur Burns endorsed the Heller approach and doubtless helped swing votes for the final version. Meanwhile Galbraith and Keyserling attacked the plan as offering next to nothing to poor people and minorities. No amount of tax cutting could dissolve "hard core" or structural unemployment, wrote Keyserling. How might a tax cut help a person with little or no income?

Heller found it difficult to answer this question. He responded that an invigorated economy could produce additional jobs. "Structural maladjustments tend to flourish in slack markets," he told the Senate Labor Committee, and "a vigorous expansion in demand helps cut structural problems down to size." Yet, despite a continued economic recovery in 1963, the unemployment rate did not fall below 5.4 percent. By then Keyserling was comparing the Kennedy approach with that of Herbert Hoover—both men seemed to believe in a "trickle down theory" of economics—that the best way to help poor people is to offer assistance to business. Or as former New Deal economist Broadus Mitchell put it, "Kennedy seems to believe that the best way to feed the sparrows is to increase the amount of grain given to horses."

In October Heller offered an explanation for the relatively high unemployment level: it was due, he said, to the increased automation of American industry. Simply stated, fewer people with technological skills were producing more goods and services than many more workers who lacked these skills. From this was drawn two implications. First of all, it was possible to have maximum production together with a high level of unemployment. Second, what was needed to correct this was a major retraining effort—once again, Heller believed the key to solving economic problems was education. Keyserling, who was emerging as an important spokesman for Democratic liberals, suggested that this was fine as far as it went, but more would be needed, and he called for large-scale spending programs to assist chronically unemployed people and minorities. In the autumn of 1963, the split between Kennedy and the Democratic left had widened.

A year after the Kennedy assassination, Heller remarked, "At the time of his death, he was a good orthodox economist." Perhaps so, but Kennedy was even more the pragmatic politician. He was

fully aware of the division in his following that had resulted from
his sponsorship of the Heller tax package. In addition he had read
Michael Harrington's book, *The Other America,* and was impressed
by its demonstrations that poverty remained widespread and would
not be eliminated by fiscal measures. A manifesto of the Galbraith-
Keyserling faction, the book had become a rallying point for reformers. Hoping to heal the breach in his party while at the same time
correct social injustice, Kennedy asked Heller to present him with a
program that would deal with structural unemployment. This did
not mean, however, that less attention would be paid the tax cut—
Kennedy wanted that too. In his last meeting with Heller, on November 19, he said, "I think its important to make it clear that we're
also doing something for the middle-class man in the suburbs."

Shortly after this discussion Heller took off for a trade mission to
Japan. He learned of the assassination while on a plane over the
Pacific. The delegation returned to Washington, and soon after
Heller met with and agreed to work for Lyndon Johnson.

Johnson's political training and economic instincts were quite
different from those of Kennedy, and for that matter so was his
personality. Temperamentally and ideologically closer to the New
Deal-Fair Deal tradition than to the New Frontier, he inclined toward large-scale spending programs to stimulate growth, halt recessions, and cut back on unemployment. Rhetoric and symbolic gestures aside, he was more of an activist than Kennedy, less fearful
of budgetary deficits, and more willing to risk inflation in order to
have growth. Heller claims that Johnson, like Kennedy, was a "modern president" in that he accepted the essential tenets of the new
economics, and he did voice his intention to redeem the Kennedy
pledges. "No act of ours could more fittingly continue the work of
President Kennedy than the early passage of the tax bill for which
he fought all this long year," said Johnson in his first address to
Congress.

In order to obtain sufficient conservative votes in the Senate,
Johnson had to pledge himself to keep spending down and in fact
cut into the preliminary Kennedy budget estimates. From his post
at M.I.T., Samuelson argued that this would all but negate the
impact of the tax cuts. If consumers and businesses spend an additional amount due to the tax measure—say, $5 billion—while at the
same time government expenditures were sliced by that amount,
net spending would be about the same as it would have been without the tax measure and the budget decreases. Heller explained

this to Johnson, and while the new President understood the economics, he had to instruct his Chairman on the politics of the situation. "If you don't get this budget down to around 100 billion dollars," he told Heller, "you won't pee one drop." Heller persisted, however, enlisting the aid of Agriculture Secretary Freeman and Labor Secretary Willard Wirtz. Johnson realized what was happening, and he called Heller to the Oval Office. "Tell them to lay off, Walter. Tell them to quit lobbying. I'm for them. I know they have good programs and the economy needs to have money pumped in. I want an expanding economy too, and I'd like a budget at 108 billion dollars. They don't need to waste my time and theirs with their memos and phone calls."

Heller came around to Johnson's position and assisted in trimming the proposed budget to $97.9 billion, lower even than the Republicans had demanded. The tax measure passed the Senate and was signed into law on February 26, 1964. With this, it might be said the New Frontier had come to its conclusion, and now Lyndon Johnson's Great Society would begin.

Toward the end of the decade Heller would write that the willingness of Kennedy and Johnson "to use, for the first time, the full range of modern economic tools, underlies the unbroken U.S. expansion since early 1961." This expansion had, "in its first five years, created over seven million new jobs, doubled profits, increased the nation's real output by a third, and closed the $50 billion gap between actual and potential production that plagued the American economy in 1961."

Can all, or even most, of this spectacular performance be credited to the Heller programs? Some monetarists claim that the Federal Reserve's policy of lowering the discount rate and increasing the money supply was the prime factor in the advance. Milton Friedman went further; in a debate with Heller he said that "so far as I know, there has been no empirical demonstration that the tax cut had any effect on the total flow of income in the U.S." This aside, there is reason to believe the economy's strong performance in the 1960s was due at least as much to such factors as the strong antiinflationary bias established during the Eisenhower era, recovery from the 1960 recession, Galbraithian spending programs, and increased military budgets.

Paul Samuelson, who played a major role in helping formulate such concepts as fiscal drag and the performance gap—and who was one of Heller's strongest supporters throughout his tenure as Chairman—said as much. In his 1967 debate with Arthur Burns, he remarked that Eisenhower "created conditions which were helpful to the long expansion which we have had in the 1960's and which perhaps we are still having." He based this upon the fact that Eisenhower had set out in 1959 to balance the budget the following fiscal year and at the same time delivered a strong antiinflation message. He managed to achieve a small surplus, though the price was the third recession of his Administration. More important, together with the Federal Reserve, he had dealt a smashing blow to those businesses and labor unions that since World War II had operated on the assumption that inflation could not be overcome. The Consumer Price Index rose by 1.5 percent in 1960 and a scant 0.7 percent the following year. But there was clear underutilization of machines and workers. The unemployment rate in December 1960 was 6.6 percent, more than twice what it had been when Eisenhower took office. The prime lending rate was 4½ percent; in early 1953 it had been 3 percent. Had the benefits been worth the price? Eisenhower thought so and in his memoirs wrote: "Critics overlooked the inflationary psychology which prevailed during the mid-fifties and which I thought it necessary to defeat." Friedman agreed, noting that this was the last period during which the White House made a serious effort at keeping inflation in check.

But whatever the judgment on this issue, the economy was positioned for a bounceback from the 1961 recession. Acting upon Heller's advice, Kennedy proposed an investment tax credit for businesses willing to expand their capacities and modernize their plants, which added to the demands for capital goods. This approach can hardly be considered an innovation of the new economics, however. During the 1953 depression, Arthur Burns had instructed Eisenhower on the merits of investment tax credits, and the following year, over the protests of liberal Democrats, businessmen were offered such credits which, according to some economists, reduced corporate taxes by $3 billion. The credits were effective in the mid-1950s, and they also worked in 1962.

In early 1962 Heller recommended support of what he termed "Guideposts for Noninflationary Wage and Price Behavior." He wanted business and unions to agree to keep their price increases and wage demands at around the 3.5 percent level. The guideposts were effective for the most part, but a good deal of the credit for their success accrued to the noninflationary psychology inherited from the Eisenhower period. That April, Kennedy blasted many steel companies for having increased their prices over the guideline limits. The steelmen backtracked and the rest of the business community got the message. Large corporations hesitated before increasing their prices, in fear of attacks from the White House. As a result, Kennedy achieved a reputation of being antibusiness—one that surely was undeserved—but in the process the prices of consumer goods were kept lower than they might otherwise have been.

Finally, it could be argued that the Kennedy-Johnson prosperity was more a product of old-fashioned spending programs than of tax cuts—that the federal government, not the consumer and newly-liberated businessmen, was the author of the prosperity of the 1960s.

Total federal spending in 1960, the last year of the Eisenhower Administration, came to $92 billion. During his presidency Eisenhower had increased spending by $24 billion, or $3 billion per year on the average. The spending figure for 1964, when the tax cut was enacted, was $119 billion, which means that during the first four years of the Kennedy-Johnson Administration spending rose by $27 billion, or close to $7 billion per year. In the next four years federal spending rose to $179 billion, an average increase of $15 billion a year. In the Kennedy-Johnson era national defense expenditures went from $46 billion to $80 billion, spending on the space program rose from $401 million to $4.7 billion, and education and manpower spending went from $1.1 billion to $6.7 billion. In 1960 federal expenditures on health were $756 million, and in 1968, $9.6 billion. Had an analyst of 1960 been given these figures and nothing else, he might have assumed that the two most important developments of the Kennedy-Johnson years had been the heightening of Cold War tensions and enactment of the Galbraithian agenda for social reforms. He might also have concluded that the stimulus provided by these spending programs had enabled the economy to operate at a high level of production throughout the eight years.

Once they got used to one another, Kennedy and Heller formed a close relationship. The President got along well with academics, and Heller's brand of pragmatic economics appealed to his instincts, even while he was wary of new economic ideology. As a result, Heller became one of the strong men of the New Frontier, and he continues to defend its policies today. Johnson was a different kind of person, one with an innate distrust of most professors, whom he suspected of being more interested in abstract theories than in real problems. Also, he had inherited his Cabinet and staff from Kennedy. These were J.F.K. people, and both he and they knew it. In order to assure both the reality and appearance of continuity, it was important to Johnson that these people remain in his Administration, and he was particularly interested in retaining Heller's services.

Johnson had an easier time with him than with other New Frontiersmen. For one thing, Heller was a midwesterner and not a member of the original inner circle. Furthermore, the two men had developed a mutual respect for one another while Johnson was vice-president. Other than this, however, there was little about Heller the economist that would have appealed to a Lyndon Johnson who achieved the presidency on his own.

Johnson always had been more concerned with federal spending programs than with tax revision, with a massive enlargement of the federal sector rather than an invigoration of the private one. Kennedy and Heller were involved with the working out of the new economics; Johnson was more interested in completing the structure of the New Deal. And the new President preferred Washington insiders to academic outsiders. Had the choice been his initially, Johnson might have selected as Chairman someone like Keyserling —perhaps it would have been Keyserling himself, for the two men shared many of the same ideas, personality traits, and experiences. As it was, he and Heller did their best to work well with one another. For the most part, they were successful in this.

Johnson made clear his domestic priorities in his State of the Union Address delivered in early January. "This administration today, here and now, declares unconditional war on poverty in America." Earlier Heller had told him of Kennedy's interest in the subject, and, according to Johnson, asked, "Did I want the Council of Economic Advisors to develop a program to attack poverty?" The President told Heller to "push ahead full tilt," so that work on it had begun before the official "declaration of war."

The Johnson antipoverty program involved many departments and White House staffers, but the President had no need for instruction or advice on how to allocate funds for welfare programs. From the first it appeared Heller would be ranked among the conservatives in this area. Although he joined with Galbraith to recommend the establishment of a new antipoverty agency, in all other matters he advocated a slower approach than Johnson wanted. On several occasions his recommendations for the establishment of pilot projects prior to the implementation of full-scale programs were brushed aside by a President anxious to get the job underway as rapidly as possible. Johnson agreed with Heller's suggestion that local agencies be used as much as possible in order to prevent waste and inefficiencies, but in practice most of the power was centralized in the White House. By mid-spring it was common knowledge that Jack Valenti and other old Johnson hands had more to say about the antipoverty war than did any of the New Frontiersmen, and the Kennedy people started to leave Washington for other jobs. Heller still had access to the White House, but as Johnson's grip on the presidency tightened and he became more secure in his office, Heller and the few remaining New Frontiersmen lost much of their remaining influence.

Shortly after the 1964 election Heller circulated a series of memoranda, which later on came to be known as the "Heller Plan." More in the way of suggestions than a fully worked-out program, it combined his notions regarding proper tax policy with a new approach to the war on poverty.

Throughout the summer Heller had spoken of a coming budget surplus, even in the face of Great Society spending programs, that would be made possible by continued economic expansion and the higher tax revenues it would bring. "Our federal tax system is so powerful that—even after reducing our income taxes by about 12 billion dollars—on the average, each year, it generates about 5 billion dollars more revenue than it did the year before," he told a reporter in late June. This extra money, pouring into the Treasury, would constitute a fiscal drag were it not put back into the economy. In the Kennedy years Heller had recommended tax cuts as the best and most efficient means of eliminating fiscal drag and enabling the economy to operate at the peak of its capacity. With a different President and altered priorities, Heller shifted ground; now he argued that the money could best be employed in the war against poverty. Thus, he recommended returning a major portion of the "fiscal dividend" to the states, on the understanding the money would be used to pay for social welfare and educational programs. Johnson was interested in the idea but ultimately rejected it. Heller remained on good terms with Johnson, but their relationship continued to be quite different from what it had been with Kennedy.

Heller resigned from the Council in November and returned to Minnesota. Perhaps he would have done so had Kennedy lived, for his health was frail and the toll of seven-day weeks and ten-hour days was severe. As it was, Heller had remained in the Johnson

White House longer than most of the New Frontiersmen, and he left Washington with a greatly enhanced reputation; from that time on, Heller would never lack a public or professional forum. One financial journal claimed that he had "helped raise the prestige of economists to a new high," while another said he was "clearly one of the nation's leading economic thinkers." The economy's performance seemed to justify this praise. That November the unemployment rate slipped below 5 percent for the first time in almost eight years, while for 1964 as a whole the Consumer Price Index rose by a bare 1.2 percent.

Heller received credit for this performance. The new economics was an almost unqualified success. The nation was confident and strong and seemed likely to remain so. Lyndon Johnson's massive electoral victory over Republican Barry Goldwater that November gave the impression that the nation was unified politically and clear in its social, political, and foreign policy goals. Never again would the outlook appear so bright as it did when Walter Heller returned to his post at the University of Minnesota.

He was succeeded as Chairman by Gardner Ackley, a member of the Council who formerly had been an economics professor at the University of Michigan. Ackley was a practitioner of the new economics and, as Heller had been for four years before, had a respectable though minor reputation within the profession. He had little opportunity to influence and educate Johnson—or to enhance that reputation—for the President did not feel the need for instruction. Nonprofessionals in the White House picked up some of the ideas set down by Heller and Samuelson and concluded that additional strains on the economy would not result in major inflation but would instead serve as a spur to greater productivity. Part of the increased tax take would be used to fight the war against poverty and the rest to bring the fighting in Vietnam to a successful conclusion.

They miscalculated. Inflationary pressures started to build in 1965 and continued on into the following year. "Were it not for Vietnam," wrote Heller later on, "early 1966 would have found us comfortably contemplating the form and size of the fiscal dividend needed to keep us on the road to full employment, rather than considering what further actions might be needed to ease the strain on our productive capacity, and deal with the vexing and perplexing problem of inflation."

By then John Galbraith was calling for withdrawal from Vietnam, while those who supported the war said that inflation could be controlled by cutbacks in antipoverty programs. True to his training, inclination, and experience, Heller said the nation needed a temporary increase in taxes. "Taxes, once enacted, can go into effect almost immediately through the withholding and current payment system. Further they are much more quickly reversible. A temporary, highly visible surtax could be—and, I believe would be—removed very quickly to act as an economic stimulant after Vietnam." Thus, Heller remained a believer in fine tuning, with tax manipulation his primary weapon.

As it happened, the Administration rejected all three recommendations. The involvement in Vietnam deepened, increased funding was provided for the war on poverty, and the tax boost was not enacted until mid-1968, by which time the inflation rate was over 5 percent and headed upward. This delay in tax revision was what CEA member Kermit Gorden later called "the worst economic mistake since the end of World War II." To some it appeared to have discredited the new economics, but Heller passionately denied this. Along with Ackley, Samuelson, and others he has persistently recommended higher taxes, to no avail.

With the exception of Samuelson, Heller had become the most vocal, visible, and prominent of the new economists. He was a regular contributor to the *Wall Street Journal* and a member of *Time* magazine's editorial board. He also was honored by election to the presidency of the American Economic Association. More times even than Samuelson or Galbraith, he was called upon by the press and television programs to respond to criticisms of the new economics hurled forth by monetarists like Friedman and George Stigler. But he also became a director at Arthur Burns's National Bureau, yet another indication of Heller's abilities at maintaining connections and friendships in many camps.

Unlike Samuelson, Heller has retained his old beliefs insofar as prescriptions for the economy are concerned; his faith in tax cuts as a panacea for many ills remains strong. He was slow in understanding the rapid inflationary buildup in 1973, which he calls "the year of infamy in inflation forecasting," noting that "we were caught with our parameters down." The crippling inflation of 1973-1974—in the latter year the annualized rate came to over 12 percent—dealt a blow to the reputations of economists, new as well as old. President Ford's initial impulse was to cut spending and balance the budget, and there was talk of a tax boost. Heller and most of the new economists strongly disagreed with this approach. The new inflation was quite different from that of the late 1960s, he said. At that time the economy was functioning at close to full capacity, while there was much slack in 1974. Thus he argued for tax reductions. "Income and payroll tax cuts applied with skill and statesmanship can do double duty, not only righting some of the wrongs of inflation but becoming part of a social contract in which real income losses of wage earnings that cannot be recaptured in the bargaining process are consciously restored though the (un)taxing process." Heller applauded when Ford switched his ground, and he wrote in favor of the tax cut passed in 1975. But it didn't go far enough, he argued. "What is needed is a major *net* continuing cut of perhaps $20 to $25 billion so that we will not only *get* but *keep* the economy moving."

The Ford tax cut did not dampen inflationary pressure to any great extent. The rate did decline, but this was due more to recessionary forces and a tight money policy than anything else. By the mid-1970s the new economics was being eclipsed. Monetarists, budget balancers, and a variety of anti-Keynesians now came to center stage. Milton Friedman attracted a wider audience than ever before, while Galbraith called for mandatory controls and Samuelson slowly edged toward that position from the sidelines.

This is not to say that tax cutting as an economic weapon was completely discarded. Jimmy Carter's tax cut of 1978 was larger even than Ford's and in some respects more sweeping than the Kennedy-Johnson measure of 1964. But it was sponsored and passed not so much to stimulate the economy and end fiscal drag as to rectify distortions in the rates caused by runaway inflation. Furthermore, it came at a time when Social Security rates were raised. Thus, many Americans were more heavily taxed in 1979 than they had been the previous year.

Heller took note of this in one of his *Wall Street Journal* articles, in which he deplored Carter's fiscal management. By then, however, other tax reformers were given more notice by the press and the public. From California, Howard Jarvis led a crusade to cut property taxes, while economist Arthur Laffer argued that massive income tax reductions would prove as stimulating in the late 1970s as they had in the mid-1960s. Both men and their followers were identified with the right wing of the Republican Party. Ironically, Heller found himself in the ideological company of Ronald Reagan, not Edward Kennedy, in 1979 and 1980. The world had changed more than he, but he was still quite a distance from the New Frontier.

Heller has not lost any of his major platforms, but he clearly lacks the kind of grip on the public imagination he possessed in the

1960s. The confident belief many Americans had in their futures, the certainties regarding economic manipulation, the belief that fine tuning could bring about a limitless era of prosperity without inflation had passed. Heller understands this and recently has moderated some of his views to incorporate an appreciation of the importance of monetary policy. He has even conceded that, under special circumstances, some controls may be necessary to keep the economy in balance.

On leaving the White House in triumph in 1964, Heller issued a manifesto for the new economics, which was as much a cry of triumph as anything else. "Part of the political economist's strength, then, lies in an ever-broadening base of economic theory, statistics, and research," he wrote. "In political economics, the day of the Neanderthal Man—indeed, the day of the pre-Keynesian Man—is past."

If nothing else, the traumatic experiences of the 1970s indicated that the profession's body of knowledge is at the very least incomplete, contradictory, and flawed. It no longer is certain that Keynes is the best guide to follow in an age of chronic stagflation. Galbraith urges the nation to transcend Keynes; Milton Friedman confidently states that non-Keynesian approaches to problems are needed, and he recommends programs Heller would categorize as Neanderthal. Heller remains where he was in the 1960s—in the ideological middle of American economic thought. It is a position, however, that has badly eroded since then.

The Walter Heller who writes and speaks today is more cautious and less self-confident than the person who left the White House in 1964. He is likely to remain so until the current malaise ends or until he and other new economists come up with plausible prescriptions for current problems. "Looking toward the future, many economists draw the lesson not that one should keep the economy's motor idling, but rather that one should provide it with safety devices and heavy shock absorbers," he wrote in a recent book, implying that the basic design is fine, but that minor modifications and alterations are required. He isn't clear yet about the nature and role of these devices and shock absorbers, however, and he has no plan for a new structure. Toward the end of the decade Heller could offer only more of the same. "In other words, it is a call for better planning, better data, and faster conversion of knowledge into policy."

7

MILTON FRIEDMAN

"To keep the fish that they carried on long journeys lively and fresh, sea captains used to introduce an eel into the barrel. In the economics profession, Milton Friedman is that eel."

This was the way Samuelson described Friedman's role in the late 1960s. It is a vivid image, and one that is fair, for no American economist—not even Galbraith—has been the source of so much contention since the end of World War II. In a period when a large majority of economists accepted Keynesianism and when Samuelson's version of that doctrine ruled among undergraduates, Friedman led the counterattack, as a champion of the older truths and some might say the new conservatism. Witty, often eloquent, and supremely logical, he is the most important critic of the new economics.

Samuelson believes that without Friedman's leadership the conservatives within the profession would not have been able to attract much attention, and he implies that once he is gone from the scene, the movement will become less respectable, more diffuse, and might even evaporate. Certainly Friedman was responsible for bringing many conservative points of view out of academia and into the public arena. Like Samuelson he is a columnist for *Newsweek,* and he has been the subject of cover stories in all the important news magazines—and even a *Playboy* interview. At the same time he is greatly respected within the profession for his originality and theoretical contributions. For years a friendly antagonist, Samuelson often has claimed that Friedman's "style surpasses his integrity," by which he means that the conservative often ignores evidence and relies more upon his powers of persuasion than the actual merits of his case.

That Friedman is a formidable debater is obvious to anyone who has seen him in action. Except for Galbraith in his prime, no liberal could match him in felicity of expression, charm, and utter conviction. "I wish I was as sure of anything as Milton is about everything," said one admiring colleague, and Friedman's son told a reporter that he had been brought up to believe that argument is the best way to develop ideas. This would become evident in 1979 and 1980, when Friedman hosted on television a series of programs entitled "Free to Choose," in which he developed many of his more familiar points. Half of each program was devoted to a confrontation between him and several critics and supporters, encounters he clearly relished, even when having to concede points and alter earlier statements. ("Free to Choose" was, at least in part, a response to Galbraith's earlier effort. Ironically, the Friedman programs were sponsored by large corporations and appeared on public television, while Friedman blasted away at corporate practices and indicated that the government had no place setting up television and radio stations).

There are other distinguished conservative economists, but none of them have filled the leadership role before the American people as well as has Friedman. In addition, he is an acknowledged original scholar in many fields, some arcane, others popular and political, and has achieved a professional reputation that has eluded Galbraith. In a paper delivered before a meeting of conservative economists, Karl Brunner and Allan Meltzer opened by noting, "None of the participants in the current discussion of monetary or macro-theory has contributed more than Milton Friedman to the revival of monetary theory and its development as a lively, perhaps the liveliest, area of active research in economics." Harry Johnson believes that the "intellectual revival of the quantity theory" has been "almost exclusively the work of Milton Friedman." Henry Wallich credits him with "almost singlehandedly" changing economic thinking on the issue of money. In his text Samuelson indicates that Friedman is one of the nation's most important intellectuals, and goes on to say that "people of all political persuasions" should read his most popular work, *Capitalism and Freedom*. Before they do so, however, Samuelson suggests they ask themselves whether anyone today can seriously oppose Social Security, farm legislation, pure food and drug regulation, the licensing of doctors and teachers, minimum wages, and a host of other programs and policies set down and administered by government. "Can a man of good will oppose Pope Paul IV's encyclical naming central planning as a key to economic development?" Samuelson surely considered Friedman as a man of good will, yet this is precisely what he has been doing for more than four decades.

How might this be explained? Friedman often has remarked that good intentions by themselves are worthless unless accompanied by intelligent policies and that those who attempt to resolve important social and economic problems through governmental actions either fail or create new difficulties more perplexing and damaging than the original ones. Furthermore, he denies that planning is the best means for creating conditions under which economic growth is maximized. A people who hope to achieve prosperity by giving up some of their freedoms usually wind up with neither. This, Friedman suggests, is a key point of difference between liberalism and his brand of conservatism. The former holds that economic development is a prerequisite for liberty, while Friedman contends that without liberty there can be no consistent economic growth. This concern for liberty, both for its own sake and as a vital ingredient in a successful economy, is at the kernel of "Friedmanism."

So is individualism. Friedman's heroes are the workers who seek no special privileges from unions, the businessmen who are not afraid of competition and do not ask for protection against it, and the citizens who do not require favors of government. No other major American economist—not even Galbraith—is as critical as he of labor union practices, corporate manipulation of the economy, and big government. All of these seek guarantees for their constituents in the form of benefiits to be paid for by other elements of society. In *American Capitalism*, Galbraith celebrated the emergence of countervailing power in the economy; throughout his life, Friedman has called for the elimination or at least the curbing of all forms of ingrained corporate power, be they in the hands of government, business, or labor.

The striving of individuals for success is the engine that powers

American capitalism. Thus the businessman will try to produce the finest possible product for the lowest possible price and will attempt to understand the desires of consumers and give them what they want (and not, says Friedman, what some bureaucrat has decided they need). The worker will do the best he can in the hope of increasing his wages (and will not become slovenly in the knowledge that he has union-protected rights and privileges). Government will have limited powers, and so taxes will be lower, providing business with more funds for expansion and workers with more money with which to make purchases.

With the freedom to succeed and prosper also comes the freedom for workers, businessmen, and others to fail. Friedman's approach might result in misery for the losers in the economic race. He appreciates this and has offered several proposals to ease their burdens, most of which involve the use of tax incentives to spur them on. Friedman also believes that government assistance programs that have proliferated since the New Deal have eroded the sense of obligation Americans once felt for one another and their communities. At one time people who needed assistance turned to churches, settlement houses, and private charities, all of which were supported by middle class and wealthy individuals. Now they seek help from the government, while those who formerly contributed money and time now simply pay taxes. Also, in the past, people had more of a sense of responsibility for their own actions, and this too has changed since the New Deal. Friedman even attributes the rise of criminal actions to this alteration in the social structure: "If a man feels he has no responsibility for his own deficiencies, he is likely to take out his frustrations on society as a whole, even if it involves lawless acts."

It should not be thought that Friedman is insensitive to suffering simply because he opposes welfare programs. While most of the new economists who indicate great concern for poor people had middle class backgrounds, Friedman is one of the few leaders of the profession whose origins were truly proletarian. None of the individuals discussed in this book had a more difficult time of it in his early life than did Friedman or encountered more obstacles to professional success. To a degree his life is a textbook example of the working out of the American dream—from rags to riches—that is inferentially celebrated in many of his essays. Friedman's sympathies often are with the wretched, but he would do little more than offer them the means whereby they could help themselves out of their miseries. As for his brand of economics, it appeals most to people who, like himself, have managed to climb the ladder of success. Friedman often traces his ideological roots to the classicists, especially Adam Smith. Emotionally, however, he is in debt to Horatio Alger.

Friedman was born in Brooklyn in 1912. His parents, like those of Arthur Burns, had emigrated to America from the area which then was Austria-Hungary shortly after the turn of the century. Jeno Saul Friedman was a petty merchant and his wife, Ethel, a seamstress. Both worked at low-paying jobs, of which there were many in the New York of that time. (Friedman would later observe that his parents had come to America in the hope of finding work and that there wouldn't have been much of that had there been a minimum wage law in effect at that time.) The Friedmans saved as much of their earnings as they could, and in 1913, when Milton was one year old, they moved to Rahway, New Jersey, where they opened a small dry goods store which his mother ran while his father worked in Manhattan. The store was not a huge success, but it provided the family with a living after Jeno Friedman died in 1927.

Milton attended Rahway High School, where he excelled in mathematics. He graduated the following year and, given the nature of his finances, decided to accept a $300 scholarship offered him by nearby Rutgers University. Since his family could not afford to give him much help during the depression years, he worked his way through school at a variety of jobs, from being a waiter in a local restaurant to a salesman in a department store.

At Rutgers Friedman first majored in mathematics, but soon he was attracted to economics. In part this resulted from the temper of the times—as already shown, the Great Depression was an incubator for economists. But in addition to this Friedman was influenced by two of his instructors. One of these was Arthur Burns, who taught economic statistics at Rutgers while consolidating his beachhead at the National Bureau. The other was Homer Jones, then completing his doctoral work at the University of Chicago. From Burns he gained an appreciation of the complexities of he business cycle and insights into how his twin interests in mathematics and economics might be combined, while Jones helped Friedman obtain a graduate scholarship at Chicago.

Chicago was one of the great breeding grounds for economists in this period. George Stigler and Allen Wallis were fellow students with Friedman, and Paul Samuelson would arrive there as a fresh-

1. Leading media personality as well as contentious economist, John K. Galbraith appeared often on television. Here he is seen being interviewed by talk show host Dick Cavett.

2. Paul Samuelson of M.I.T. has advised presidents, pioneered in several areas of theory, won the Nobel Prize, and is the author of the most influential text in the subject.

3. John Connally, shown here with his mentor, Lyndon Johnson, switched parties and became President Richard Nixon's chief spokesman for economic policy and Secretary of the Treasury.

4. President Carter's CEA Chairman, Charles Schultze, was a Washington veteran who tended to remain in the background during his term in office.

5. G. William Miller, who served President Carter as Chairman of the Federal Reserve Board and later as Secretary of the Treasury, was an able technician who came a cropper when it was learned he was involved with irregularities while leader of the Textron Corporation.

6. As President Ford's Secretary of the Treasury, William Simon became the harsh, often abrasive and contentious advocate of conservatism and enemy of government regulation.

7. Milton Friedman, America's leading monetarist, is congratulated by King Karl Gustaf of Sweden for winning the Nobel Prize in Economics.

8. President Nixon and Paul McCracken, as the latter assumed the post of Chairman of the Council of Economic Advisers.

9. James Schlesinger's puritanical approach to economics attracted both President Ford and President Carter, but both men eventually had to dismiss him.

10. Gerald Ford and his economic soothsayers, from left to right, Arthur Burns, Alan Greenspan, Frank Zarb, Rogers Morton, William Seidman, and James Lynn.

11. Alfred Kahn, Jimmy Carter's chief inflation fighter, became the symbol of deregulation and an attempt to utilize microcconomics in the search for a stable society.

12. The Nixon economics brain trust—Paul McCracken, John Connally, Arthur Burns, and George Schultz.

13. President Johnson and Walter Heller, the Chairman of the Council of Economic Advisers and one of the last New Frontiersmen to leave Washington.

14. A Washington veteran at the time of his nomination as CEA Chairman, Leon Keyserling is shown with Mary Kingsburg Sinkhovitch and Mrs. Roosevelt during a discussion of postwar housing problems.

15. W. Michael Blumenthal, fiscal conservative who spent more than twenty years in big business, part of the time as chief executive officer at the Bendix Corporation, was Jimmy Carter's first Treasury Secretary.

16. President Johnson and John Kenneth Galbraith in a happier mood, before Galbraith came out in opposition to Johnson's renomination.

man the following year. Many had been attracted to Chicago by members of its economics faculty and in particular its star, Frank Knight.

Then 48 years old and at the height of his powers, Knight was among other things a leading defender of the business community at a time when it was under severe attacks. In his influential microeconomic treatise, *Risk, Uncertainty and Profit*, Knight justified the concepts of the marketplace and consumer sovereignty and of free enterprise in general. By the late 1920s he had emerged as one of Thorstein Veblen's leading critics, a "militant expositor of neo-classicism."

Friedman was in Knight's class when the New Deal began. While defending the concepts of deficit spending and unbalanced budgets to bring the nation out of the depression, Knight was critical of the New Deal, fearing that Roosevelt would increase the powers of government so as to restrain freedoms and stifle capitalism. Shaken by the depression, he was now unsure of the validity of economic analysis in general and spent more time tearing apart arguments of liberal economists than in setting down his own thoughts. This was understandable, for at that time he was one of the few major economists willing to defend unpopular conservative ideas in a period of expanding Keynesian influence. Knight was not a particularly good teacher, but he had an important impact upon Friedman and others of his generation, many of whom digested his ideas and imitated his style. In 1935 Friedman joined with Stigler, Wallis, and Homer Jones to edit a collection of Knight's essays, which was characteristically entitled *The Ethics of Competition*.

Henry Simons, who was also at Chicago during this period, had more of an influence on Friedman's thinking. As much a social commentator as an economist, Simons was on his way to becoming a leading critic of Keynesianism, but his major interest was the elimination of monopolies, which he believed the source of most of the nation's problems—concentration of power in the hands of government, labor unions, or corporations prevented the economy from developing naturally and freely and so should be opposed. Simons would simplify the tax code, reform the monetary system so as to prevent manipulations by government of the money supply, and remove all tariffs and related barriers to commerce, all of which anticipated and influenced Friedman's thoughts. Simons's ideas on the proper relationship of government with the economy also appealed to Friedman. The true liberal, said Simons, wanted government to establish the rules under which the economic system would function, but did not think it should interfere in order to help one group or another. In his book *Economic Policy for a Free Society*, he wrote that "the liberal creed" should call for the state "to provide a stable framework of rules within which enterprise and competition may effectively control and direct the production and distribution of goods," and nothing more. Rules were fair, he said, in that they apply equally to all. "Authorities," on the other hand, were not, for they twisted rules for the benefit of one faction or another. The respect for law and the mistrust of politicians, central to Friedman's philosophy, was at the core of Simon's as well.

Friedman also took Jacob Viner's course in economic theory. A conservative economist with an encyclopedic knowledge of history and who did not suffer fools gladly, Viner both frightened and inspired those graduate students who attended his seminars. To Friedman the course was "an absolute eye-opener," and "one of the greatest intellectual experiences of my life." He served as an assistant to Henry Schultz, who was doing important research in the area of economic statistics, and some of whose efforts dovetailed with those of Burns at the National Bureau. The combined influence of these men upon Friedman was immeasurable. By the end of the 1932-1933 academic year, he was a confirmed "Chicagoan."

He was also broke. Unable to remain in school, Friedman faced the possibility of having to abandon his studies. Then, with Arthur Burns's help, he obtained a $1,500 a year fellowship at Columbia. Given his interests in economic statistics, there also was the possibility of assignments at the National Bureau. Friedman gratefully accepted, moved to New York, and began work on his doctorate.

As might have been expected, Friedman came under the influence of Wesley Clair Mitchell, and while he found his work on business cycle theory "illuminating," Friedman was not attuned at that time with Mitchell's institutional approach. Rather, he was far more interested in the researches being conducted by another of his mentors, Harold Hotelling, a brilliant mathematical economist who then was attempting to calculate the true net costs of public works.

While Columbia did not possess a strong ideological tinge, it was more of a centrist school than Chicago and less Keynesian than Harvard. Most of the department's liberals—including Rex Tugwell and Leon Keyserling—had left for positions in Washington, and many of those who remained were engaged in theoretical work that had no direct application to the problems posed by the depression.

Friedman felt comfortable at Columbia, where for the first time in his life he had a measure of economic security. Furthermore, like most Jewish academics of that period he had been concerned about cracking the anti-Semitic barrier that existed in the profession. Now he had obtained what appeared to be a good launching pad for his career. Still, he was not one of the rising stars on Morningside Heights. Nor had he demonstrated the brilliance that marked Samuelson's graduate years. In the mid-1930s Milton Friedman was a hard-working, intelligent, and ambitious economist laboring in a specialized area, which is to say that there were dozens of others like him in the nation's leading graduate schools, and all of them scrambling for the same limited number of positions. His publications record was undistinguished. As was and is the case with most such manuscripts, his M.A. thesis, which dealt with the "Factors Influencing Railroad Stock Prices," was generally ignored. Friedman's first scholarly article, a study of Arthur Pigou's methods for measuring demand elasticities from budgetary data, came out in 1935 and caused no discernible stir within the profession.

In that year Friedman took a leave of absence from Columbia to accept a research post in Washington. One of the fact-finding branches of the New Deal, the National Resources Committee, was preparing a study of consumption patterns in the hope that from them might be gleaned ideas as to how to end the depression. Out of this work came a book, *Consumer Expenditures in the United States*, which reads more like one of the scientific treatises published by the National Bureau than the kind of argumentative works he would produce later on.

Friedman's instinctive dislike of bureaucracies was intensified by his Washington experiences. It was a pleasant enough assignment; his salary was good, and Friedman enjoyed the company of Rose Director, the economist sister of Aaron Director of the University of Chicago, who also worked on the study. But he had no intention of remaining in Washington longer than was necessary, and so maintained his Chicago and New York connections, hoping to receive a call to return to academia, preferably as a faculty member.

In 1937 Simon Kuznets, then one of the leaders the the National Bureau, offered Friedman a post there. Kuznets was involved in a study of the income of professionals and required assistance. In addition the Bureau needed a new general secretary for its Conference on Income and Wealth, a post of some influence in the selection of studies and scholars. Friedman accepted the offer and eventually took over most of the work on the professional study from Kuznets in addition to editing the manuscripts of others.

Friedman had obtained an important toehold within the profession. In the late 1930s it appeared he would concentrate his attention upon research in technical economics and produce the kinds of studies admired by his peers for their elegance but ignored by almost everyone else for their lack of readability. The United States Printing office had committed itself to the publication of *Consumer Expenditures,* several of his statistics-laden articles had appeared in journals, and he offered courses in mathematical economics at Columbia. With all of this, his ideological commitment to free enterprise was growing and maturing. His marriage in 1938 to Rose Director brought him still closer to the Chicago tradition, and so for that matter did an aspect of his research at the National Bureau.

Those who remember Friedman as he was in this period speak of his constant insistence upon scholarly detachment, and a few reflect that this usually appeared in his criticisms of liberal economists who were sympathetic with the social objectives of the New Deal. Economists should strive for objectivity, he thought, and seek to make the discipline as value-free and scientific as possible. Terms like "decent wages" and "unjust profits" simply did not belong in their lexicon. This position was one that might have been expected from a free enterpriser at a time when that creed was in eclipse and its believers had little in the way of political power. But more important, perhaps, was the fact that Friedman was a member of the National Bureau, where Wesley Clair Mitchell had always insisted that ideology had to be kept out of research publications, and had shown the way in his own scholarly output.

In Friedman's view, his report on professional incomes was both scientific and in the Mitchell tradition, while others at the National Bureau disagreed. Friedman had found a large gap between the incomes of physicians and dentists, which he described and documented with care and precision. He believed this due in large part to monopoly practices of the medical profession, but it could not be demonstrated, at least not in a statistical, scientific way, as defined by the National Bureau. So he presented his views in a circumspect fashion. Clearly one reason for the higher incomes of doctors was the relative shortage of practitioners. This might be due to greater innate abilities required of physicians or a shortage of training facilities. "A third possible explanation is that the difference in ease of entry reflects a deliberate policy of limiting the total number of

physicians to prevent so-called 'overcrowding' of the profession,"
wrote Friedman in his final draft. Attempting to placate purists at
the National Bureau, he went on to say that "An adequate judgement of this explanation would be exceedingly difficult and is well
outside the scope of this study," and he suggested it might be found
in "an analysis of the motives, acts, and influence" of the American
Medical Association and other groups involved in regulating the
profession.

The report caused consternation and debate at the National Bureau. Some said it wasn't scholarly enough for their tastes, that
Friedman hadn't demonstrated the validity of his conclusions.
Others might have been concerned about implied criticisms of the
A.M.A. Might this not endanger outside support for other National
Bureau publications? Mitchell disagreed with both contentions and
supported publication. But he also believed that all National Bureau
books should be acceptable to most of the members, or at least that
disagreements should be minimized. Not only was the book's future
in doubt, but without publication Friedman could not receive his
Ph.D., and so his professional future was clouded.

In the midst of all this Friedman received an invitation to become a visiting professor at the University of Wisconsin for the
1940-1941 academic year. Harold Groves, who it will be recalled
was Walter Heller's mentor there, helped arrange for the appointment, and so the Friedmans left the contention at the National Bureau for what appeared to be a promising future in Madison.

For a while all went smoothly. Friedman received and accepted
a long-term appointment, and it seemed he had found a permanent academic niche. At the time, however, the department was in
the midst of a major upheaval. One faction, generally conservative
in ideology, wanted to join the School of Business, while the liberals,
including Groves, wanted to remain in the College of Liberal Arts.
Friedman agreed with Groves, and the conservatives protested his
appointment, which became a symbol of the contention between the
factions. Although the public discussions were civilized for the most
part, a note of anti-Semitism quickly was heard. In private, some of
the conservatives argued that there was no room on the campus for
another Jew (Wisconsin had one on the faculty) and that Friedman, a pushy New Yorker, had to go because he "didn't fit in." The
arguments continued for weeks, and the situation was extremely
nasty. Led by Walter Heller, the graduate students demonstrated
in favor of his appointment, while others came out against it. Dis-

gusted and uncomfortable, Friedman withdrew his acceptance and left Wisconsin to return to the National Bureau and Columbia—and the struggle to publish his book and obtain his doctorate.

As it happened, Friedman's luck was about to change. Had he remained at Wisconsin, he might have developed into an important statistical economist with only a small audience outside of the profession, for this was his primary interest at he time and the reason he had been brought to Madison. On his return to Morningside Heights Friedman was approached by Carl Shoup, who had just received a Carnegie Foundation grant to study the relationship between inflation and tax policies. Shoup wanted Friedman to serve with Ruth Mack of the National Bureau as one of his associate directors, with special responsibilities for statistical work. Friedman accepted and for the first time started to conduct important research in the area of monetary economics. Less than a year later, however, Shoup was asked to become an economist at the U. S. Treasury's Division of Tax Research. He took the post, on condition that he could continue his Carnegie Corporation work there and in addition bring his staff to Washington. The Treasury agreed, and so once again Friedman went to work for the federal bureaucracy, though at a higher level than he had occupied at the National Resources Committee.

Now he was asked to provide testimony before congressional committees and later on help formulate wartime tax measures. Walter Heller, who served for a while as one of his assistants, recalled that Friedman seemed to blossom in Washington. This is understandable. The wartime capital was an exciting place, he was in a policy-making post involved with critical research and in an area of economics that enabled him to combine his mathematical and statistical expertise with his ideological inclinations. "His technical work was brilliant," said Heller, "and his clashes with the late Senator Taft about taxes were something to see."

Friedman played a small role in the debate as to the best means to contain inflation. A large group (which included John Galbraith) argued for wage and price controls. Others, many of whom followed recommendations of Keynes, thought forced savings and higher income taxes would cut deeply into civilian expenditures. Friedman, Shoup, and Mack argued for this approach in their book, *Taxing to Prevent Inflation*, which was published in 1943. Controls would be cumbersome and difficult to enforce, as well as requiring a large bureaucracy at a time when professional and skilled labor was scarce. In addition, they tended to distort the economy and create black markets. But while Friedman preferred taxes to controls, he wasn't certain they should be levied on earnings. A Chicago colleague, Allen Wallis, headed a statistical team at the Division of War Research at Columbia, where he developed an alternate approach to the problem, one that involved a tax on spending, not income. Now Friedman came out in favor of a "spendings tax," which not only would discourage civilian purchases but result in a higher level of savings and so incorporate elements of the Keynesian program. Friedman was willing to bend on the issue; he conceded that in times of national danger forms of controls and drastic mobilization might be needed. But his aversion to bureaucracies and preference for the open workings of the marketplace increased during the war.

The great debates regarding tax policies had ended by 1943, and Friedman was ready to move on. In addition he was anxious to resolve the matter of publication of his book on professional incomes and so complete work on his doctorate. When Wallis offered him a post at the Division of War Research, he accepted. For the next two years Friedman was engaged in the development of statistical tools for use in the design of military ordnance, and he also revised his manuscript and prepared for an academic career after the war.

The National Bureau finally published *Income from Independent Professional Practice* in 1945. By then much of academia knew of the conflicts the work had stirred, and the debate over its merits continued to the very end. C. Reinhold Noyes, one of the Bureau's directors, insisted on appending a note to the work, in which he disputed some of its findings, in particular those dealing with comparisons between the earnings of physicians and dentists. Without alluding to the roles of the A.M.A. and related groups, he wrote "It is doubtful that competent opinion would support the assumption that medicine and dentistry require much the same type and degree of ability, etc." Friedman had not said they did, at least in the final version, but of course he had been obliged to soften his positions and modify his prose in order to gain publication.

Clearly he was unhappy about this situation. The experiences in Wisconsin and the National Bureau, his tours of duty in Washington, and his rather difficult time of it in general must have stiffened his determination never again to be at the mercy of bureaucracies and institutions. Later on, when he enunciated his views in strong, even exaggerated fashion, he might have done so to make up for those years when he was prevented from doing this.

Friedman was awarded his Ph.D. the following year, at which time he was 34 years old. He had a growing reputation in the profession but as yet no permanent position; at the time he was an associate professor at the University of Minnesota on a short-term appointment. Then came the call to Chicago, where two years later he was promoted to full professor of economics.

At first Friedman was seen as one of Knight's allies, and by the early 1950s he was looked upon as his possible successor and standard bearer of the classical tradition. Friedman was awarded the John Bates Clark medal in 1951 (Samuelson had won it two years earlier)—a sign of his enhanced position in the profession. During the next decade he published more than a score of books and major articles on a wide variety of topics, from mathematical economics to monetary theory. These helped establish Friedman as one of the half dozen most original economists in the nation, perhaps the world.

The body of Friedman's work possesses a unifying philosophy and an internal consistency, both of which attracted others to the Chicago banner. It was not surprising, then, that by the late 1950s economists had begun referring to "Friedmanites," indicating he had become the focus of a school. But while some of his essays appeared in general interest publications, he remained virtually unknown outside of the profession and government circles. Friedman was not yet a familiar name to the kinds of people who read Galbraith's books, or even to most of those who used Samuelson's text. That recognition would come later.

Friedman's approach to the discipline is spelled out in an essay entitled: "The Methodology of Positive Economics," which appeared in 1952 and remains one of the indispensible documents in any study of the man and his beliefs. He opens by referring to the distinction between positive and normative (or regulative) science as made by John Neville Keynes, the economist father of the more famous son. Normative economics, which Freidman believes is more an art than a science, is used to realize moral values through legislation and public policies; it is concerned with "what ought to be." Positive economics, on the other hand, deals with "what is" and is employed to determine the facts of a stiuation and the context in which they exist. Thus, it should strive to be value-free, objective, and truly scientific. "Its task is to provide a system of generalizations that can be used to make correct predictions about the consequences of any change in circumstances." Some economists, Friedman suggests, confuse or muddy the distinctions between these two varieties of economics and advocate moral goals as though they were produced by dispassionate research. What is required is greater care and stress upon positive economics, for the more that is known about a problem, the clearer will be the prescription for its remedy. "Two individuals may agree upon the consequences of a particular piece of legislation. One may regard them as desirable on balance and so favor the legislation; the other, as undesirable and so oppose the legislation." But the two parts of the process should be kept apart and considered separately, with stress and primacy afforded the discovery of facts. For example, says Friedman, those who favor an increase in the minimum wages claim that by so doing poverty would be decreased without enlarging the unemployment rate, while their opponents believe that unemployment rises when wages are boosted. Before doing anything else, a determination should be made of the impact of higher minimum wage laws upon employment, and this can be accomplished through recourse to positive economics. "Agreement about the economic consequences of the legislation might not produce complete agreement about its desirability," writes Friedman, "for differences might still remain about its political or social consequences; but, given agreement on objectives, it would certainly go a long way toward producing consensus."

All of this seemed both obvious and not particularly contentious. In so stating, Friedman indicated his allegiance to the National Bureau's approach as typified in the works of Mitchell, Burns, and their kind—the mainstream of American scientific economics. But these statements also suggested that since Friedman's positive economics would be grounded upon strong research, those who would contest him had better be prepared to be as thorough as he. In future debates with his adversaries, Friedman often would marshal impressive statistical and other empirical evidence to support his conclusions, and in exchanges he would imply that those who refused to accept his views did so out of ignorance, perversity, or recourse to normative economics. He would often lay this last sin at the feet of John Galbraith, with whom he has had a running debate for three decades. "The puzzle I find on reading Galbraith," he said recently, "is how to reconcile his own *sincere* conviction in the validity of his view of the world with the almost complete failure of any other students—even those who are sympathetic with his general political orientation—to *document* its validity."

Galbraithians often respond to this kind of criticism with a paraphrase of this quotation, substituting Friedman's name for Galbraith's. And in fact, as his celebrity increased, Friedman too became a public philosopher, who shared Galbraith's tendency to employ exaggerated phrases and simplify conclusions when addressing general audiences. As his confidence and audiences grew, Friedman spoke out on a wide range of issues, many of them having little or nothing to do with economics—the volunteer army, public versus private education, and freedom of the press among others—and on such occasions his conclusions were derived more from philosophical beliefs than the operations of positive science. Too, the distinction between the scientific economist and the public figure was becoming blurred even in the early postwar period.

For all of this, Friedman retained his faith in positive economics as a means whereby one might forsee the implications of present actions, policies, and tendencies, and he posed more often as a seer than a politician. "Economics as a positive science is a body of tentatively accepted generalizations about economic phenomena that can be used to predict the consequences of changes in circumstances," he wrote. Again, this textbooklike definition does not appear to be particularly contentious, yet it was a methodological gauntlet thrown at some of the methodologies prized at the National Bureau. The painstaking fact gathering practiced there, admirable and useful though it might be, was geared primarily at obtaining an appreciation of the many complexities of the economy and not at the more important task of providing a model for predictions. Friedman cared little if the model was imperfect or did not take account of all aspects of the economy; the test was accuracy in predictions, not completeness in content. "Truly important and significant hypotheses will be found to have 'assumptions' that are wildly inaccurate descriptive representations of reality, and, in general, the more significant the theory, the more unrealistic the assumptions (in this sense)." To Friedman the reason for this was almost self-evident. "A hypothesis is important if it 'explains' much by little; that is, if it abstracts the common and crucial elements from the mass of complex and detailed circumstances surrounding the phenomena to be explained and permits valid predictions on the basis of them alone."

These two tenets—the belief in the virtues of positive science and the insistence that accurate predictions can be made from simplified assumptions—run through much of Friedman's work and may explain apparent contradictions and paradoxes in his behavior. Friedman insists on holding those who arrive at different conclusions than his to farily rigid standards of evidence, as has been seen in his criticisms of Galbraith. But he has often offered predictions based not only on flimsy evidence but also on what social scientists term counterfactual constructs. For example, in the early 1950s Friedman advocated an all-volunteer army, and he has continued to do so to the present, claiming that pay incentives would attract sufficient qualified individuals to the ranks. This may appeal to logic, but Friedman has never provided evidence to support his conclusion. On many occasions over the past three decades he has offered predictions as to what might transpire if one or another regulation was eliminated, from the pure food and drug law (many lives would be saved) to the licensing of radio and television networks (the quality of programming would increase and diversity would be encouraged). But of course there is no way of proving this on the basis of positive economics.

This tendency on Friedman's part could be discerned as early as 1946, when together with George Stigler he published *Roofs or Ceilings? The Current Housing Problem*, which argued that if all controls were eliminated the shortage of housing would be quickly ended. The authors reasoned that if the price of housing increased due to an imbalance of demand over supply, renters and buyers would be forced to settle for less space, while builders would be encouraged to construct additional units. "No complex, expensive, and expansive machinery is necessary. The rationing is conducted quietly and impersonally through the price system."

The authors offered scant evidence to support this conclusion, and what was introduced was highly selective. Their conclusions were logical, appealing, and possessed of an almost geometrical simplicity. The message was bold and forthright: when in doubt, trust the marketplace and, wherever possible, eliminate a bureaucracy. Friedman would say as much in proposing solutions to problems of international finance (he favored freely floating exchange rates and opposed the gold standard), the poor quality of education in America (he would eliminate the public schools, issue vouchers to students, and then let the schools compete for them), the chronic ills of transportation (the Interstate Commerce Commission would be

disbanded), income tax inequities (the Internal Revenue Service
would be gutted, all tax loopholes and preferential treatment would
be ended, and everyone would be taxed at a flat rate), and the many
difficulties of administering an equitable welfare program (Friedman was an early supporter of the negative income tax, which he
would substitute for all welfare programs). He did not feel the government had the right to impose morals upon the general population, even when he agreed with them. Thus, while Friedman deplored racial injustices, he did not back much of the civil rights
legislation of the 1960s and hoped that change could be brought
about through discussion, education—and the workings of the marketplace.

In setting forth these and other, similar solutions to major national problems, Friedman won the ardent support of antigovern-
ment forces, conservatives of most hues, and millions of Americans
who were convinced the system wasn't working well, that "special
interests" were in command in Washington, and that enlightened
self-interest was a more fitting engine for a free society than legislative enactments or bureaucratic decrees. Much to his distress, Friedman also was praised by bigots and reactionaries, who perceived in
his philosophical constructs justification for racial and religious discrimination, segregation, and opposition to even private measures to
alleviate poverty and economic misery. As had been the case with
other celebrity political economists, Friedman found the public
arena less polite and more demanding than were the classrooms.
Like them he was an intellectual who by force of circumstances and
desire was obliged to function in an arena in which emotions, visceral
slogans—and even antiintellectualism—often were more effective
than reasoned argument. In the early 1950s he did his best to maintain a cool demeanor and a scientific detachment in the face of growing contention, but, as the decade wore on, a strong note of passion
entered both his writings and speeches. Clearly the public Friedman
was drifting away from positive economics.*

With all of this, Friedman still lacked a prominent podium from

---

* Few college campuses were quiet during the Vietnam War, when professors and
students debated the merits of that struggle in heated and emotional fashion. On
some campuses supporters of the war had difficulties making themselves heard, as
they were shouted down and, in some cases, assaulted. This ended as the war came
to an end, but other protests continued. In the 1970s some of Friedman's appearances
were disrupted by individuals who protested his supposed aid to the Chilean junta and
other undemocratic regimes. Few of his colleagues on the political left spoke out
strongly in favor of Friedman's right to be heard. Samuelson was one of these, and
Heller another.

which to speak to the general literate public. This must have been irksome, for it appeared his brand of conservatism might receive another chance during the Eisenhower era, one that was seized upon by Burns and others, while economics was becoming a topic for general conversations. Friedman did what he could to advance himself in 1962 by publishing *Capitalism and Freedom,* which is more a collection of essays than a book, and which grew out of a series of lectures he had delivered in 1956. While the work did not become a best seller, it was read by large numbers of people who may have heard about Friedman but lacked the background and interest to plow through his scholarly articles. Partly as a result of the popularity of this work, Friedman was invited to contribute a column to *Newsweek,* where he alternated with Samuelson and Henry Wallich, his role being that of spokesman for the conservative point of view. In its paperback version, *Capitalism and Freedom* was adopted by economics professors wishing to provide a counterweight to Samuelson's text, expose their students to neoclassical ideas, or just to stir things up.

Capitalism and Freedom remains Friedman's most accessible work and the best introduction to his economic philosophy. That this is so, close to a quarter of a century after the ideas were originally presented, is a commentary on Friedman's consistency and the strengths of his beliefs. His outlook hasn't altered much in the past three decades or so; Friedman dug in his ideological heels while still a fairly young scholar and since then has hewed to pretty much the same line. His reactions to problems that have developed since then may be idiosyncratic, but they also are quite predictable.

Many reviewers noted that *Capitalism and Freedom* was squarely in the tradition established by Adam Smith in his famous *Wealth of Nations.* Both men celebrate the free market and try to demonstrate that, left to his own devices, each person attempts to maximize his benefits and that, through the workings of Smith's "invisible hand," society as a whole prospers. But Friedman's book has more in common with Smith's *The Theory of Moral Sentiments* than with the better known treatise, in that it is involved as much with ethics as with economics. In this comparatively neglected work, Smith is concerned with the necessary moral foundation for human societies. He concludes that they exist because people feel a need for companionship—we are social animals. But at the same time all people possess certain antisocial tendencies. In order to be able to live with one another, rules of conduct are required. Each member must understand his rights and obligations and realize that transgressions will be punished. This is no less the case for a society of criminals than for one of saints. "Beneficence, therefore, is less essential to the existence of society than justice. Society may subsist, though not in the most comfortable state, without beneficence, but the prevalence of injustice must utterly destroy it." Friedman echoes this sentiment in a section of *Capitalism and Freedom* entitled "Government as Rule-Maker and Umpire," in which he outlines the role government should play in a free society. Wherever and whenever possible, custom, tradition, and group standards should prevail. "But we cannot rely on custom or on this consensus alone to interpret and to enforce the rules; we need an umpire . . . to provide the means whereby we can modify the rules, and to enforce compliance with the rules on the part of those few who would otherwise not play the game." Friedman believes "the need for government in these respects arises because absolute freedom is impossible. However attractive anarchy may be as a philosophy, it is not feasible in a world of imperfect men."

One of the most important roles government plays in a free society, says Friedman, is to insure the integrity of the marketplace and make certain these "imperfect men" do not destroy or cripple it. "So long as effective freedom of exchange is maintained, the central feature of the market organization of economic activity is that it prevents one person from interfering with another in respect of most of his activities." Thus, a consumer with many producers from whom to select will be protected against coercion by any one of them. Similarly, sellers who have many customers will not be under the thumb of a single person or group. "The employee is protected from coercion by the employer because of other employers for whom he can work, and so on. And the market does this impersonally and without centralized authority." To Friedman, this is the point of having a free market: it prevents any one person or group of people from dominating others, from forcing them to accept their products or way of thinking. He believes this is why totalitarians on all parts of the political spectrum dislike free markets. "It gives people what they want instead of what a particular group thinks they ought to have. Underlying most arguments against the free market is a lack of belief in freedom itself."

Government often becomes the means whereby crusading and well-intentioned individuals attempt to impose their concepts of what is right and good upon others, who may not share in their visions or particularly want them. People who consider themselves liberals seek to protect citizens against their foolishness—or at least what appears foolish in their eyes—and imply by so doing that most Americans are either stupid or ignorant, possibly both. Thus, says Friedman in one of his more famous examples, they have made participation in the Social Security program mandatory, despite the fact that many people are capable of planning for their own futures. Furthermore, the system has backfired (as do most of them), for the very people Social Security was intended to protect suffer under it. Friedman notes that poor people pay a larger percentage of their earnings into the system than do the wealthy, and, since they do not live as long, receive fewer benefits after retirement.

Friedman believes that most modern liberals are more concerned with the redistribution of wealth than with its creation and prize egalitarianism more than freedom. Thus, they seek to tax the winners in the economic game and use the funds thus obtained to help the losers. They would provide more money for public schools in the ghettos than for those in affluent areas, for example. Friedman is sympathetic with the goals of many liberals but here as elsewhere suggests that the approach is unworkable. "One can shuffle inanimate objects around; one can compel individuals to be at certain places at certain times; but one can hardly compel individuals to put forward their best efforts. Put another way, the substitution of compulsion for co-operation changes the amount of resources available." Thus, the innovative businessman and productive worker are discouraged from functioning at their full potential by what they see as inequities, and so their total output is not what it might be. In seeking to divide the pie into equal shares by means of coercion, the liberals only succeed in shrinking the pie, so that everyone has less than might be expected under conditions of freedom."The best are often the enemy of the good," is the way Friedman put it on several occasions.

Friedman believes that, left to their own devices, without government intervention, free enterprise economies tend to expand at a more or less stable rate. This sets him apart from the Keynesians, who hold that the failure of businessmen to maintain investments at critical points in the business cycle causes recessions, and so government intervention is required to correct the imbalance. Thus, Heller and Samuelson advocated tax cuts as a means to stimulate demand, which in turn would result in larger investments by businesses. To them, a sluggish economy requires a prod to make it perform at its peak. This is backward thinking, says Friedman. Without government fiscal and monetary intervention, the economy would act to eliminate both long-term inflation and unemployment. Deviations from a smoothly running economy are the results of political and economic meddling. Thus, in order to have optimal development, steps should be taken to cut back in these areas.

Both as an economist and a moral philosopher, Friedman supported the Kennedy tax cut; he approves of all programs designed to allow people to retain more of what they earned. But he also argues that elimination of barriers to individual self-realization is a better way to accelerate the growth rate. More important, he opposes all attempts at fine tuning. Not only does he prefer the economy to work its own way, but he denies economists have the knowledge of what to prescribe, when to administer the medicine, and when to alter the treatment.

As indicated, Friedman's major contributions in positive economics dealt with monetary matters. He would later claim that his interests and viewpoints on this subject were an integral part of what he called the "Chicago Tradition" of Knight, Simons, Viner, and others, whose concern with monetary theory and policy remained strong during the 1930s, when the subject was out of favor among the Keynesians. These men developed "a subtle and relevant version" of the quantity theory of money, which held that changes in the money supply directly influenced the price level, and which "became a flexible and sensitive tool for interpreting movements in aggregate economic activity and for developing relevant policy prescriptions." His later work at the National Bureau made him more aware of the complexities of the economy and the difficulties in programming changes, while the two tours of duty in Washington sharpened Friedman's innate dislike of bureaucracies. By the time the war had ended all of these had come together to form the foundation for his subsequent work.

Friedman was drawn into the debate revolving around the passage of the Employment Act of 1946, of whose wisdom he had grave doubts. He prepared a paper that touched upon the subject and was delivered in the autumn of 1947, and that, in a somewhat revised form, appeared in the *American Economic Review* the following year as "A Monetary and Fiscal Framework for Economic Stability." In this essay Friedman states that most economists can agree upon certain fundamental long-run goals. While not defining his terms, he says these are political freedom, economic efficiency, and equality of economic power. The best way to preserve political values and achieve economic ends would be the implementation of a program marked by simplicity of design and lack of coercion in application. In this can be heard a distinct echo of Henry Simons's call for "rules" rather than "authorities" and a prefiguration of mature Friedmanism.

"Government must provide a monetary framework for a competitive order," says Friedman, and "this competitive framework should operate under the 'rule of law' rather than the discretionary authority of administrators." He concedes that this will do little to lessen the economic inequities but hopes that a "competitive order" will take care of some of them. As for the rest, he expresses his belief that the community would desire to reduce inequality even further, and his faith that "general fiscal measures (as contrasted with specific intervention) are the most desirable non-free-market means of decreasing inequality."

Friedman goes on to present a three-point program to create conditions of economic stability, in which can be found the seeds for his more-familiar, later recommendations. He would sharply curtail the powers of the Federal Reserve System to create or destroy money, a reform that would assure the population that no tinkering in this important area would take place. The second point involves the level of public expenditures. This would be determined by the public's desire for services and willingness to pay for them, and would not be a countercyclical tool. Thus, Friedman would eliminate or at least play down the role of fiscal policy in dealing with depressions. Nor would he vary welfare and Social Security payments so as to respond to the developments in the business cycle. Finally, Friedman would rely upon the personal income tax for most revenues and sharply curtail the corporate and related levies.

Most governmental expenditures would be financed through taxes or the sale of noninterest-bearing paper to banks, which would use them as a basis for reserves. The public would realize that it had to pay for what it wanted from government, either through taxes or an increase in the volume of loans, which would create inflation. There would be no shrinking from the consequences of federal spending. "Government would not issue interest-bearing securities to the public; the Federal Reserve System would not operate in the open market." Moreover, "Deficits or surpluses in government budgets would be reflected dollar for dollar in changes in the quantity of money; and conversely, the quantity of money would change only as a consequence of deficits or surpluses." Deficits would result in an increase in the money supply, while the amount of money in circulation would decline should there be a surplus.

Friedman believes that such a system would function automatically to correct imbalances during the course of the business cycle. In times of prosperity more people would have jobs and would be receiving higher incomes, while the need for welfare payments would decline. This would mean the total tax take would increase and expenditures decline, and so there would be a budget surplus. This in turn would bring about a shrinkage in the money supply that would prevent overheating and inflation. Then, as the economy headed into a slump, the tax revenues would decline while welfare payments would increase. This situation would lead to an expansion in the money supply, a stimulative measure that would pave the way for economic revival.

Friedman differs from Heller in that he would not program budget deficits in order to maximize economic growth. In any case, he is far more concerned with maintaining stability and preventing inflation and depression than with pushing the economy to its limits. "What we need is not a skillful monetary driver of the economic vehicle continually turning the steering wheel to adjust to the unexpected irregularities of the route, but some means of keeping the monetary passenger who is in the back seat as ballast from occasionally leaning over and giving the steering wheel a jerk that threatens to send the car off the road." The two men agree, however, that tax reductions are preferable to public spending as means of bringing a nation out of a slump. "Many of the programs do not come into effect until after the recession is passed," said Friedman, at a time when Heller was battling Galbraith on this very issue.

While aware that this simple approach was not flawless—there are lags between changes in the money supply and their impacts on the economy, for example—Friedman believed this to be a move "in the right direction" that provided a "more satisfactory framework on which to build future actions."

More satisfactory than what?—clearly Friedman meant to challenge the American Keynesians. Throughout the 1950s he would issue many calls to battle, which more often than not were accepted. In the course of debate, Friedmanism came to be seen as a conservative alternative to Keynesianism.

Friedman also elaborated upon his theories in scholarly articles, some of which were collected in *Essays in Positive Economics*

(1953) and *Studies in the Quantity Theory of Money* (1956). Another work, *A Theory of the Consumption Function* (1957), was published by the National Bureau. In it Friedman offered a strong defense of the quantity theory of money, writing here that "there is perhaps no other empirical relation in economics that has been observed to recur so uniformly under so wide a variety of circumstances as the relation between substantial changes over short periods in the stock of money and in prices." Friedman believes this relationship so close as to be "of the same order as many of the uniformities that form the basis of the physical sciences." In this area, as far as Friedman was concerned, economics could be considered a positive science. His version of the monetary theory became the linchpin of Friedman's economics. If it could be discredited, or even seriously challenged, the entire edifice would be undermined.

The field upon which the battle would be fought was the magisterial *A Monetary History of the United States, 1867-1960,* which he coauthored with Anna J. Schwartz, who was responsible for most of the statistical work. Certainly this is one of the half-dozen or so most important economic treatises of the postwar period. More than any other of his works, the *Monetary History* served to insure a place for Friedman in the history of economic thought but also was a major reason for his having been awarded the Nobel Prize in Economics in 1976.

The fact that this book was cast in a historical mold was as much a result of happenstance as design. In the late 1940s, when Arthur Burns realized that Wesley Mitchell would not live to complete the many projects he had underway at the National Bureau, he assigned portions of his research to various fellows, and Friedman was given a barely started effort in monetary economics. Several years later Walter Stewart, who had been a director of research at the Federal Reserve in its early days, urged Friedman to undertake an "analytical narrative" of American banking and monetary history since the Civil War. Although Friedman had not done any significant work in financial history, he decided that such research would enable him to demonstrate convincingly that the money supply and monetary policies were the key determinants for economic growth or decline, inflation or recession.

During the next decade Friedman, Schwartz, and a group of assistants dug into the monetary and financial statistics for their period and studied its politics as well. In the process, their ideas were formed and reformed. "Our foray into analytical narrative has significantly affected our statistical analysis," the authors wrote in their preface. But the work only served to strengthen their devotion to positive science. At he heart of it is the primacy of monetary forces. Personalities do not count for much when it comes to reactions to shifts in the money supply. Increase it substantially and no force available to presidents and kings will be able to prevent inflation. Decrease it sharply and recession will be unavoidable. As one reviewer put it, the book's essential message is that "money matters."

The existence of this work-in-progress was known within the profession. In a paper entitled "The Supply of Money and Changes in Prices and Output," published in 1955, one can find the germs of ideas later presented in the *Monetary History*. During the next eight years as he worked on the book, Friedman tossed off articles on monetary subjects, and through these one can see the development of his thesis. Chapter drafts were circulated to Stigler, David Meiselman, Lloyd Mints, and others of the Chicago school. Burns provided suggestions and made his contribution. Friedman acknowledged their assistance, not only in the area of expertise but also in helping frame and focus his ideas. He went so far as to imply that the *Monetary History* was not only a product of Friedman and Schwartz but a definitive statement of the thinking of the Chicago School circa 1963, the year the National Bureau and Princeton University Press released the book.

For example, he took note of the help provided by Clark Warburton, the idiosyncratic Chicago School economist and director of research for the Federal Deposit Insurance Corporation. His papers on monetary subjects, and in particular several dealing with the history of monetary thought, had anticipated and helped shape parts of the *Monetary History*. Warburton had observed that sharp declines in the money supply invariably preceded all major recessions and depressions and charged that "economists have neglected an important phase of the relation of changes in the quantity of money to prices and business profits and prospects which had been recognized by eighteenth-, nineteenth-, and early twentieth-century economists." Friedman and Schwartz drew upon his research and assistance. "His detailed and valuable contributions on several drafts have importantly affected the final version," they wrote. "In addition, time and again, as we came to some conclusion that seemed to us novel and original, we found that he had been there before."

The *Monetary History* not only became a definitive statement of

Chicago School economics but also helped expunge Keynesian ac-couterments from the dogma and provided a text with which to combat the new economists. A. James Meigs, a Chicagoan who in the early 1950s worked as a Federal Reserve economist, recalled that at that time he "accepted the quantity theory as an explanation of long-run price behavior. But I was blissfully ignorant of the possibility that money-supply changes might do much more than influence prices and interest rates. . . . We were the children of our time and had been well indoctrinated in Keynesian economics." This was all changed with the appearance of the Friedman-Schwartz book, which according to Meigs evoked "indignant in-credulity" even among the Chicagoans for its breadth of vision and depth of research.

Although the *Monetary History* is replete with charts, tables, and diagrams, there is little in the book that would puzzle a layman or student capable of going through one of Galbraith's books or even Samuelson's text. The authors trace the impact that shifts in the money supply have had on the economy and conclude that "changes in the behavior of the money stock have been closely as-sociated with changes in economic activity, money income, and prices." Moreover, "the interrelation between monetary and economic changes has been highly stable." The money supply figures, then, provide the best lead indicator for aggregate economic activity. It is more than that, however. "One can regard the mon-etary events partly as shocks that trigger a cyclical reaction mechan-ism." Change the money supply, then, and you will soon see a ripple effect throughout the economy.

Changes in the money supply in the late nineteenth and early twentieth centuries resulted from discoveries of precious metals, political decisions, foreign trade, and shifts in international invest-ments. The recessions and booms of this period can be traced to one or more of these factors, writes Friedman, and all contributed to the declining price levels of the 1880s and early 1890s and the inflation that began close to the end of the nineteenth century. These factors continued to exercize an influence on the money supply after 1914, but with the establishment of the Federal Reserve System in that year came a major change in the creation and shrinkage of the monetary base. Friedman traces the activities of the central bank in the 1920s, concentrating upon the philosophy and policies of Benjamin Strong, head of the New York Bank, who comes close to being the "hero" of the work. A devoted monetarist and a man of substantial influence in the banking community, Strong understood that recessions can be halted by expanding the money supply. He died in 1928. Friedman writes that "if Strong had still been alive and head of the New York Bank in the fall of 1930, he would very likely have recognized the oncoming liquidity crisis for what it was, would have been prepared by experience and conviction to take strenuous and appropriate measures to head it off, and would have had the standing to carry the System with him." This is as close as Friedman would come to saying that personalities do matter in history—but only if they prescribe the proper medicine and convince the patient to take it, and it is the medicine, not the doctor, that affects the cure.

This section provides the background for the heart of the book, "The Great Contraction," which deals with the period from 1929 to 1933. This is a monetarist interpretation of the causes for the Great Depression and, by inference, a critique of the body of New Deal practices. Later on the chapter would be published separately in paperback form and find its way into college courses in American history. Just as some professors employed *Capitalism and Freedom* as a counterweight to Samuelson, so others used *The Great Contraction* to balance Galbraith's *The Great Crash*.

Friedman contends that the Federal Reserve reduced the money supply from 1927 to 1929 in an attempt to curb speculation on Wall Street and that this led to an economic slowdown, the outlines of which were evident in mid-1929. Thus, the market's crash in October was caused in part by a growing realization that the nation was entering a slump. But there was no banking panic. The ratio of bank deposits to currency in circulation remained high. The situation appeared to have stabilized by late 1930 when, in mid-December, the Bank of the United States in New York failed, and this collapse resulted in a major run on banks and a major liquidity crisis. The money supply then declined sharply, at a time when monetarists believed the Federal Reserve should have been pumping additional funds into the system to bring a halt to the deflation and save the banks. George Harrison, Strong's successor in New York, urged this course of action, but he lacked the forceful personality and influence needed to sway the other members. "Stand patters" noted that most of the failed banks were not members of the System, and so the Federal Reserve had no responsibility to save them. In addition, few of them understood monetary theory, since most of the governors were political appointees. Thus, the money supply continued to shrink, and the crisis worsened.

Great Britain went off the gold standard in September 1931, and this resulted in an outflow of the metal from the American monetary system, as Europeans started to hoard it. Now the money supply declined more rapidly than before. Bank failures increased, the exodus of gold quickened, and the Federal Reserve's reactions were half-hearted, inadequate, and at times counterproductive. What was needed, said Friedman, was a stable monetary base. Hence, the central bank should have poured money into the system. Instead it provided an early version of fine tuning which failed utterly. Manipulation of interest rates and open market operations often succeeded in making matters worse. Between 1929 and 1933, according to Friedman, the nation's money supply shrank by more than one-third. Over two-thirds of the decline came after Britain abandoned gold, and this coincided with the most severe period of the slump.

The onset of the Great Depression is for Friedman both the classic example of the power of money and his best illustration of how changes in its supply can affect the economy. Elsewhere he wrote that "I know of no severe depression in any country or any time that was not accompanied by a sharp decline in the stock of money and equally of no sharp decline in the stock of money that was not accompanied by a severe depression."

This flew in the face of much of liberal historigraphy regarding the depression. Galbraith, Arthur Schlesinger, and others of their persuasion hadn't considered the money supply an important factor in the late 1920s and 1930s. Most college texts held that the collapse had been caused by sharp business practices in the 1920s, and that Roosevelt's spending programs had helped stabilize matters in the 1930s, after which World War II spending brought the nation back to prosperity. In Friedman's view none of this makes sense. The depression was brought on by a shrinkage of the money supply from 1929 to 1933. All of the New Deal programs could have been scrapped, as far as he was concerned, for the good they did. Had the money supply been expanded in the 1930s, prosperity would have returned. A rapid increase in supply of money from 1938 to 1941, and not the onset of the war, provided the necessary stimulation that brought about economic recovery. Thus, the experiences of the 1930s did not demonstrate that American capitalism was weak or about to crumble. "The Great Depression in the United States, far from being a sign of the inherent instability of the private enterprise system, is a testament as to how much harm can be done by mistakes on the part of a few men when they wield vast power over the monetary system of a country." Or in the words used in *Capitalism and Freedom,* the depression resulted from the substitution of authorities for rules.

The villain here is the Federal Reserve. Friedman would take from the central bank the power to manipulate the money supply. "I would specify that the Reserve System shall see to it that the total stock of money so defined rises month by month, and indeed, so far as possible, day by day, at an annual rate of X percent, where X is some number between 3 and 5." Had this been the monetary policy from 1929 to 1933, Friedman implies, there would have been no Great Depression—for the Great Contraction would not have taken place and triggered it.

The *Monetary History* stirred a heated debate within the profession. While recognizing it as a major effort, liberal critics charged Friedman with having inferred sweeping conclusions from inadequate or incomplete data. Samuelson wrote that the "implied proof" of a "simple, controllable, causal relationship" between the money supply and the rise and fall of the gross national product was "unconvincing." But he added that Friedman had obliged him to reconsider his opinions. "Contrary to some of my earlier views," he wrote, "I believe that monetary and credit policies have great potency to stimulate, stabilize, or depress a modern economy." Economic historians charged that Friedman had not considered the impact of nonmonetary factors on the economy. Nor had he examined fully the effects that changes in the interest rates had upon the demand for money, preferring instead to concentrate upon the Federal Reserve and the supply side of the picture.

M. I. T. economist Peter Temin went over much of the material Friedman had used and concluded that this was a major flaw in the book. Temin found no evidence of deflationary banking policies from the time of the stock market crash of 1929 to the British abandonment of gold two years later and absolves the Federal Reserve of a great deal of the blame Friedman had heaped upon it. In his book, *Did Monetary Forces Cause the Great Depression?*, he concludes that the answer must be, "not proven." Alluding to Friedman, Temin warns that any economist "who uses this conclusion or any other conclusion about the Depression as a basis for economic policy recommendations essentially is performing an act of faith."

The release of the *Monetary History* and the debates surrounding it coincided with the 1964 presidential election. Although a Republican, Friedman had had little direct contact with national politics in the 1950s and early 1960s. Burns had not called him to Washington during the Eisenhower years, and there is no reason to believe Friedman wanted a post in the capital. Certainly no Republican candidate in his adult lifetime had espoused his kind of ideology. In early 1964, however, Friedman had a meeting with Senator Barry Goldwater, and he emerged to tell reporters that "there is no candidate now on the scene that I'd sooner support." Shortly thereafter he submitted position papers for Goldwater's consideration and defended the candidate's economic statements in articles and on television and radio programs. Political analysts assumed Friedman was playing a role in the Goldwater camp similar to that of Samuelson or Heller in Kennedy's 1960 campaign and that, if Goldwater were elected, Friedman would become his chairman of the Council of Economic Advisors.

They were incorrect on both counts. Friedman did not join the campaign organization as a fulltime staffer and had only occasional contacts with Goldwater. He did not presume to "educate the candidate," as Heller had done for Kennedy four years earlier. Also, Friedman must have known he lacked the political tact necessary in a high Washington post and was too contentious to be considered for one. In any case he, like Samuelson, preferred to speak out on a variety of issues from his own podium. Economist G. Warren Nutter of the University of Vermont, one of Friedman's former students, was Goldwater's closest advisor in this area, and he probably would have been the first choice for the chairmanship had Goldwater defeated Johnson.

Friedman devoted an increasingly large portion of his time and energies to advocacy and less to scholarship after publication of the *Monetary History* and the 1964 campaign. It was as if he realized that the body of his doctrine was almost complete and that his future role should be that of a popularizer. In addition, the failures of some Great Society programs, the antiwar protests, and the growing feeling within the country that government had failed in many areas contributed to his belief that a turn to the political right was in the making. Also, he was impelled to speak out against the new economics, which to him was anathema. He mocked Heller's efforts at fine tuning through a tax cut, observing that the measure wasn't enacted until two years after it was suggested. "The 1964 tax cut was said to be an absolute necessity in 1962. It was stressed again in 1963, and it was finally enacted in 1964." Friedman concluded that "it's very hard to say that the New Economics has accomplished very much of anything, except getting a great deal of publicity."

Friedman's advice was sought by several prominent Republican presidential candidates. His appearances before congressional committees were more numerous than ever before, and they usually were well attended, for Friedman could be entertaining and stimulating as well as informative. During the 1968 campaign he provided position papers and ideas for Richard Nixon and became one of his unofficial defenders on television panel and interview shows. After Nixon's victory Friedman made it clear he wanted no post in Washington. The reason, said one magazine, was that "he is too brilliant, too idiosyncratic, too iconoclastic, too right wing in his politics. . . ." But he did help several of his students, colleagues, and fellow monetarists obtain key positions in the new Administration, and in addition other Nixon appointees had a distinct Friedmanesque tinge to their economic and social ideologies.

The Nixon men afforded Friedman's ideas respect and attention. This is not to suggest they were confirmed monetarists or that *Capitalism and Freedom* became required reading in the Oval Office. Rather, in late 1968 Friedman had reason to believe the time had arrived for a testing of his theories, and he was eager to see the coming to power of what he considered would be the first truly Republican Administration since Herbert Hoover gave way to Franklin Roosevelt in 1933.

Writing in *Newsweek* in December of 1968, he sketched the failures of the New Frontier and Great Society, observing the Democrats had left the economy in far worse shape than it had been in when Eisenhower left office eight years earlier. The Nixonians would have to clean up the mess, from inflation to an adverse balance of payments situation to a swollen and unbalanced budget. "In each area the New Economics had managed in eight years to turn a comfortable, easy situation into a near-crisis, to squander assets and multiply liabilities." Of course, he had solutions to all of these problems, developed and refined for more than two decades. "Many a New Economist may well have secretly sighed in relief when the election returns were in," he concluded. "What a mess to have to straighten out! What a legacy to leave the opposition!"

8

THE PRESIDENT'S OTHER MEN

DURING THE 1968 PRESIDENTIAL SEASON most literate Americans knew the general outlooks of three economists: Paul Samuelson. John Kenneth Galbraith, and Milton Friedman. To call them economists was like categorizing Walter Cronkite as a newsman—that label both stated and understated their roles. Never before had the celebrity of major economists been so high. These men had international reputations greater than those of many senators, congressmen, and governors who hoped for a major party nomination.

The potential candidates knew how Arthur Burns and Walter Heller had exercized power during the Eisenhower and Kennedy-Johnson years. All of them sought the advice of an important, well-known economist, and some of the leading academics received "bids" from several. Newspaper columnists, who a generation earlier had speculated about the possible composition of presidential cabinets now also analyzed campaigns on the basis of which economist was working with which candidate. Such leaders of the profession as Kenneth Arrow, William Baumol, William Fellner, Hendrick Houthakker, Robert Solow, and James Tobin were wooed assiduously. Harvard, Yale, Stanford, Chicago, and other leading universities buzzed with rumors as to which distinguished scholar would be off to Washington in the winter. Deans and department chairmen welcomed such talk and approved leaves of absence and reduced teaching loads with alacrity. Economics had become a "glamour subject" in academia, attracting some of the best graduate students in the nation. To have a former Chairman of the CEA on one's faculty was the ambition of many university presidents, and most would settle for a member or two on the Council. The call to Washington, then, was something to celebrate.

There was little expectation that Friedman, Galbraith, or Samuelson would accept a government post in 1969—no more than Cronkite would consider entering the Cabinet. These men had more power and influence outside of government than in it and in any case were unwilling to relinquish their independence. Heller had no driving ambitions in this direction; he was content to remain at Minnesota, making forays to Washington several times a year to testify before congressional committees. Leon Keyserling, a vigorous and feisty 60 years old, might have welcomed some kind of political role, but it seemed hardly likely that he would receive a bid in 1969. Throughout the nation, dozens of prominent economists had their bags packed, awaiting the call that would mean celebrity and excitement and perhaps give them a chance to put their theories into practice.

Arthur Burns, 64 years old that year, was about to retire both from Columbia and the National Bureau. But not from the public spotlight. There would be the usual consultantships, special projects, speeches, and articles, and the honors distinguished scholars had come to expect. Burns's position in the profession was unique. Throughout the 1960s he had gravitated to the ideological center of American economics, allying himself at different times with moderates of both the Keynesian and monetarist schools, all the while maintaining the respect of both. While Friedman had talked often of the need to separate normative from scientific economics, Burns actually had done so—or at least this was the view of a large majority of his peers.

That he had conservative inclinations was obvious, but Burns was always ready to jettison ideological baggage when the occasion demanded. More to the point, he was adept at keeping his political leanings separate from policy prescriptions, while maintaining the image of a disinterested scientist. Where Friedman was likely to

begin an explanation with phrases like, "It's really quite simple
. . ." or "All that is required is . . ." Burns would puff thoughtfully
on his pipe, clear his throat, and enter upon a lengthy exposition,
the moral of which often appeared to be that the problem was complex and subtle and admitted of a wide variety of treatments, no
one of which could be guaranteed. Friedman acted as though he
had the answers to major problems. So did Galbraith. In contrast,
Burns was always adding new data to his mix, shifting judgments as
he progressed.

Burns saw merit in some aspects of the new economics and had
spoken out forcefully in favor of the 1964 tax cut. Later on he would
be one of Heller's most influential supporters in the call for a tax
surcharge to fight inflation. He agreed with Friedman's contention
that the new economists failed to appreciate the key role played by the
money supply in causing inflations and recessions, but Burns was
not a pure and simple monetarist. For example, he noted that
changes in the money supply were not the best lead indicator for
the economy—better still were initial claims for unemployment com-
pensation, new orders for capital goods, and stock prices. By accepting portions of the arguments of both camps and exhibiting a willingness to alter his views, Burns managed to become the liberals'
favorite conservative and the conservatives' favorite liberal. Each
camp wooed him, each flattered him, and all wanted his support.
But Burns remained very much his own man. It was typical of him,
noted one reporter, that he parted his hair squarely down the
middle.

Throughout the Kennedy-Johnson years Burns served as one of
the Republicans' leading economists-in-residence and wise men,
one clearly associated with the party's centrist elements. As such
he had nothing to do with the Goldwater campaign. Burns ex-
pressed doubts as to the viability of some of the candidate's programs, especially his recommendations for drastic changes in Social
Security, the welfare program, and the tax codes. All forms of
radicalism were alien to Burns's personality and economics, and
Goldwater was the most radical candidate put forth by a major
party in his lifetime. Burns remained on good terms with several
of Goldwater's economic advisors, but the distance between him
and Friedman grew during the campaign, and their differences
sharpened during the next four years.

After the debacle Burns drew closer to Richard Nixon, now considered the frontrunner for the 1968 nomination. The two men had

worked well together during the Eisenhower years, and their relationship deepened in the 1960s. This was somewhat surprising given their disparate personalities and interests and may have resulted from traits they shared. Nixon was as pragmatic and eclectic in politics as Burns was in economics, and both had an instinctive feel for the centrist position. But there were differences too. Burns's positions on issues developed out of an accumulation of evidence and practice, while Nixon, a political animal, tended to go where the votes could be found. In time their differences would become more important than those matters on which they agreed, but in 1968 Burns helped Nixon frame his economic ideas, especially in the campaign against inflation.

That Burns would have a role to play in the new Administration was evident, but what that would be was difficult to fathom in the aftermath of the Nixon victory. The White House would later say that Burns had been targeted for the Federal Reserve Board chairmanship from the start, but the present Chairman, William McChesney Martin, would not retire for another two years. In the interim, he was to serve as Counsellor to the President, a position created for him that would carry Cabinet rank and special responsibilities. Burns would advise Nixon on a variety of issues but have no direct administrative powers.

At the time, however, it appeared otherwise. Nixon was expected to concentrate on foreign affairs, especially on ending the Vietnam War. He had never shown much interest in domestic matters and would have to delegate responsibilities in this area. The Washington press corps analyzed his Cabinet appointees and concluded that this was where Burns would fit best—he would be in charge of Nixon's domestic program, with emphasis on keeping the economy on a steady course and bringing down the inflation rate. This was Burns's view of his job too. Considering his close relationship with Nixon and the status of other White House economics experts, it seemed reasonable.

As for Burns's initial economic prescription, it was standard and familiar, designed both to appeal to Republican conservative instincts and bring a swift halt to inflationary pressures. In essence, he called for what amounted to a replay of the 1953-1954 experience, at which time he had been CEA Chairman. Burns recommended a slowdown in the growth of the money supply and cutbacks in federal spending to bring the budget closer to balance. He expected Chairman Martin to cooperate in the monetary area and thought the elimination of many Great Society programs, combined with a quick conclusion of the Vietnam War, would make possible a lower level of government expenditures. As part of this package, Burns would retain the Johnson 10 percent tax surcharge, due to expire in 1969, not only to help narrow the budget deficit but also to keep a lid on consumer expenditures.

Taken as a whole, this program would dampen the inflation rate, which Burns considered his immediate economic problem. Prices rose at a rate of 4.7 percent in 1968, the highest since the Korean War, and the Consumer Price Index was climbing by more than 7.2 percent at year-end. Through the proper blend of fiscal and monetary policies, Burns hoped to slash that rate below 4 percent by 1970.

That this approach ran the risk of causing a recession was obvious, but Burns was willing to take the chance, believing as he did that inflationary pressures were so strong and had become so ingrained that powerful medicine was needed. He expected any recession that began in 1969 to be a short one, after which the economy would recover nicely—in time for the 1970 congressional elections.

The Friedmanites offered an alternate approach, one that amounted to almost complete reliance upon monetary policy. Specifically, Friedman thought the Federal Reserve should lower the rate of growth of the money supply from its current level of 11 percent to about 7 percent and keep it there for a year or so. Then the rate should be lowered again, this time to 4 or 5 percent, where it should remain. If this were done, said Friedman, the tight-money medicine would work its way through the economy, and there would be a slowdown of inflation in the second half of 1969. There need be no serious recession, he said in 1968. Rather, the economy could experience a "soft landing."

As expected, Friedman gave little heed to the inflationary psychology of the period; this would be dissolved by tight money. He approved of plans to cut federal spending but also wanted lower taxes and in particular opposed attempts to retain the Johnson surcharge. "Taxes and spending are now too high, not too low. The urgent need is to cut both," he wrote, conceding that "this will not be easy."

Galbraith also ran true to form. Recognizing political realities, he knew his formulas would have no place in this Administration. Galbraith predicted the Burns approach would fail. There were only two ways to bring an end to the kind of ingrained inflation that existed in early 1969: a serious depression or wage and price controls. Since the nation would not tolerate the former, the only alternative would be an "incomes policy," and Galbraith recommended strictly enforced federal guidelines such as those employed by Kennedy and Johnson. He knew, of course, that Nixon had said he would have none of this. As for Burns, he was a longtime opponent of controls, believing they distorted the economy, created the illusion of stability but not the reality, and prevented fiscal and monetary medicine from working their ways through the economy. In the last days of the Johnson presidency, as Burns prepared to assume a leadership position on the economic front, there seemed little chance he would alter his convictions on this issue.

Paul McCracken, the new Chairman of the CEA, was even more strongly opposed to all forms of federal controls, which he viewed as counterproductive and distortive of the economy. The Chicagoans welcomed the nomination, especially when McCracken told reporters that, while he was not a Friedmanite, he was "Friedmanesque" in his approaches to problems. But he was also a centrist by temperament. In 1956 he had been recommended as a Council appointee by outgoing Chairman Burns, and during the next four years he delivered many of Burns's ideas to the White House. Finally, the selection was applauded by new economists. Heller called it "a fine appointment" while Samuelson thought Nixon had "done well" in naming him.

McCracken was not a prolific scholar or a particularly original thinker. A small man, unimpressive in either appearance or speech, he had a talent for making friends and reducing complex problems to their components. He was more a technician than a theorist, and few expected him to become a strongman in the new Administration.

McCracken went far on what he had. In 1937 he graduated William Penn, a small Iowa college, and then taught for three years at Berea; both were undergraduate institutions and neither could claim any particular academic distinction. That McCracken was not bitten by the Keynesian bug in this period is understandable, since he was so distant from the scenes of conflict and debate.

Unwilling to settle for this, he enrolled at Harvard in 1941 and received an M. A. the following year. During the war he served as staff economist at the Department of Commerce and afterward he returned to Harvard to enroll for the doctorate, supporting himself by working as an economist and eventually director of research at the Minneapolis branch of the Federal Reserve. McCracken received his degree in 1948, at which time he was named to an assistant professorship at the University of Michigan School of Business Administration. This was a prestigious institution, but there remained within the profession that prejudice against those economists who held appointments in business schools; with few exceptions, they were considered second-class citizens.

This did not bother McCracken, for he was not a research-oriented social scientist. Over the years he had produced few scholarly papers and instead delivered scores of speeches dealing with such matters as where the economy was headed over the coming year and what it would mean for a particular industry. McCracken achieved a reputation as an intelligent forecaster, and it was for this reason Burns had plucked him for the Council in 1956.

McCracken supported Nixon in 1960 but at the same time retained his friendships with moderate Democrats. After the Republican defeat he was invited by Samuelson to prepare reports for incoming President Kennedy's consideration. Throughout the 1960s he would return to Washington to serve on commissions and testify at hearings. McCracken was not considered a prominent economist in this decade, but he had managed to emerge from anonymity. He became a consultant to such leading firms as the Bank of New York and the Commercial Credit Corporation and in addition was a familiar figure at such business groups as the National Industrial Conference Board and the American Bankers Association. McCracken progressed in academia as well; in 1966 he was named Edmund Ezra Day University Professor in Business Administration at Michigan.

All of this provided McCracken with a major podium from which to speak out on national and international issues, and so he did. From them can be sketched a picture of a moderate monetarist, one who would reject the label of Chicagoan. He subscribed to Friedman's belief that changes in the money supply strongly affect the economy's overall performance and held that a gradual dampening of the rate of growth could result in a lower rate of inflation without an accompanying recession. But he also approved the notion of "full employment budgets" as set down by the new economists in the 1960s. This held that deficits could be tolerated—and even encouraged—if they were the results of attempts to stimulate the economy to full employment.

McCracken would not accept fine tuning. Like Friedman he

preferred economic instruments that worked automatically with a minimum of manipulation. In an article written for the Republicans in the 1968 campaign, he said that "fiscal and monetary policies have themselves been a major source of erratic movements in the economy, and the first requirement for improving our economic performance is that these policies themselves be operated in a more even-handed and steady manner." On occasion government might have to intervene in fiscal and monetary areas, but on the whole adjustments should be made by self-regulatory devices. McCracken would not go as far as Friedman in what he termed an "abdication to automaticity." Rather, he issued a "call for learning to operate these instruments of policy with more sophistication and exactitude, and within substantially narrower tolerances."

It is a rare person who can weave together arguments of Friedman and Heller and present them in Burnsian cadences. This was McCracken's forte, but it hardly was the kind of talent that would win him a presidential audience for long. When Nixon announced the appointment, he described McCracken as "a centrist, a man who is pragmatic in his economics." So he was. But his salient qualities —flexibility, good humor, and open mindedness—would prove liabilities in the Nixon White House. The incoming President had always been fascinated by men who shared his instincts for power and drama and combined them with qualities he appeared to lack— magnetism, grace, and intellectual elegance. Although it could not have been realized at the time, McCracken was destined to play a secondary role in this Administration.

Being a centrist implies that one is between opposite forces on either side, and such was the position McCracken occupied in early 1969. He could not hope to dominate the middle, however, for Burns had preempted it years earlier. Burns had sponsored McCracken for the chairmanship in the belief that he would speak in favor of his programs in the Nixon White House as he had under Eisenhower. He was to help guard against challenges from the left flank, which was represented by Daniel Patrick Moynihan. Burns distrusted Moynihan's ideas, disliked his flamboyant manner, and saw in him a rival for power and influence.

Described by Nixon as "a thoughtful liberal," Moynihan had been named to the White House staff over Burns's objections. Nixon was capitivated by Moynihan, who urged upon him a program of social activism which, if implemented, could further unbalance the budget. Burns was more concerned with counteracting the Moyni-

han personality than in combating his programs, for he knew they
ran counter to Nixon's essential conservatism. He also believed that
in any contest with Moynihan he could count on the support of
Administration Friedmanites, not only on ideological grounds but
because he had carefully selected and recommended most of them.

George Shultz, the new Labor Secretary, was one of those who
passed the Burns muster. Like McCracken he was a business economist, a well-respected mediator of labor-management disputes.
Shultz was believed a conservative with monetarist leanings, somewhat to the right of most Nixonians. He had been selected for the
Cabinet for several reasons. Burns believed Nixon would need a
Labor Secretary who was known and respected by union leaders
and one with great persuasive talents. He also assumed Shultz
would accept the Burns prescriptions, which is to say that he would
be willing to advocate a short, sharp recession as the price to be
paid for containing inflation in the initial year of the Nixon Administration. Such a person might be able to obtain the understanding,
if not the support, of organized labor. Thus, Burns believed Shultz
had fine qualities that would be utilized in a limited area, that he
would serve alongside McCracken as one of his lieutenants.

Nixon had met Shultz on one or two occasions and had formed
no strong opinion of him. The two men had come into brief contact
during the second Eisenhower Administration, when Shultz served
for a while as consultant to the Labor Department, but they were
never close.

During the summer and autumn of 1968 Shultz had been on
leave to write a book, and so he played no important role in the
campaign. In fact, he had rejected overtures to chair study groups
and coordinate efforts. Given the practice of distributing political
plums to the worthy, he had no reason to expect a job offer from
Nixon. After the campaign he helped prepare position papers on
labor-management relations and wage-price policies and then returned to his researches.

Burns called Shultz with the offer of the Labor portfolio in early
December, and it was immediately accepted. The announcement
was well received, with Shultz being praised for his fairness and
intelligence by both George Meany and Henry Ford II. He was
seen as one of the better selections in a somewhat lackluster
Cabinet. But few thought he would have any influence outside of
his department. In this regard and several others he proved one of
the major surprises of the Nixon era. Except for Henry Kissinger,

no Nixonian emerged from that Administration with so enhanced a reputation as did George Shultz. This surprised even Burns, who clearly had underestimated his talents for impressing powerful leaders. Furthermore, Shultz's commitment to monetarism proved deeper than Burns had imagined it to have been. Not only would he prove capable of balancing Moynihan, but Shultz outlasted him and in the end eclipsed even Burns.

Shultz's interests and inclinations may have been inherited. His father, Birl, had founded the New York Stock Exchange Institute, a school that trained people for jobs in the securities industry. George attended private schools and entered Princeton in 1938, where he majored in economics. He had arrived too late to participate in the ferment of the early Keynesian revolution, was at the wrong place, and had an improper background to share in the excitement. A large and robust man, he was an athlete and activist, not a scholar. He entered college with probusiness proclivities and left the same way.

After wartime service with the marines, Shultz enrolled at M. I. T. for a doctorate in industrial economics and while a graduate student also taught the fundamentals course to undergraduates. He was a talented teacher and a promising scholar, who in both classroom and library was more concerned with empirical evidence than abstract theory and econometrics. Shultz was awarded the Ph.D. in 1949, at which time he became an assistant professor of industrial relations at M. I. T. This was a major academic plum; around this time the school began its drive to surpass Harvard in economics, and the junior faculty was selected with this in mind. Shultz was not quite 30 years old and already had been singled out as a comer in the field.

Shultz's dissertation, a study of wage determination in the men's shoe industry, was hardly calculated to win for him a general audience or national celebrity, but it did provide the beginnings of an academic reputation. More important, perhaps, its high quality was noted by Charles Myers, a leading scholar in the field, who selected Shultz as his coauthor for a more general work. Published in 1951 as *The Dynamics of a Labor Market: A Study of the Impact of Employment Changes on Labor Mobility, Job Satisfaction, and Company and Union Practices*, it became a standard text in college courses and gave Shultz's career another boost.

The most important message of the book is that academic economists often have difficulties in appreciating the nature of many labor-management disputes, because they attempt to understand a complex social phenomenon with imperfect and limited tools. Specifically, they assume the existence of economic man, when he seldom appears. "Thus, with workers not interested wholly in wages, with employers not acting as the marginal analysis assumes they do, and with unions unable and unwilling to consider the volume of employment as relevant to their wage decisions, some of the basic premises of economic analysis appear to be weakened." Furthermore, both union and management appreciate this situation. Within most industries and in most bargaining situations, each side had a clear appreciation of the values, needs, strengths, and weaknesses of the other. Outsiders—be they arbitrators, mediators, or governments—who attempt to interfere and try to impose settlements usually wind up doing mischief and often escalate minor skirmishes into major confrontations. By implication, then, Myers and Shultz rejected federal intervention in the collective bargaining process and in general would limit the role played by mediators and arbitrators as well.

Shultz's views became known by unions and managements, which appreciated his apparent modesty and even-handedness. Out of this came invitations to serve on arbitration panels and, in 1954, a post as acting director of the industrial relations program at M. I. T. The following year he received a leave of absence to serve as Council of Economic Advisors senior staff economist, where he met and impressed Arthur Burns. Shultz accepted a professorship at the University of Chicago Graduate School of Business in 1957 and five years later succeeded Friedmanite Allen Wallis as its dean. By then he was fairly well known within the profession.

In the 1950s Shultz's belief that government should not interfere in the collective bargaining process had broadened to encompass Friedmanite views on a wide variety of issues. Despite this, his work on arbitration panels enabled him to maintain contacts within the labor movement and among liberals. He was a conservative—moreso and with greater convictions than McCracken—who gave the appearance of being a centrist.

Shultz usually could be counted upon to advocate laissez-faire solutions to outstanding problems, and this helps explain his popularity with big labor, something the Galbraithians had no difficulty in understanding. Union leaders joined with business executives in applauding his calls for open and unrestricted collective bargaining. To those critics who would limit labor's right to strike, Shultz replied that "some strikes are part of the price we pay for collective bargaining," and, furthermore, "the public has vital interests in allowing people to strike." While union leaders approved of such statements, businessmen liked the way he castigated the Kennedy Administration when, in 1962, it forced the steel industry to back down from a round of price increases.

Shultz also criticized Kennedy's attempts to establish wage-price guidelines, claiming they not only distorted the economy but were an impingement upon personal liberties. It was a "myth," he said, "that government can set forth guideposts for union and company behavior that will make a constructive contribution to solving the problem of full employment without inflation." Furthermore, "the American economy is much too complex and market forces too powerful for the application of a single wage-price guideline." These were themes he would stress in 1970-1971, when he served as leader of the Friedmanite forces within the official family.

These three men were key figures in determining economic policy in the early months of the new Administration. Treasury Secretary David Kennedy, who might have been expected to make a contribution, soon proved one of the weakest figures in the Cabinet and was content to go along with the others. Nixon rarely met with his Bureau of the Budget Director Robert Mayo. Arthur Burns was in command, thought the Washington press corps, and the struggle against inflation would be conducted under his leadership and with his policies.

There were three essential ingredients in the Burns strategy. In the first place, Burns counted on the Federal Reserve to tighten the monetary screws through open market operations and increasing the discount rate. Chairman Martin had spoken out repeatedly of the need for an all-out campaign against inflation and could be relied upon to do his part. Next, under his direction the federal budget would have to be brought under control. This meant there should be no new spending programs, and most of the old ones would either be phased out or their appropriations slashed. This not only would cut back on aggregate demand but would obviate the need to finance a deficit. If all went according to plan, there would be a slowdown in the inflation rate well before the end of the year. Thus, the third part of Burns' approach was freedom of the marketplace; there would be no recourse to wage-price guidelines in the Nixon Administration, if for no other reason than a belief that fiscal and monetary policies, if properly administered, could perform the job in 1969. Then, once inflation was defeated, the economy would roll along on its own, with no fine tuning. This not only would resolve a major national problem but deal a crushing blow to the new economics and the Galbraithians and vindicate Burns's eclectic approach to problems.

It was a program that Nixon endorsed. "I do not go along with the suggestion that inflation can be effectively controlled by exhorting labor and management to follow certain guidelines," he said in late January. "So the primary responsibility for controlling inflation rests with the national administration and its handling of fiscal and monetary affairs."

That winter and early spring it appeared the first part of the Burns program was well underway. As expected, the Federal Reserve cut back on the increase in the money supply; during the first four months of 1969 it expanded at an annualized rate of 4.3 percent, as opposed to the 6.8 percent increase for 1968. Already businessmen were complaining about the tightness of money and difficulties in obtaining credit. In addition, the Federal Reserve increased the discount rate to 6 percent, a height which hadn't been seen since just before the stock market crash of 1929. The financial markets were jittery, and there was talk of a new panic on Wall Street. Even Friedman was disturbed by what seemed to him a heavy-handed approach. "It would be a major blunder for the Fed to step still harder on the monetary brakes," he wrote in May. "That would risk turning orderly restraint into a severe economic contraction."

On this front at least, the Burns formula for an orchestrated recession seemed to be working. Most lead indicators were falling into line, predicting the onset of an economic decline. Yet there was no sign inflation was coming under control. During the first half of the year, the Consumer Price Index (CPI) rose at an annualized rate of 5.8 percent, a sizable increase over the 1968 figure of 4.7 percent. This was due, said the Friedmanites, to the big jump in the money supply in the second half of 1968. In their thinking, the CPI lagged six months or so behind shifts in the money supply. Given a continued stringent attitude at the Fed, prices surely would decline.

But they didn't. In the second half of 1969 the central bank tightened the screws. The money supply expanded by only 0.6 percent on an annualized basis. The nation entered its recession. Unemployment rose, and on Wall Street stock prices collapsed. Yet the

CPI inched upward, and the inflation rate for 1969 on the whole was 6.1 percent, its worst showing since the immediate postwar period. By year's end the economy was beset by advancing inflation and developing recession, something both the classicists and Keynesians had thought unlikely.

"Stagflation" had been born.

Writing in August, Friedman said that prices soon would turn downward as a result of heavy-handed Federal Reserve policies. The recession would deepen, he thought, and to prevent this some monetary expansion was required. This hardly seemed likely. "If the rate of price rise has not begun to abate by the fourth quarter of the year, it will be time to ask us for an explanation." But he had none to offer at that time.

Had he been of a mind to do so, Burns might have provided one. Nixon had placed too much reliance on monetary policies, and had refused to take his fiscal prescription seriously. Burns had told him both would be required, and his advice had gone unheeded.

In a major address on inflation delivered in March 1969, Nixon had said that "only a combined policy of a strong budget surplus and monetary restraint can now be effective in cooling inflation, and in ultimately reducing the restrictive interest rates forced on us by past policies." The last Johnson budget had come in at a surplus of $3.2 billion. In January Nixon had said his budget for fiscal 1970 would show a surplus of $3.4 billion. But now he backtracked; due to a variety of reasons, that figure would have to be halved.

Over the next few months, as new spending programs were announced, analysts started to project a deficit. Administration spokesmen denied this, claiming that reduced Vietnam spending would more than compensate for new allocations elsewhere. In the end, however, the budget was in deficit by $2.8 billion. This did not result from a decline in federal receipts but rather from an enormous increase in spending. Under Burns's direction, federal expenditures were supposed to decline; in fact, they rose by $12.1 billion over the figure for fiscal 1969.

The reason for all this was that in the tug-of-war for Nixon's support, the "spenders" defeated the "cutters," with most of their victories taking place in domestic rather than foreign areas. Nixon did agree to cuts in national defense spending, as he started to wind down the Vietnam War, though Burns and his allies had asked for more than they got. In addition there would be lower appropriations for the space effort. But spending on social welfare programs—including many Great Society measures—increased sharply, and this more than compensated for economies elsewhere.

By midyear, Washington columnists were reporting that in the "battle of the professors," Burns had been defeated by Moynihan. Nixon had taken up Moynihan's proposal for direct cash payments to poor people in the place of the cumbersome welfare apparatus, and had this been passed, along with other new social programs, the Nixon record in this area would have matched that of Johnson in terms of new spending. At a time when many Americans probably thought of Nixon as a person who was a "hawk" in foreign affairs and an opponent of liberal domestic programs to benefit the nation's poor people, the opposite was closer to the truth—at least in mid-1969. For despite all that he had told Burns prior to the inauguration and the campaign rhetoric, Nixon did not intend to permit his political enemies and historians to say that his arrival in Washington was accompanied by the onset of a new recession.

The Friedmanites in his entourage were telling Nixon that stringent Federal Reserve policies threatened the nation with recession while bringing down the inflation rate. Moynihan and his group believed that new spending programs would stimulate the economy and not result in inflation. Burns continued to believe the Federal Reserve was on course and that additional cuts in the budget were needed, while holding that recession was unavoidable. Who could have blamed Nixon—who after all was not economically sophisticated—for preferring to believe Moynihan rather than Burns? To this should be added his fascination for this dazzling and articulate addition to his inner circle; Moynihan was like a peacock in a flock of pigeons. After a short meeting with him, Nixon was reported to have remarked that "four minutes with Pat is worth four hours of Arthur Burns," and Burns soon heard of this.

It had not worked out the way Burns thought it would. His position at the White House had eroded, his policy recommendations given short shrift, and his alliances were jumbled. McCracken, who had been deemed a likely supporter, talked much of the need for tight money and little of budget balancing. In interviews and speeches he echoed the Friedmanite line, that a soft landing was probable given the current rate of monetary expansion. Within the Cabinet Shultz was busily consolidating his position, maneuvering for a position close to that of the President, and at midyear he generally favored the Moynihan approach of substituting direct payments to indigent people for that of disbursements by the welfare system. Burns had found two allies in Treasury Secretary Kennedy and Budget Director Mayo, but neither man was a match for Moynihan. Increasingly Burns was viewed not only as a dour bearer of bad news but as a boring Cassandra.

Yet Richard Nixon had never been a man who easily abandoned old friends, especially those who stood by him during his darkest periods. In August Burns managed to convince him that a 75 percent cutback in federal construction projects would be a dramatic way of demonstrating the Administration's dedication to budget balancing. The news was to be released at the Governors' Conference in Colorado Springs the following month, with Burns there to handle the explanations.

Then followed a period of confusion and political dealings. Fearful of the adverse economic impacts on the states, Vice President Spiro Agnew, who was charged with bringing the news to Republican governors, told them that there would be a six-month delay before the cuts went into effect. On hearing of this an angry Burns told Nixon that this would undercut all of his efforts at ending inflation, that a delay would only convince the governors and others that Nixon had no true commitment to the fight. To this Agnew responded that the governors were more fearful of recession than inflation and that as a group they would oppose the move.

Nixon waffled. He told the press that there would be an immediate cutback in new federal construction but also said that "the states and localities will, of course, be given due notice, so that they can adjust their affairs properly." This was taken as a way of saying that the cuts might never go into effect, and the governors took it as such.

By early autumn Burns realized that the program he had presented Nixon for ending inflation by means of a mild recession had been distorted out of recognition and that his influence in the White House had declined considerably. The only other ways of dealing with rising prices were methods put forth by the Friedmanites on the one side and the Galbraithians on the other. As for the former group, the figures showed that stringent monetary policies by themselves hadn't worked, and in any case Burns had never accepted the efficacy of pure and simple Friedmanism—or for that matter, of any other doctrine. The alternative was wage and price controls or strict guidelines—an incomes policy, which Galbraith had advocated for decades. In what was one of the most significant and unanticipated shifts of attitude on the part of any major economist in the postwar period, Arthur Burns, the master pragmatist, started talking of the benefits of an incomes policy.

He did not convert to Galbraithianism but characteristically incorporated this device into his own structure. Burns thought guidelines might be useful to keep inflation in check temporarily, while fiscal and monetary medicines were taking hold—they could provide a bandage of sorts over the inflationary wounds, to be discarded once the healing process was well underway. Later on, Burns would say, "We should not close our minds to the possibility that an incomes policy, provided it stopped well short of direct wage and price controls and was used merely as a supplement to overall fiscal and monetary measures, might speed us through this transitional period of cost-push inflation." This hardly was a Galbraithian statement, but it was a long way from what Burns had advocated in the 1960s.

Nixon rejected the notion but in a fashion that indicated he was keeping his options open. In mid-October he still talked of the need to "gently, but firmly, apply the brakes" of fiscal and monetary policies. Controls were not to be considered, and Nixon rejected the notion of guidelines such as those employed by Kennedy and Johnson. "They collapsed back in 1966 because they failed to get to the root of the problem," and nothing that had happened since then had changed his mind. The President did issue a call for "self-restraint," however. He asked unions and corporations to behave in such ways as to promote "a return to price stability," and suggested that consumers limit their use of credit "so as to reduce the pressures that help drive prices out of sight."

What if self-restraint failed, as almost everyone expected it would? Nixon offered no alternative that summer. But in retrospect it can be seen that this rather weak approach easily might be replaced by "jawboning," which in turn could give way to a Burnsian variety of incomes policy.

This was a period of growing confusion and uncertainties. Burns continued to view inflation as the nation's major economic problem, but by autumn his indicators told him the forthcoming recession would be deeper and last longer than he originally had believed. Now he joined with Shultz and McCracken in urging a let-up in the rate of money supply growth. Shultz advocated talks on the matter with Federal Reserve Board Chairman Martin, while McCracken told reporters that "a time was bound to come when students of monetary policy would start to raise questions about whether the tough course has been held long enough." But while Shultz continued to believe monetary policy was paramount, the CEA Chairman was starting to have doubts. "Demand is beginning to slow up," he noted, and still there were no clear signs that inflationary pressures were abating. McCracken talked less of the certainty of a "soft landing" and the ability of the Nixonians to "clean up the mess" left by the new economists. He conceded the possibility of higher unemployment and more and longer strikes, as well as social protests resulting from the continuing war and developing recession. When asked whether the outlook for business was good, bad, or indifferent, McCracken replied, "In all seriousness, I'm tempted to answer, 'Yes.'"

Such an outlook hardly endeared McCracken to Nixon. The President, who continued to devote only a small portion of his time and attention to economic matters, much preferred Shultz's assurances that all was going according to plan. Burns wanted to change direction, and McCracken was gloomy, while Shultz offered certainties, optimism, and conservative doctrine. Little wonder, then, that Shultz's star rose in the Nixon White House. If his "game plan" were accepted, then the President would have a great degree of leeway in political decisions affecting economic planning.

Nixon's devotion to the Shultz forecast may help explain his acceptance of a hodgepodge tax measure in late 1969, one that contained contradictions but would be appealing as a campaign document for the following year. The bill ended investment tax credits (and so would discourage capital formation and deepen and prolong the recession but would enable the Republicans to claim they were bringing new moneys into the Treasury), while at the same time it lowered rates and increased personal exemptions (which further unbalanced the budget and stimulated the very kind of spending Nixon earlier had deplored but which would be welcomed by voters). The tax plan, and the President's confidence in early 1970 that all was proceeding well, was the best testimony to Shultz's high standing at that time.

Burns had been bested by Shultz and Moynihan in the contest for a place at Nixon's right hand, and in late 1969 he was "promoted out of the White House," having been nominated by Nixon to succeed Martin as head of the Federal Reserve. Friedman, who had been one of Martin's chief critics, hailed the appointment of his old friend. "He is the right man in the right place at the right time," wrote Friedman in early February. He continued to believe that Martin's tight money policy would assure a recession in 1970, but felt that Burns would ease up gradually, and so create conditions for a stable 1971.

Although Friedman did not know it at the time, the Fed already had decided to expand the money supply, and Burns accelerated it. The money supply was enlarged by 7.2 percent in the first half—which Friedman called "excessive." He had difficulty understanding Burns's intentions, for while such a policy might shorten the recession, it all but assured another bout of inflation for 1971.

Burns, who enjoyed his new independence, knew exactly what he was doing. By pumping up the money supply he not only was helping mitigate the effects of the recession and shortening its duration but placing pressures in the White House to make the kinds of budgetary cuts he had advocated. Without the institution of a restrictive fiscal policy to balance the monetary expansion, there indeed might be the kind of inflation Friedman anticipated. Burns's power and prestige increased as the year wore on. In June, when it seemed the stock market would crash in the wake of the Penn Central collapse, Burns acted swiftly to calm fears and assure the business community the Fed was prepared to act as lender of last resort. Not since the days of the elder J. P. Morgan had any American banker, public or private, played so important a role in a financial crisis. Businessmen and bankers appreciated this. Burns always had a constituency in this group, and now it was even larger and more devoted.

Shultz, who in June was elevated to the newly created post of Director of the Office of Management and Budget (the assistant presidency that Burns once thought would be his), appreciated what was happening. Unless budget cuts were made there would develop in late 1970 an irresistible inflationary situation, at which time demands for wage and price controls would escalate—from Burns as well as from the Galbraithians. Earlier in the year Congress had passed the Economic Stabilization Act, under the terms of which the President was given the power to impose controls. Nixon had said that he neither wanted that option nor intended to exercise it, but the possibility that if subjected to sufficient pressures he would do just that did exist.

In retrospect one can discern signs that Nixon's gradual shift away from monetarism and toward acceptance of some form of incomes policy was continuing, even while he saluted Shultz and spoke of the horrors of controls. In an address delivered on June 22 he spoke of the inadequacies of controls and how they "never get at the real cause of inflation." Toward the end of the speech Nixon said, "I will not take the nation down the road of wage and price controls, however politically expedient that may seem." But in between these statements he announced that henceforth the CEA would issue "inflation alerts," which would "spotlight the significant areas of wage and price increases and objectively analyze their impact on the price level." This was quite different from the jawboning practiced by Kennedy and Johnson. McCracken would draw attention to increases after they went into effect, and presumably fear of being exposed as "unpatriotic" would lead some unions and businessmen to reconsider wage and price boosts. Nor was there any talk of federal actions other than exposure. The alert policy didn't bother the Friedmanites, while those favoring controls felt frustrated. Still, a beginning had been made, and the monetarist facade was cracking.

The situation worsened that summer and autumn. Although there were signs that inflation was finally abating, this had been accomplished at a price of economic decline and increasing misery. Both the unemployment and inflation rates were around 5.5 percent, with every fractional decline in price increases matched by a boost in joblessness. In September a Democratic study group led by Walter Heller sketched "a disturbing picture of accelerated and unduly prolonged inflation; soaring interest rates and financial disruptions; a stagnation of production and jobs, the cost of which continues to grow; policies that have remained long on hopes and short on accomplishments." To this, the Nixonians answered that they had inherited much of this situation from the Johnson Administration and that progress was being made in correcting the economic abuses of a decade.

With all of this the President's popularity remained steady, with rises and declines attributed more to Vietnam-related issues and reactions to "law and order" appeals than to the course of the economy. In a November 1970 poll, 57 percent of those responding gave Nixon an "approved" rating, against 59 percent who did so after his first month in office. On the eve of the congressional elections, other polls indicated that voters were more concerned with foreign policy and social issues than they were with those relating to inflation and recession.

Most commentators had expected the Republicans to do poorly that year. Yet the G. O. P. lost only nine House seats and actually gained two in the Senate. But the party lost eleven state houses, and analysts observed that in these races the economic issues predominated.

The election results may have helped nudge Nixon further from the monetarist position and closer to that espoused by Burns. In his first major economic address after the elections, delivered before a friendly National Association of Manufacturers group on December 4, Nixon stressed the importance of measures taken to stimulate growth and alluded to an agreement with the Federal Reserve: "I have been assured by Dr. Arthur Burns that the independent Federal Reserve System will provide fully for the increasing monetary needs of the economy. I am confident this commitment will be kept." On his part, Nixon announced plans to revive the housing industry and increase the petroleum supplies through new allocations. Engaging in a bit of jawboning, he added, "This is the moment for business and labor to make a special effort to exercize restraint in price and wage decisions." Significantly, there was no renewed pledge to avoid wage and price controls and fewer references to the importance of the free and open marketplace than were customary in a Nixon speech to such an audience.

Burns's response came a few days later, in an address at Pepperdine College. After praising the President's "stern warning to business and labor to exercize restraint in pricing and wage demands," he demonstrated that the Fed indeed was independent. Burns called for the establishment of "a high-level price and wage review board which, while lacking enforcement power, would have broad authority to investigate, advise, and recommend on price and wage changes."

There was a nice logic in Burns's position. If the monetarists were right, then Nixonian jawboning would not be necessary—prices would decline due to a lack of demand, this caused by changes in the money supply the previous year. If they remained where they were, or even rose in the face of declining demand, it would mean that the Galbraithian argument had merit. Burns had no hard-and-fast commitment to either camp; he usually went where the evidence led him. And at this juncture he was headed left.

Comparing and commenting on the two speeches, *New York Times* business writer Leonard Silk noted that "We are witnessing the emergence of what should go down in the history books as the Accord of 1970." In return for an expansionary Federal Reserve policy, the President would take a more interventionist stance in the economy; he too would move to the left.

This situation was duly noted by Milton Friedman. "Talk about stopping inflation has given way to talk about stimulating employment. Talk about nonintervention in prices and wages has given way to jawboning. Talk about 'gradualism' has given way to talk about 'activism.'" He deplored all of this, in such ways as to sharpen the differences between his position at that newly taken by Nixon. In earlier statements Friedman had indicated that the steady-as-she-goes policy might bring about a gradual end to inflation while sparing the nation the pains of a serious recession. Now he said the current downturn had been unavoidable; it was the price paid to halt the inflationary spiral and in any case was close to its conclusion. Why did Friedman believe an upturn was in the making? The Fed's expansionist monetary policies would accomplish this.

Friedman already had chastised Burns for his espousal of an incomes policy; now his criticisms were harsher. The money supply expanded at a rate of 13 percent per annum in the first two months of the year, better than double the 1970 rate, and for the rest of the first half the expansion was a fraction below 12 percent. This sharp reversal of the 1970 experience would whipsaw the economy. "Erratic monetary growth almost always produces erratic economic growth," wrote Friedman. The economy would recover in 1971; unemployment would decline. But there would be further inflation in the future and a greater dislocation than the economy had experienced in the 1968-1970 period. Friedman called upon Burns to moderate the growth of the money supply and asked Nixon to renew his fight against inflation.

There is no evidence that Nixon and Burns ever came to the kind of accord described by Silk, or that their economic outlooks meshed as well as Friedman supposed they did. But whatever harmony existed between the two men started to break down in early July, when in a report delivered before the Joint Economic Committee Burns both criticized Administration handling of the economy and moved yet further in the direction of controls. As had been his practice, Burns used the occasion to lecture the legislators on the niceties of economic reality and theory as viewed through his particular prism. This much had been expected, but few present could have guessed just how far Burns had traveled down the Galbraithian road.

Burns opened by observing that the Administration had succeeded in turning the the economy around. There was evidence of renewed economic growth; the recession was ending. And prices were rising as well. But the dollar was weak in international markets and capital spending remained sluggish. A major reason for these problems, he said, was the budget deficit, which in fiscal 1971 came to more than $20 billion. "Many influential citizens in the business and financial community view this situation with alarm, so that the large budget deficits have become an important psychological factor contributing both to inflationary expectations and to high interest rates." In Burns's view, then, the Administration was largely responsible for many of the economic ailments of the time. Burns had advocated spending cuts while in the White House and, now that he had his independent podium, he demanded them as a price for further recovery.

Burns could not have expected any meaningful response on this score; spending would rise in fiscal 1972, and so the situation would worsen. With this in mind, Burns analyzed the current malaise. "A year or two ago it was generally expected that extensive slack in resource use, such as we have been experiencing, would lead to significant moderation in the inflationary spiral. This has not happened, either here or abroad." The old notion, which Burns had shared with such polar opposites as Friedman and Keyserling, had been that most inflations were caused by excessive demands. To the monetarists, this meant that too much money was chasing too few goods, and they would solve the problem by cutting back on the money supply. Keyserling would accept the diagnosis but offer a different cure: increase the production of goods and services so that all demands would be filled. The Keynesians, who advocated deficit spending to cure recessions, accepted the need for budget surpluses to remedy inflationary demands, and Burns would go along with this. But he also observed that none of these people and groups had a plausible explanation for stagflation. "Despite much idle industrial capacity, commodity prices continue to rise rapidly. And the experience of other industrial countries, particularly Canada and Great Britain, shouts warnings that even a long stretch of high and rising unemployment may not suffice to check the inflationary process." Prices were rising at a time when the demands for goods and services had softened. To a classicist this was akin to a repeal of the law of gravity. Dogmatists might elect to make adjustments in their theories to fit changes in fact or observation—or simply to ignore realities. Burns took a different route: quite simply he scrapped his now outworn beliefs.

"The rules of economics are not working in quite the way they used to," he told the legislators.

It would be hyperbolic to claim that this statement by a major practitioner marked a turning point in the history of American economic thought. Yet along with Samuelson, Burns occupies a position at the ideological center, with Friedman at one extreme and Galbraith at the other. Now that the center was crumbling, unable to provide a program for meeting stagflation, one might have assumed that given their reputations and proclivities Burns would look to his right for new approaches and Samuelson to his left. For months economists wondered how long it would take Samuelson to embrace Galbraithianism. Such a move had not been expected from Burns, and here it was. Without having first become a hard-and-fast Keynesian, Burns appeared to have leapfrogged into the camp of the post-Keynesians.

Once again, Burns asked for some form of incomes policy. The current inflation was not of the demand-pull variety, he said, but rather had been caused by rising costs in the face of diminishing demands. Powerful unions asked for higher wages even while unemployment was rising, and corporations gave in to their demands, knowing the costs could be passed on in the form of higher prices to consumers accustomed to inflation. In a section that might have been written from or by Galbraith, Burns observed, "Labor seems to have become more insistent, more vigorous, and more confident in pursuing its demands, while resistance of businessmen to these demands appears to have weakened—perhaps because they fear the loss of market position that would be caused by a long strike or because they believe that their competitors too will give in to similar wage demands." Such a situation cannot be remedied rapidly by traditional monetary and fiscal policies—the kind the Administration counted upon. Once adopted, economic controls would "free the American economy from the hesitations that are now restraining its great energy."

That the White House was furious at this apparent defection soon became obvious. Not only was Burns winning converts in Congress, but even Paul McCracken was bending, conceding that some form of incomes policy might be salutary. CEA member Herbert Stein, whose influence had grown steadily during the past two years, was also coming around on this issue. Only George Shultz would argue forcefully for the Friedman approach, but such was his influence over Nixon by then that this sufficed.

The President was hurt; not only had he been challenged by an important and influential official but by one who he had considered a friend, a man he had elevated to his present post. Something had to be done either to change Burns's mind or silence him. Nixon realized it would be foolhardy to try to argue economics with Burns or issue an appeal to loyalty under the present circumstances. So he took another path. Charles Colson, who already had a reputation as one of the President's most effective hatchet men, was assigned the task of "getting Burns."

Within days Colson had floated a rumor to the effect that, while advocating cutbacks in federal spending, Burns had been lobbying to obtain a pay raise for himself of $20,000 a year. In addition, there was talk in Washington of attempts to curb the Federal Reserve System's independence, either through the introduction of new legislation or expanding the Board to include several new Nixon selections. Immediately the financial community responded. The stock market sold off, and the White House was deluged with protests. Burns was viewed as a leading defender of fiscal integrity. Was the President trying to "pack" the Federal Reserve, and, if so, toward what end? Some Administration insiders recalled that on more than one occasion Burns had recommended pay *cuts* for officials in high visibility posts—including that of Federal Reserve Board chairman.

Nixon had not expected so strong and negative a reaction. Moreover, he realized that, unless something were done quickly, the situation could get out of hand. From an independent podium Burns might mount a campaign for an incomes policy and speak out forcefully against Administration policies. No Friedmanite in the Administration—not even Shultz—could match him in power of intellect, reputation, and support from the business community. Thus, Nixon disavowed the attacks, defended Burns, and offered other gestures of reconciliation. They seemed to work. "This just proves what a decent and warm man the President is," Burns said to William Safire, the White House speechwriter who acted as go-between. "We have to work more closely together now."

But Burns did not mean to end his campaign for an incomes policy. Realizing he lacked the kind of leverage within the Oval Office needed for such an advocacy, he formed an alliance with one who had Nixon's ear and almost constant attention. In the spring and early summer of 1971, Burns converted Treasury Secretary John Connally to his way of thinking.

Connally was no stranger to Washington, where he had served as Navy Secretary in the Kennedy Administration and before that as aide to Senator Lyndon Johnson. Impressive in both appearance and manner, he tended to dominate any gathering he was in. His nicknames—"the silver knight" and "Big John"—indicate the prevalent view of him in 1971. He was colorful and, like Moynihan before him, stood out in the rather grey crowd that surrounded Nixon. As has been indicated, the President was fascinated by such men, and, though Connally was a Democrat, thought of him as a possible successor. "Every Cabinet should have at least one potential President in it," he had complained in 1970. "Mine doesn't." This changed with Connally's arrival.

Some thought Connally lacked the credentials to fill the position. Although a lawyer and businessman with extensive interests, he had no direct banking experience, much less demonstrated skills in framing fiscal policies. This concerned some legislators, but Connally seemed sublimely confident of his ability to absorb as much information as he would need on the job. At heart he was an expansionist; during the confirmation hearings he seemed more concerned with stimulating the economy than with controlling inflation. Connally was flustered only once—when asked what he would do to hold back prices. He advocated easy money, budget deficits if necessary, and increased federal spending as cures for almost all ailments, and all of these were standard Democratic remedies. Afterwards he conceded that he lacked the "capacity to create the models." "What I'm going to do, very frankly, is get advice from all sides," he added, "and there are other considerations, I think, that have to be applied."

The forthcoming election was one of these. The economy was sluggish, the dollar weak, stock prices were declining, while inflation raged. Nixon was slipping at the polls; several of them indicated he would have trouble defeating Senator Edmund Muskie, who at the time appeared the likely Democratic nominee for 1972. The tides were running against the Administration, and Nixon realized he had to do something dramatic to change their direction. A new approach would be required.

Ideologically and temperamentally the President remained close to George Shultz, who in June assured him the recession was ending and that inflation would pose no great problem during the forthcoming campaign. Shultz had nothing novel to offer by way of policy. Neither did McCracken, who continued to edge his way toward acceptance of an incomes policy and in the process lost support among the Friedmanites and gained little elsewhere. Connally understood what was happening; a vacuum existed that he was well suited to fill.

This was the background for the marriage of convenience between Connally and Burns. Perhaps there were no two men in high echelon government more dissimilar than these two. Yet Burns's prescription for an incomes policy meshed well with Connally's penchant for action. The Federal Reserve Board Chairman needed someone to sell his ideas, and the Treasury Secretary required a program he could support but was ill-equipped to frame. And on his part, Nixon was prepared to accept Burnsian economics as presented by John Connally.

Shultz appreciated the situation and started to adjust to it. By late July he was speaking less of the virtues of free enterprise and starting to consider a monetarist rationale for a temporary incomes policy. By mid-August all the pieces were in place, and the scene set for high economic drama.

The President convened an economic summit at Camp David on Friday, August 13. Connally, Burns, Shultz, McCracken, and a dozen or so other advisors and experts were present. So was William Safire, who was charged with framing a major address based upon decisions reached at the conference. Of those present, only he has written a detailed record of the sessions, and from what is known of the personalities and their positions, it rings true.

According to Safire, Nixon opened the conference with an indication of what he expected to happen. "Circumstances change," he said. "In this discussion, nobody is bound by past positions." To underline this, he asked Connally to make the first presentation.

The Secretary offered a three-point program that was bold, dramatic—and contradictory. In order to staunch the outflow of dollars, he would take the nation off the gold reserve standard. The dollar would be permitted to float freely against other currencies, its value determined by forces of supply and demand. This was a long-standing Friedmanite proposition, which Connally embraced whole-heartedly.

Given the situation at the time, it was evident the dollar would decline against most foreign currencies. This would make American products less expensive in terms of other currencies and discourage Americans from importing goods, since their prices would now be higher when stated in terms of dollars. If all went well, then, imports would decline and exports expand, in this way correcting a serious balance of trade problem. But this program ran the risk of creating an international liquidity crisis and crippling the dollar as a major international currency at a time when no substitute existed. Under the worst of circumstances, the move could trigger a crisis similar to that of 1931—which opened the world depression of the 1930s.

To underline his resolve to correct the balance of trade problem, Connally would impose new import taxes—which amounted to higher tariffs—and take other measures to keep foreign goods out of the United States. That this would invite retaliation by foreigners was equally obvious.

The Secretary came out in favor of a wage-price freeze, which by then was conventional enough. But his third point involved the creation of new jobs by reinstatement of the investment tax credit and removal of excise taxes on automobiles. With one hand he would put a cap on prices and with the other stimulate the economy in such a way as to create new inflationary pressures. That this would set the stage for an eventual blowoff was obvious, at least to economists present. But to politicians the prospect of steady prices and more jobs was enticing.

Nixon indicated his approval, with the understanding that they would be combined with budget cuts and that the wage-price freeze would remain in force for only a brief period, perhaps three months or so. The President clearly found the idea of enforcing an incomes policy distasteful and would underscore this several times during the meetings. If America was to have a Galbraithian future, it would be one administered by men who had Friedmanite souls. It was a recipe for failure.

Shultz had prepared himself for this and was able to fall back to a strong defensive position, one that enhanced his standing with the President. He would provide Nixon with a rationale that would ease the pain. Earlier Shultz had said that controls invariably failed, but now he modified his position. Under a special set of circumstances such policies might prove beneficial. In particular, the inflationary engine had to be slowing, monetary policy should be tight, and the government dedicated to balancing the budget through expenditure cuts. Finally, there should be sufficient play in the economy to permit productivity gains, which is to say the economy should be in a mild recession.

Imagine a balloon from which air is slowly leaking. Place pressures on it and the deflation will accelerate. Similarly, wage and price controls will perform well, said Shultz, when deflation is taking place—on such occasions they will accelerate the process. And such was the situation the economy found itself in August of 1971.

So Shultz was willing to go along with the Connally proposal plus the Nixon amendment. In his presentation he came out in favor of an across-the-board freeze of a short duration. How long should it last? asked Nixon. "A freeze will stop when labor blows it up with a strike," was Shultz's reply. "Don't worry about getting rid of it—labor will do that for you." (Shultz knew that AFL-CIO President George Meany had long believed that wage-price freezes usually benefit management more than they did labor, and he could be counted upon not only to oppose the Connally plan, but test it when conditions were ripe.)

Burns had his victory, but he had no difficulties in reconciling with his former adversary. Though one of the first converts to the incomes policy, he had always favored it as a temporary measure, to be used because all else failed—and the rules no longer seemed to work. Now he said, "There is a remarkable similarity between George's thinking and my own," and appeared to be sincere. Like Shultz he favored a three-month freeze "which would have shock value, and give us the time to work out the machinery to deal with stabilization." Unlike Shultz he expected controls would be needed thereafter, but at least both men agreed that the policy would have an initial run of a fixed period of time. The most ardent defender of wage and price controls at the Camp David meeting was a most reluctant Galbraithian, if even that.

With this out of the way, all went smoothly. Other discussions were devoted to details, ancillary operations, and politics. Meanwhile Safire began work on the speech, which the President delivered on the evening of Sunday, August 15. It had been billed as an important address, which Washington reporters anticipated would be concerned with the dollar-gold problem. Few supposed Nixon would spring a major surprise that evening.

After a brief introduction, the President announced a wide program of economic incentives for businesses, a speedup in personal tax exemptions, a $4.7 billion federal spending cut, postponement of pay raised for federal workers, and a 10 percent cut in foreign aid. Then he proclaimed his conversion to an incomes policy. "The time has come for decisive action—action that will break the vicious circle of spiraling prices and costs." Toward that end, "I am today ordering a freeze on all prices and wages throughout the United States for a period of ninety days. In addition, I call upon corporations to extend the wage-price freeze to all dividends."

Having said this, Nixon assured the nation he hadn't altered his views regarding the benefits of an open marketplace. The freeze would be temporary. "To put the strong, vigorous American economy into a permanent straightjacket would be to lock in unfairness; it would stifle the expansion of our free enterprise system." No large bureaucracy would be enlisted to administer this program. Instead, a small Cost of Living Council would coordinate work by existing agencies and plan for ways to achieve "continued price and wage stability after the ninety-day freeze is over."

A temporary, barely enforced, admittedly underfunded program was to be put into place by people who did not believe in it. The following day Nixon anounced that Connally would head the Cost of Living Council, but the executive director—the person who would do all of the actual work—would be Arnold Weber, a Friedmanite from the University of Chicago who previously had served with Shultz as codirector of the Office of Management and Budget. From the first Connally paid little attention to the CLC, while Weber gave the impression of counting the days until he could close shop.

The remainder of the speech was concerned with strengthening the dollar, with stress on the closing of the gold window and measures to hold down imports. But insofar as most Americans were concerned, the wage-price freeze was paramount. While the overseas press analyzed the new role of the dollar (and American tourists had difficulties exchanging their greenbacks and travelers checks for local currencies), the American newspapers focused on the wage-price freeze and its implications.

As might have been anticipated, Friedman strongly opposed the action. He discounted Nixon's pledge to end controls as swiftly as possible. In his view, the President's change of direction was permanent. "He has a tiger by the tail. Reluctant as he was to grasp it, he will find it hard to let go. The outcome, I fear, will be a further movement toward the kind of detailed control of prices and wages that Mr. Nixon has resisted so courageously for so long."

Shultz had said that George Meany would have more to do with ending the freeze than would anyone in government, and the following day the AFL-CIO chief denounced it as being "patently discriminatory against working men and women." Shultz was sent to union headquarters to reason with Meany. "I am a defender of free collective bargaining," he said, "And there are times when I feel among the last who feel this way." Thus, he told Meany, in effect, that he didn't like controls either. After the meeting ended Meany said that Shultz "tried to explain the program as forward looking, but he didn't convince anyone in the room."

Paul Samuelson sensed what was on Shultz's mind. He conceded that the program would stimulate the economy and would help crack inflationary psychology. But it clearly was probusiness and antilabor. "This is worse than a crime; it is a blunder." And for this reason if nothing else, it would not work. "The success of the wage-price freeze depends crucially on the pressure of public opinion," and in a short period—when Americans realized that while wages were being held down profits would advance—the controls would break down. Samuelson suspected that what Nixon was to dub the New Economic Policy was a sham. "Every nation of the West can make a 90-day freeze work." It was what happened afterwards that counted, and in this case there would be nothing. Disagreeing completely with Friedman, Samuelson believed the freeze would be only an interlude, certainly not a major change of heart or direction.

Samuelson read the signs correctly. As Meany had predicted, businessmen placed a lid on wage increases while their profits rose as the economy continued to recover from the recession. The labor leader flatly predicted a confrontation over what he called "socialism for the wealthy" and "a one-sided redistribution of the public wealth." But opinion was on the side of controls, moreso than any of the Nixonians had expected it would be. On October 4, the President claimed a victory on the economy front and offered more of the same: "Phase II," which would be a continuation of "our program of wage and price restraint." While specific guidelines were not mentioned, he later indicated that price increases on the order of from 2 to 3 percent would be tolerated.

Finding a proper formula for wage increases was more difficult. A Pay Board, which functioned under the Cost of Living Council and comprised labor, management, and public members, debated the issue through the autumn, without much agreement. On Nov-

ember 5, with the labor representatives opposed, the Board voted
in favor of a guideline of 5.5 percent. Three weeks later, after
threats of a national soft coal strike, the Pay Board approved a 16
percent wage package for the miners. The ice had been broken, as
Shultz had said it would be, by organized labor. Other large increases followed. While the White House insisted the freeze remained in place, in fact it had been replaced by a rapid thaw.

Nixon had claimed the primary purpose of this exercise in controls had been to halt the growth of inflation, and the rate of price
increases did decline somewhat. During the first eight months of
1971 the annualized advance in the Consumer Price Index came to
3.8 percent, while, during Phase I, the advance was on the order of
3.2 percent. Those who believed in controls claimed that these
figures showed that an incomes policy could work even when administered by nonbelievers. The Friedmanites countered that inflationary pressures had abated somewhat by August, this the after-
effect of the recession, and that that the decline in the advance
should be attributed to monetary factors alone.

Friedman predicted a continued expansion that would prompt
and accompany a new round of inflation. This would result not
from the workings of the New Economic Policy, but from Arthur
Burns's activities at the Federal Reserve. In order to spur economic
recovery, the central bank had expanded the money supply at an
annualized rate of 10 percent during the first eight months of the
year. The price for this would be higher prices in late 1972, by
which time the NEP would be in shambles.

After the August speech, however, the increase in the money
supply was slowed appreciably—for the rest of 1971 the advance
came to 1 percent. Presumably this was done to mitigate some of
the effects of the earlier expansion and to present a common front
with the Cost of Living Council. Then, in the first three quarters of
1972, the expansion was on the order of 8 percent. Friedman then
charged that the central bank was more interested in orchestrating
a Republican victory at the polls than with providing the setting for
orderly economic growth without inflation.

Whatever the reason, the economy seemed in good shape in
1972, and on Election Day both the unemployment and inflation
rates were declining. If this had been the goal of the NEP as Friedman claimed it was, that it should be said that "Nixonomics" succeeded. But after the election all pretense at controls ended. The
price was paid the following year. Due to a wide variety of factors,

from disappointing harvests to a major boost in oil prices to even a change in the migratory habits of anchovies—prices rose sharply. The inflation rate for 1973 would come to an amazing 8.8 percent, at a time when unemployment was a shade below 5 percent. This was stagflation with a vengeance.

Mired in Watergate, the Nixonians lacked the time, interest, and abilities to deal with this situation. Furthermore, mainstream pragmatic economics provided few ideas and programs that were useful. Arthur Burns said the new inflation resulted from "special factors" that unfortunately defied anticipation and the remedy for which fell outside the pale of conventional treatments. Samuelson devoted his energies to analyzing the problem, setting forth piecemeal palliatives, but in the end had no programmatic approach to suggest, and the same held true for Heller and other new economists.

The economic rumblings of the Nixon years had shaken up the profession. The Galbraithian stream became a river, while the Friedmanites—despite their failures—won new support and prestige. The center continued to crumble. Any new Administration would find its potential economic soothsayers in a far more militant mood than they had been in the 1950s and 1960s. As the nation moved to extremes, so did the economists of the 1970s. A new generation, which not only is post-Keynesian but also may be post-Friedmanite as well, started to emerge, and their ideologies remain somewhat nebulous. As yet there are no intellectual giants, no rallying cries, and not even a major text. Those who gained power at the White House utilized conservative rhetoric, but some of them did so while groping toward new or alternate ways of dealing with problems, which could not be classified either as conservative or liberal and contained elements of both.

9

OLD REMEDIES
AND NEW PROBLEMS

Although the Nixonian experiment with wage and price controls came to its official end in April 1974, it in fact had suffered from neglect for over a year and a half. Most restraints already had been lifted, and only a handful of industries—machine tools, steel, and health care among them—were being monitored with any care. Certainly the President disliked his incomes policy. In his memoirs he conceded the program had been politically inspired and "wrong" from the start. "The piper must always be paid, and there was an unquestionably high price for tampering with the orthodox economic mechanisms."

Opponents of wage and price controls often argued that they create distortions in the economy and result in unequal sacrifices. Manufacturers will not produce goods on which the profit margins are low, inventory policies will be determined as much by responses to regulations as by market conditions, and incentives are stifled. Moreover, the effects of yet another bureaucracy and the creation of artificial shortages only add to inflation.

Throughout the life of the experiment, George Meany regularly observed that more attention was being paid to wage controls than to keeping a lid on prices. Most Nixonians denied this, but not Shultz. An Administration loyalist in almost all other issues, he kept up a continual criticism of the incomes policy within the Cabinet. Controls, said Shultz, impede economic growth while doing next to nothing to dampen demand. When they are lifted, labor and management increase prices to meet that demand, which in fact has been sharpened by the development of shortages. Thus, an incomes policy turns out to be a destabilizing mechanism, for which Shultz had no use.

Those who rejected controls were obliged to present their alternatives, and so they did. Friedman continued to argue that market forces could bring the economy into balance once the monetary situation was stabilized. Some of his followers claimed Nixon had proven to be a "closet Keynesian" and that a real believer in monetarism had yet to take office in the postwar period. Monitoring the situation carefully from the other side, the Galbraithians charged that the Nixonians were scuttling the New Economic Policy. These men derived little comfort from the prospect of a second Nixon Administration, but most were convinced that their turn would come. The structure of the American economy was such that neither Friedmanism nor a return to the new economics could deal with inflation. Government-directed coercion would be required, and this might be expected once a liberal Democrat took command at the White House.

As the Nixonians had anticipated, the economy appeared in fine shape for the 1972 elections. Under Arthur Burns's direction the Federal Reserve had accelerated the growth of the money supply, which by Election Day was expanding at an annualized rate of more than 10 percent. This was a harbinger of future inflation but a stimulant for 1972. Administration programs helped boost the economy so as to more than compensate for decreases in war-related expenditures. The gross national product that year came to $1.16 trillion, almost $100 billion more than it had been in 1971. The inflation rate was 3.4 percent and steady, while unemployment, though historically high at 5.6 percent, was declining. The economy seemed to have responded well to a classic blend of conventional fiscal and monetary policies augmented by soft wage and price controls.

The reputation of mainstream economists remained high—at least in Washington. Inflation was a problem and unemployment scandalous, but economic science would provide politicians with rational explanations and offer them alternatives to resolve difficulties.

Despite Vietnam, the trade imbalance, and the weakness of the dollar, the belief remained that the United States was the master of its economic destiny, "the leader of the free world." Mainstream economists would help politicians chart their courses; they would sketch trade-offs in policies, frame questions, and even provide answers. Their toolboxes were well stocked, and their instruments constantly being improved. Additions were made to knowledge even when old prescriptions failed, so that fresh medicines would work better the next time around. Or so it was assumed.

Nineteen seventy-two was the last year in which this might be said.

Everything seemed to fall apart in 1973. At the time many economists observed that this was the result of an unfortunate and nonrepetitive set of developments that affected many societies, paving the way not only for the worse recession since the end of the war but "the Great Inflation," also a world-wide phenomenon. According to them, it would have been unrealistic to expect the expansion of the 1960s and early 1970s to continue for much longer. Strains were showing in 1971-1972; there would have been a recession in 1973 even had there been no OPEC price increases, embargo, and poor harvests. These served to turn what could have been a mild downturn into a disaster. But the likelihood of such a convergence of negative forces occurring again was slight, so they said. In other words, the old tools of economic analysis still worked and should not be discarded. The aberration of 1973 was like poison in the system of a healthy, predictable beast. All would be well again once it worked its way through the body or was absorbed.

At first this was a popular belief, one that served to soothe tempers and even create a mood of wary optimism. But then, as there was no clear recovery, as OPEC seemed to grow more powerful and wealth was sucked out of the United States, skepticism and fear set in. Many of the more cheerful prognostications were revised downward, and other, more radical, economists received the kind of hearing they had lacked in previous years. Some of them observed that OPEC could remain a major determinant of America's destiny for decades and that its motivation was geopolitical and religious as well as economic, and so would not bow to the old, immutable "laws." Furthermore, several other raw materials cartels were in the process of formation, among them copper, bauxite, nitrates, and even coffee, and these too would have destabilizing impacts on world economies. The convulsions of 1973-1974 brought home the realization that the postwar era had ended.

That the United States had become dependent upon many countries for a wide variety of raw materials had been well publicized. The popular view was that, like all advanced countries, America imported raw materials and exported manufactured goods. But now it appeared laggard in this area as well. Once the leader in most areas of capital equipment, toward the end of the decade, the United States imported more machinery than it exported.

What had caused this? In addition to the more obvious reasons, there was a score of others, and each analyst drew together his own mix from the pile. The productivity of American workers had not kept pace with that of their European and Japanese counterparts, ran one argument, while another blamed the powerful and expanding multinational corporations for many of the more severe ailments that beset the American economy. For the most part, however, right wing, monetarist economists placed the blame on government meddling, while from left wing Keynesians and post-Keynesians came calls for central planning.

The Friedmanites talked of excessive regulations that were stifling the entrepreneurial instinct and destroying the profit motive. Environmental costs had become a major source of inflationary pressures, they said, while calling for an end to reformist attempts to "place businesses in a regulatory straightjacket." High taxes for misbegotten social programs were decimating the middle class, the producer of most of the nation's wealth, and this too had to end. The Friedmanites fixed most of the nation's economic woes on the reformers, not the foreigners. Friedman himself claimed that, if all controls on energy were abandoned and prices left to market forces, OPEC would be smashed within a matter of months.

The "responsible left," led by Galbraithians, said that industrial concentration was leading to a variety of economic fascism and that this was throttling the economy while at the same time causing inflation. Exorbitant "windfall" profits made by the large oil companies had to be taxed heavily, and there was some talk of nationalizing the industry. The post-Keynesians spoke easily of the need for government control of leading sectors of the economy and of a coming socialism for the United States. While the Friedmanites claimed that all or at least most of the economic problems could be rectified by a return to a market economy, their opponents on the left countered by claiming that if nothing else, the experience of 1973 had demonstrated that market conditions no longer were determined by the law of supply and demand, and that rigorous controls were needed.

The inflation rate for 1973 came to 8.8 percent while unemployment was 4.9 percent, and at the time both figures were considered intolerable. In early 1974 Nixon stated his belief that the recession would end in the second quarter, after which growth would resume and inflation be moderated. In late April he predicted, "There will be a very good year in 1975 and the best year in our history in 1976." Few believed him.

To compound the problem, America faced a major constitutional crisis around this time. As a result of Watergate-related pressures and a near-certainty Nixon would be impeached, all attention was focused on the political process, while the economy was ignored. Around this time Galbraith was purported to have said that Watergate itself was a "coverup"—for the inept handling of the economy. He thought little better could be expected of a Ford presidency.

Nixon resigned from office on August 9, and Gerald Ford immediately took the oath of office, telling the American people that "our long national nightmare is over." He was referring, of course, to the recent constitutional crisis. The nation's economic maladies would not be so swiftly eliminated. On the day Ford took office the inflation rate was 12.2 percent and unemployment stood at 5.3 percent, with both figures rising. Not since 1933, when Herbert Hoover gave way to Franklin Roosevelt, had a new President taken command at so critical a time for the economy.

In an address to Congress delivered three days after being sworn in, Ford spoke of the need to restore trust to government and conquer inflation. As was to be expected from a man who was even more of a conservative than Nixon, he asked for greater fiscal restraint. This was not empty rhetoric; during his two-and-a-half years in office, Ford would veto more spending appropriations than any President since Coolidge. But his conservatism was instinctive, not cerebral. Though hardly an economic illiterate, on assuming office Ford lacked a strong grasp of more than the fundamentals of economic science. Unafraid to admit his shortcomings, understanding he had a large reservoir of good will at his command, and knowing a dramatic ploy when he heard of one, Ford called for an "economic summit" to discuss and analyze the nation's problems and come up with solutions. He would draw together many of the nation's top businessmen, labor leaders, and politicians—and the major economists—in a conference, which would turn out to be a public seminar on economics.

Other Presidents had asked for advice on the subject but always in private meetings. This conference would be different. The economists would have an opportunity to lecture the President on what he should do, Ford would be there to listen and perhaps ask questions, and the public would watch the entire event on television and read about it the next day in their newspapers. Of course, the economists would be speaking not only to Ford and his advisors but to millions of Americans who never before had been reached by such men or heard such ideas.

The nation's leading economists often appeared on television, but for the most part on Sunday afternoon interview programs with relatively small followings. Now they were to be provided with a national spotlight. If handled correctly, the conference could have been one of the more important educational events in the history of the discipline.

The sessions were scheduled to begin on September 27. What initially was supposed to be a relatively small affair ballooned into a major media event, with over 800 "participants" and as many newsmen, technicians, and onlookers crowding the International Ballroom at the Washington Hilton and overflowing into the halls and lobbies. The President was there to hear many of the papers, and the public that watched the conference on television could see him puffing thoughtfully on his pipe, listening attentively, and taking notes. Later on some of his aides spoke to reporters and television personalities regarding their impressions of the meetings. By then it was clear that what had started out as an educational forum had been transformed into a television program.

The impact the conference might have had was blunted by a series of unrelated developments. Ford had pardoned Nixon by the time the conferees had gathered and with this act lost a good measure of his support. There were controversies surrounding the nomination of Nelson Rockefeller to become Vice President and talk of White House feuds between Nixon holdovers and the new Ford assistants. The President had been defeated in his first attempt to economize, a move to stop pay raises for federal employees. To further complicate matters, Senator Edward Kennedy had just announced he would not be a candidate for the Democratic presidential nomination in 1976, and this news dominated political discussions in the lobbies. Those who weren't interested in such matters spoke of the problems of Mrs. Ford, who had entered a hospital for treatment of a breast cancer and was under the knife at the first session. In other words, there was more on the minds of conferees than economics.

As is customary at such gatherings, much of the important work was completed prior to the public meetings. At a "pre-summit" conference, 28 of the nation's leading economists—among whom were Samuelson, Burns, Galbraith, Friedman, Heller, McCracken, and others whose ideas are discussed in this work—met to exchange ideas. Although the meetings were private, news of the talks appeared in the press. Clearly none of these mainstream economists had come up with original or new ideas to deal with the current malaise. Samuelson, who was one of the last to speak, indicated as much in an anecdote he told of the leadership decisions at the World War I battle of Passchendaele. British General Robertson had committed his troops to an almost certain disaster. When later asked why he had done so, the General replied, "I had to do something." Thus, Samuelson implied that economists of his persuasion—the liberal centrists—had no magic formula, no clear way out of the stagflation. This is not to suggest a concession that the new economics had failed or was obsolete. Rather, he and others like him would have to rummage around for other tools to use in the fight, and some of these were found in the conservative bag. One of the clearest lessons of the conference was that a swing to the right from the center was taking place.

This might be seen in the paper delivered by Walter Heller, the quintessential new economist. Much of what he had to say might have been anticipated. Heller advised the President to urge the Federal Reserve to ease its tight money policy, abandon the illusion that minor budget cuts would have much of an effect on economic performance, and reject the notion that a major increase in unemployment would cut deeply into inflation. He also asked Ford to be sensitive to the needs of the poor, the young, and minorities. None of this was new, at least from this particular source. Heller went further, however, calling for an end to "outmoded restrictions on the economy" such as import quotas, fair trade laws, and "over-regulation of railroads and airlines." This had been a long-standing Republican battle cry, and it sounded a trifle strange coming from a new economist. Heller believed that, if this were done, increased competition would result in lower prices and contribute toward bringing the current inflation to an end.

Paul McCracken, now back in academia, believed centrist economics had reached a dead end of sorts. "The conventional wisdom of the Keynesian era was that unemployment was usually worse than a little inflation—and I thoroughly agree with that—and that inflation can always be cured with mildly restrictive policies where necessary. Well, we tried that in 1970-71, and it was a bust," he conceded. "To say that we should try that again is merely to apply outmoded wisdom." In McCracken's view, "The economics profession became a bit too smug about a decade ago. We really thought we knew the answers. Well, we know better now."

Paul Samuelson was somewhat more hopeful, but most of his recommendations were of the kind McCracken had indicated had been tried and found wanting. Samuelson did urge the President to reject radical solutions and simplistic models from whatever quarter they came. Jawboning, rather than an incomes policy, would provide Ford not only with an opportunity to curb inflationary price increases but also a chance to exercise political leadership. And Samuelson thought the President might seek advice from a different group of economists than those usually found in the White House. He urged Ford to utilize the talents of microeconomists, who could help him seek "reform in energy, agriculture and regulatory areas to relieve inflation."

Samuelson's advocacy of microeconomic solutions contained within it a tacit concession that macroeconomic remedies were insufficient to deal with the problems posed by stagflation. Heller's new interest in the regulatory process was in this vein, for this was a particularly important aspect of microeconomic analysis. McCracken's deep gloom and criticism of the profession applied to the macroeconomists—the people who had provided advice and guidance since the end of World War II—and in it was an implied endorsement of attempts to use the micro-approach. This was a growing sentiment among mainstream economists. "We are doing everything we can macro-economically—and it does not look to be enough," said Sidney James, a White House economist. He too was seeking another vehicle. "We are getting into micro-economics in a big way," he told reporters.

Those economists whose names were known to the literate public were by and large involved in the macro area. They were concerned with such large aggregates as gross national product, the unemployment and inflation rates, the position of the dollar in world finance—in general, the performance of the economy as a whole. Their attention was focused on "the big picture," and prescriptions were organized with this in mind. Thus, they spoke of "stimulating the economy" and "preventing a resurgence of inflation." They did so with a tacit understanding that each aggregate was composed of a large number of specific units—the forest consists of trees—and in order to understand the former one must first study the latter. All of the major soothsayers concerned themselves with aggregates, for it is from these that one can draw philosophical and political generalizations and prescribe for a nation and even a world. The line between macroeconomics and political philosophy was thin and, in the case of some practitioners, all but nonexistent. Still, the work of all the major macroeconomists—Samuelson, Keyserling, Heller, and even Galbraith—had roots in the study of the nuts and bolts of the economy, the domain of the microeconomists.

Several microeconomists not only were well known in the business an union worlds but had excellent reputations within the profession. In the nature of things, however, they had less exposure in Washington and in the popular media than did the prominent macroeconomists. For the most part they were unknown to the lay public—a book on where the economy was headed might interest many readers, but one on the economics of the wood pulp industry would hardly attract much of an audience. The Chairman of the CEA would inform a President of the effects of trade deficits on inflation and unemployment; his microeconomic colleague would be sought out by makers of men's shoes wanting to know how an alteration in tariff rates or exchange controls would impact on their sales, or by titanium dealers interested in finding out how new antipollution regulations would affect demand and price for the metal. Where macroeconomics was political and philosophical, microeconomics tended toward the practical.

Wassily Leontief of Harvard, a Nobel Prize winner and a giant within the profession, was perhaps the most prominent microeconomist. Leontief was best known for his work in input-output analysis. He would construct giant models of the economy, or parts of it, from which practitioners could discover how changes in one industry—say, automobile production—would affect another—lumber, for example. Leontief was a supreme empiricist, even moreso than Arthur Burns, but he also was an apostle of central planning.

By using his models, one could control the flow of materials and predict oversupplies and bottlenecks, which he thought were primary causes of recession and inflation. Leontief provided some of the raw material from which Galbraith constructed his post-Keynesian visions. Literate Americans knew Galbraith and many of them had read his books and articles; few knew of Leontief, and fewer still had gone through his early masterpiece, *The Structure of the American Economy, 1919-1929.* But now he and others of his particular breed were coming into prominence, if for no other reason than that the macroeconomists had run out of answers.

For decades Leontief had criticized macroeconomists for having formulated principles and prescribed policies on weak empirical grounds, but these sentiments usually appeared in scholarly papers or talks at professional meetings. Now his feelings on the subject were printed in the national press, and many Americans learned for the first time of Leontief and his specialty. "The macro-economists work by disregarding details," he told a *Newsweek* interviewer. "This aggregate approach was developed for pedagogical reasons— so that even the President could understand the economy. There's a lot of fancy methodology, but the macro-economists get indigestion if you give them facts." Even more damning was evidence that their "practical prescriptions" had failed to alleviate even the symptoms of the ailment. "Their systems didn't perform as expected," said Leontief. "It is clear the macro-economists couldn't contribute a dime to the energy crisis."

Leontief implied that stagflation might be alleviated through recourse to microeconomic tools. For example, Heller had spoken of the need to deregulate important segments of the economy—a policy that might eliminate some of Leontief's bottlenecks and so relieve inflationary pressures. Microeconomist Hendrick Houthakker of Harvard, whose talents had barely been employed when he served as a member of the CEA under McCracken, had for years been working on this problem. Now he presented a list of 45 specific proposals to accomplish just this, and these ranged from eliminating steel import quotas to the abolition of the Interstate Commerce Commission. Thomas Moore, a microeconomist at the Hoover Institution and one of the Washington conferees, presented a 32-point program similar to Houthakker's. Moore would eliminate "rigidities" that prevented the flow of goods and services, and he spoke of a sclerosis of an economy overburdened by regulations. Economists of his speciality would explore all aspects of the system and recommend measures to free latent energies. It was a piecemeal approach but one that could promise at least limited benefits.

Moreover, it was well suited to the ideological climate of the time. This was a period during which many evinced a kind of sullen anger. Much in America had gone wrong during the past decade or so. Old verities had been challenged, respected institutions rejected, and the national fabric rendered. Social analysts called for "a time of healing," but there also was a need for scapegoats. Ever since the New Deal, conservatives had been wary of government's exercise of power over the economy, and some of them—the Friedmanites in particular—rejected monopolistic practices of businessmen and unions. Many liberals came to view government as their enemy during the Vietnam War and the Nixon years; even while asking for additional social programs, they were troubled regarding the power of the Washington bureaucracy. This was joined to a generations-old distrust of big business. During the civil rights struggle, when some unions opposed quotas for minority workers and suspension of seniority rules, a split developed between these liberals and a segment of the union leadership. Thus, for different reasons, and in different ways, both conservatives and liberals had become critical of large institutions—governments, corporations, and unions. "Small is beautiful," a slogan of some splinter elements in the profession, drew approval from Friedmanites who called for free enterprise and liberals who criticized big business and aspects of big government.

With all of their differences and disagreements regarding objectives, tactics, and even style, these individuals could unite to try to curb the government's penchant for overregulation and monopoly practices in the private sector. They might be on opposite sides in debates regarding continuation of nuclear power generation and the merits of certain environmental restrictions, but they joined forces in criticizing the Civil Aeronautics Board and the Interstate Commerce Commission for eliminating competition, forbidding rate cutting, and protecting the firms they were supposed to control.

The political unity could not provide a substitute for economic theory, however. Thomas Moore understood that microeconomic solutions to specific problems were of limited value if applied in a macroeconomic void. Scientific economists might reject normative objectives; without them political economists would be lost. For example, it was one thing to discover the impact of lower tariffs on a shoe plant in western Massachusetts, and quite another to deter-

mine whether or not it was important for the United States to have
its own shoe industry. "We can't do away with macro-economic
policies," said Moore. "But perhaps we can make the macro-
economic policies more effective through microeconomic steps."
Little more than this could be expected from this branch of the
discipline.

Arthur Burns, one of the few leading soothsayers who remained
wedded to the micro approach even while venturing successfully
into the macro area, continued to believe the old rules weren't
working as they had in the past, and increasingly he sought the
reasons for this in studies of the components of the economy. In
different ways his sentiments were echoed by Samuelson, Mc-
Cracken, Heller, and other centrists, all of whom turned to investigations of specific industries, the operations of government agencies,
and the machinations of corporations and unions. They agreed the
world of Adam Smith no longer existed, and to a large degree that
of John Maynard Keynes was also fading. What was required was
a new Smith or Keynes, and there simply was no such person in the
center. Thus, they went about restudying the components that went
into making their philosophies, as though hoping to find something
there that would enable them to refashion their systems in a more
workable way.

The situation was different at the polar extremes of conventional
economics. On the left were the Galbraithians, while the Friedmanites were on the right. Each camp had a strong, famous, charismatic leader, one their followers believed might prove to be the
Keynes of the 1970s. For years the Galbraithians had been claiming
that a new stage in capitalist development had been reached, and
for this reason the old solutions no longer applied. While others at
the economic summit believed inflation could not be brought under
control for years, Galbraith confidently claimed that strong wage
and price controls, combined with a tax increase and tight money,
would take the inflation rate down to 3 or 4 percent in less than a
year. Friedman offered a prescription as simple as Galbraith's,
though he did not promise as fast a resolution of problems. "There
is only one way to cure the disease of inflation: slow down the rate
of increase of total dollar spending." He continued to reject all
attempts at imposing an incomes policy. "Wage and price controls
are no part of the cure. On the contrary, they are one of the most
damaging parts of the disease."

Beyond the pale of conventional economics were fringe elements. On the left, for example, was the Ad Hoc Committee for National Teach-ins on the Economic Crisis of Monopoly Capitalism, which called the summit a "charade" that served only to "disguise and avoid the fundamental economic issues confronting the American people." A group known collectively as "libertarians" were to Friedman's right. These economists would eliminate all forms of government and rely exclusively upon market forces to resolve problems. That each group grew larger and gained national spokesmen in the late 1970s is another comment on the growing weaknesses of mainstream economics in our time.

The new President was the kind of man who shunned all extremes. That he would reject the advice both of Galbraith and Friedman was evident from the start. He was seeking some form of middle-of-the-road consensus. Such publications as the *Wall Street Journal, Fortune,* and *Business Week* noted that one consensus appeared to be forming slightly to the right of center. The "buzz words" at the Washington summit were "gradual" and "moderate." "At this point there can be a gradual move," said Shultz. "Rapid monetary expansion in the present inflationary environment would add fuel to the fires of inflation and thus worsen our economic troubles," added Burns. The Federal Reserve had tried to apply the monetary brakes "firmly enough to get results" but at the same time he was "mindful of the need to allow the supply of money and credit to keep expanding moderately." Even Friedman counseled Ford to "apply the cure gradually." All three continued to hold that inflation, not recession, was the nation's number one economic problem.

The public opinion polls of this period indicated that economists were not alone in their shift to the right. The number of Americans who accepted the label of "conservative" was far greater than that of Americans who called themselves "liberal." There was a growing sentiment for balanced budgets and less welfare spending. One heard more of the need for "prudence" and "restraint" and fewer cries for social justice. Some polls showed an increasing sentiment in favor of accepting a recession as a price for obtaining a lower inflation rate. Galbraith would later criticize this as the revenge taken by the rich against the poor, but, whatever it was, the move away from social activism and reform was in full swing.

It could be seen in politics too. The only strong presidential hopeful on the left, Edward Kennedy, had taken himself out of the 1976 race, and with this the hopes of Galbraithians for national

power all but vanished. That Gerald Ford was a fiscal and monetary conservative was beyond question. The selection of Jimmy
Carter as the Democratic Party's nominee two years after the Washington summit reflected not only a rejection of politics as practiced
in that city, but a search for moderation and a turning away from
the social reformism that had characterized the party's presidential
leadership since the early 1930s. Carter's victory would bring to
office a man who rightly was deemed the most conservative Democratic chief executive since Grover Cleveland, one who had more in
common insofar as his economics was concerned with Gerald Ford
than he had with the party's 1972 nominee, Senator George Mc-
Govern.

These two presidents of the stagflation era yearned for approaches to the economy that would harmonize with the kind of
moderate or conservative sentiments they felt the times demanded.
In addition, they would need a concrete program that would realize the objectives of that philosophy. Finally, Ford and Carter had
to discover economists to create the new program and then present
it to the White House, Congress, and the American people. Keyserling had performed this task for Truman and Burns had done so for
Eisenhower. Heller continued to claim that he had schooled Kennedy in the new economics. But there was no such package available in the 1970s and no original, forceful economist who might
create and merchandize it.

Yet some of the elements clearly were present. Ford, Carter, and
the people who helped nominate them clearly wanted a watered-
down version of Friedmanism or at least some program that would
be considered conservative. At the same time the renewed interest in
microeconomic policies might easily provide instrumentalities for
its realization. They meshed well. Conservatives generally preferred
decentralized decision making, an end to regulatory bottlenecks,
and a pragmatic approach to problems, and so did some of the more
prominent and original microeconomists. How might they be
wedded? Which economists could perform the task and symbolize
this approach the way Heller did for the new economics of the
1960s? More to the point, would this formulation be effective in
dealing with stagflation and related problems?

William Simon, who was Secretary of the Treasury at the time,
came close to epitomizing this emerging conservative philosophy.
At the end of the Washington summit he was named to chair a new
Economic Policy Board, which was to consolidate and coordinate

domestic and international efforts at restoring economic equilibrium. The President said that, together with Secretary of State
Henry Kissinger, Simon would meet with representatives of other
industrial nations to develop "a coordinated plan to cope with a
world energy crisis and world economic dislocations." Ford told
the conferees that Simon would be his "principal spokesman on
matters of economic policy." In effect, he was to become an assistant President for domestic affairs and function in that capacity
in somewhat the same way Kissinger did in the international arena.

Simon had achieved the status Arthur Burns had hoped to have
in the Nixon Administration and which had eluded him. While
Burns was one of America's most distinguished and respected economists, William Simon was not even a member of the guild and
had far less academic training in economics than any major advisor
on that subject since the end of World War II. Rather than considering this a drawback, Simon believed it an asset—he would not be
blinded by old dogmas and had not been polluted by liberal
economics as taught in the schools. In his best-selling book, *A Time
for Truth,* he made clear his disdain for academic economists.
Simon contrasted the "impecunious Ph.D.s who destroyed the
economy" with the "successful but Ph.D.-less financiers who fought
to save the economy" and in so doing, located a scapegoat for stagflation.

Simon was born in 1927 in Paterson, New Jersey, the son of an
insurance broker and a mother who died when he was a child. Although he later wrote that his father made only a "modest living,"
Simon did not suffer during the Great Depression. Later on he
attended a private school, where he was an indifferent student but
an excellent swimmer. Rather than go on to college, he joined the
Army in 1946 and swam for its team in the Pacific Olympics. Upon
his discharge in 1948, Simon enrolled at Lafayette College, where
according to his own account he spent more time in competitive
swimming, card playing, and partying than in studies. For a while
he considered going on to law school, but the combination of low
grades, a lack of interest in intellectual activity, and financial
pressures led Simon to seek employment when he graduated in
1952. He took a position as a management trainee at Union
Securities, a Wall Street brokerage, where he discovered a latent
interest in finance and economics. Simon developed a study program
for himself and pursued it with an intensity he had never before dem-

onstrated. He also proved an aggressive and skilled financier and was moved into more responsible and better-paid posts.

His experiences and studies gave him a respect for the market-place and a distrust of impediments to open and free exchanges. In 1957 he became a vice president at Weeden & Co., a maverick financial house that was to challenge the New York Stock Exchange, claiming it exercised monopoly powers in its sphere and, further-more, that that monopoly was protected and sanctioned by govern-ment. Simon played no direct role in this challenge, but the atmos-phere at Weeden must have been such as to further deepen his free market beliefs.

In 1964 Simon left Weeden for a partnership at Salomon Brothers and within a few years had earned a reputation as one of the Street's most astute dealers in government securities, at a time when the market was booming and the financial outlook appeared more promising than at anytime since the 1920s. Soon he was elevated to a senior partnership and had become a wealthy man—toward the end of his stay at Salomon, Simon was earning well over two million dollars a year.

As an expert in the field, Simon's advice was sought by trusts, funds, and government agencies. His work took him to Washing-ton, where he provided advice for the Federal National Mortgage Association and the Department of Housing and Urban Develop-ment. In the process he made high-level political contacts and developed both an interest for government and a distaste for bureaucrats, whom he believed far less intelligent and able than their counterparts in the financial arena. At one point he became a member of the Technical Debt Advisory Committee to assist New York in structuring its debt and marketing its securities. Working with figures provided by Comptroller Abraham Beame, Simon and his colleagues assumed all was well. "It never occurred to us to disbelieve those figures, which always indicated that New York would be able to repay its debt."

Simon was a conservative Republican who in 1968 supported Nixon. Not only was the candidate a Wall Street lawyer, but his associate and chief advisor was John Mitchell, perhaps the financial district's most prominent bond attorney. Simon supported Nixon again in 1972, with even greater zeal since he feared what might transpire if Democrat George McGovern were elected. In late September of that year he was asked if he would be willing to serve

as Secretary of Housing and Urban Development. Simon was interested but heard nothing further for almost two months. Then
he was asked to meet with Nixon to discuss his new position, that of
Deputy Secretary of the Treasury, serving under George Shultz.

By then Shultz had emerged as Nixon's chief advisor on domestic
affairs—the role Simon would achieve under Ford—and so left most
of the actual work at the department to the new man. Simon immediately impressed Shultz and others with whom he came into
contact with his ability to work around the clock and absorb
difficult, technical materials. While winning the respect of his staff
assistants, he became known as one of the Administration's leading
antibureaucrats. "He is like nobody I have ever seen in the bureaucracy," said one official. "He can cut red tape, cut across administrative lines, and get things done in a way you have to see to believe."
But his bluntness offended others. "Simon has a lot to learn about
the Federal Government," said a White House staffer. "He has a
tendency to want to run everything, and he likes to see things
happen fast. Granted he can break bottlenecks, but he sometimes
breaks the bottles in the process."

Shultz was tired, worn-out, and frustrated. He had fought a successful rear-guard action against Nixon's incomes policy, but there
seemed little else he could accomplish in the White House. Perhaps
Simon could do better—he at least was fresh, young, and vigorous,
and the times might be right for a blunt, forthright approach from
an apparent antipolitician. And he was optimistic as well; this too
would be beneficial. In December Simon became director of the
Federal Energy Office, charged with seeking solutions to energy
problems in the aftermath of the OPEC price boosts and the embargo. "I suppose there are people who might call this a no-win
situation," he said at the time. "But that never bothers me. I would
say what we have here is an infinitely soluble problem. And I enjoy
getting things done."

Simon became the subject of magazine and newspaper profiles
and television interviews. He held regular (some said continual)
press conferences and even seemed to enjoy giving testimony
before congressional committees. Where Shultz preferred to do his
work behind closed doors, Simon relished attention. Part of the
reason derived from his outgoing personality and the need to
dramatize the energy crisis. But Simon also had a missionary approach. Where Friedman and Shultz defended the free market in

cerebral terms, Simon was less sophisticated and a visceral believer in the capitalistic system, a man who held to certainties at a time when there seemed few of his breed remaining. In a period of cynicism he was a believable patriot. Simon told reporters he had little doubt the American people could work their way out of the energy crisis. "We have the capacity and the resources to meet our energy needs if we only take the proper steps and take them now." Other Administration figures, the President included, had said as much, but none could match Simon for fervor and transparent sincerity. Furthermore, he had been on Wall Street, and not in Washington, at the time of the Watergate break-in. The White House, still recovering from the scandal, needed such people. The nation remained in a conservative mood, but there were few credible conservatives left to capitalize upon the situation. Little wonder, then, that Simon was named to succeed Shultz when the latter stepped down.

Although Simon identified the energy crisis as one of the nation's major problems and a cause for stagflation, his chief culprit was not OPEC. Rather, like Friedman, Simon focused his attention upon the federal government which, under the guidance of collectivist liberals, had both destroyed the economy and eroded American freedoms.

Inflation resulted from irresponsible fiscal and monetary policies and the misbegotten belief the nation somehow could "spend itself into prosperity." "Much of today's inflation can be traced directly to excessive government spending," he said. This brought him into direct conflict with Roy Ash, director of the Office of Management and Budget, who claimed federal spending had been reduced to the bone, that congressional mandates, costs of ongoing programs, and interest on the national debt accounted for most of the spending, and that these could not be touched. Simon called this a "cop-out." "We've got to quit saying there's nothing we can do about it." He continued to criticize bureaucratic mismanagement and wasteful excesses and to promise reforms. But federal spending increased, the budget remained out of balance, and under Ford the nation suffered its largest peacetime deficit.

Simon blamed congressional liberals for much of this. Each legislator was out to grab as much as he could for his constituents, and few had any scruples regarding conserving funds. They insisted upon wealth-redistribution and antibusiness legislation that stifled initiative, increased waste, contributed to inflation, and reduced employment and productivity. Conventional politicians could do little when confronted with "a tidal wave of egalitarian projects and proposals for increasingly authoritarian controls over the economy, and the best and most principled among them merely find themselves saying no."

Something could be done to fight red tape and outmoded regulations—the tape could be cut, the regulations amended or eliminated. This alone would bring about a sizable decline in the inflation rate. Referring to a CEA estimate that regulations cost Americans $130 billion a year in added charges, Simon warned of the harms caused by an omnipresent bureaucracy. "They exercised control over every aspect of the operations, not only of interstate transportation, power generation, the securities market, electronic communications, and the maritime, automobile, drug, food, agriculture, and defense industries, but of small business as well." Regulations, many of them unrealistic or protective of special interests, often cause disharmonies and frustrate the desires of businessmen to perform efficiently. The Interstate Commerce Commission, one of Simon's chief villains, had 40 trillion individual rates with 400,000 new tariff schedules out every year. Was it any wonder that railroaders had difficulties operating efficiently and within the law? Under ICC rules truckers were obliged to travel 30 percent of the time without cargoes, and this cost consumers between $5 and $10 billion a year in higher prices. Airlines with interstate routes were crippled by rigid tariff regulations that forbade them from lowering prices or competing with one another. Simon attacked the minimum wage law for aggravating teenage unemployment, the housing codes for inflating the prices of dwellings, the complicated tax code for encouraging cheating, and the many health and safety codes under which the automobile industry operated for adding hundreds of dollars to the cost of new cars.

Simon spoke with passion and verve. The time was right for attacks upon government, and the nation needed scapegoats for stagflation. Four decades earlier Franklin Roosevelt had blamed the business system for many of the problems of depression; now William Simon located the causes of stagflation in a mindless bureaucracy that was strangling free enterprise.

The enemy had a face. Simon attacked academics who attempted to implant anticapitalist doctrines in the minds of their students, and he called upon the business community to withdraw support from those institutions that retained such individuals.

America's major universities are today churning out young collectivists by legions, and it is irrational for businessmen to support them. Conversely, business money must flow generously to those colleges and universities which do offer their students an opportunity to become well educated not only in collectivist theory but in conservative and Libertarian principles as well.

Galbraith, "who came out of the closet in 1973 to confess he was a 'new socialist,'" was one of Simon's whipping boys, a symbol of what was wrong with American economic thought, but there were many more, all of whom had to be challenged by a new, vigorous, unashamed conservatism.

Simon's approach not only was antiacademic but smacked of antiintellectualism as well. He appealed to the instincts of visceral conservatives, not the brains of the kind of people who were attracted by the arguments of Burns or McCracken. Simon described himself as a spokesman who was fighting for "a certain constituency that went virtually unrepresented in our allegedly representative government—those millions of Americans who may not have understood the complexities of our economic problems but who knew full well that their taxes were oppressive, that the government was growing steadily more authoritarian, and that their voice was virtually unheard in Washington." He became what amounted to a right-wing populist, offering the traditional conservative values and classic remedies of hard work, sacrifice, and frugality as the means by which inflation could be checked. Simon hoped he could touch an American instinct for individualism and self-reliance as well as of community and economic morality, and he did so in a way not experienced in the upper reaches of federal government for decades. Still, none of his ideas was original. Rather, he drew some of them from the Friedmanites and other conservatives. Burns had criticized the minimum wage laws for many years and William Packard, a businessman who served under Nixon in the Defense Department, sounded the call against liberal academics who received corporation support. Simon brought their ideas together and packaged them. But he was not a manufacturer of doctrine.

The Administration program presented after the summit bore Simon's brand. Rejecting much of the advice given him there, Ford announced a crusade to "Whip Inflation Now" (WIN), the slogan for which came from a White House assistant but whose content was undiluted William Simon. The President called for federal spending cuts of more than $5 billion combined with a 5 percent tax increase that would fall hardest on many middle- and upper-class individuals. This proposal was made at a time when the economy was fast slipping into what promised to be a major recession. The WIN program clearly was a double-edged attempt to stifle consumer demand and, had it gained congressional approval, would have served to deepen the economic decline without a commensurate reduction in the inflation rate.

The new economists and even moderates quickly observed that conventional theory demanded precisely the opposite kind of prescription, namely, tax reduction and continued spending so as to soften the impact of recession. The current inflation was of the "cost-push" variety, caused in large part by increased prices for raw materials, petroleum, and foodstuffs in particular. The WIN program was geared to slice into demand, which in the autumn of 1974 already was quite weak. It contained no provision for stepping up production. Thus, it would result in economic decline with few benefits. Even conservative critics, eager to grasp at most programs to curb inflation, agreed with this diagnosis. Friedman thought little of the WIN program and continued to recommend an easing of the money supply—an inflationary move—to mitigate the effects of the recession. Burns said that "action to reduce income taxes temporarily is an appropriate course at the present time," and Mc-Cracken concurred. Yet Simon continued to press for the WIN program to the very end. The nation had to realize that "neither man nor government can continue for a sustained period of time to spend more than he receives," and that the way to correct this imbalance would be to cut back on spending and increase income, which was precisely what the WIN program set out to accomplish.

Late in the year, when it became evident that the recession would be more serious than had been anticipated, Ford dropped the strategy and started to stress spending programs and talk of tax cuts. The budget deficit for fiscal 1975 was over $44 billion, a peacetime record, as expenditures far outran recession-shrunken tax revenues. Simon fell from favor and was distraught. For a while it appeared he might either resign or be forced from office. In any case, he clearly had lost a good measure of the influence he had had at the time of the Washington summit. Later on, a reporter told White

House press secretary Ron Nessen that in despair Simon talked of resigning and joining with George Wallace and Ronald Reagan to fight increased government spending.

Simon's brand of moralistic economics received its clearest test during the New York fiscal crisis of 1975. That the city had been spending far more money than it took in through taxes had been evident for months, even years. Now it was on the verge of what amounted to municipal bankruptcy, and Mayor Abraham Beame turned to Washington for help. Burns was willing to have the Federal Reserve mount a rescue effort, but only after certain conditions had been met—all other sources of funds had been exhausted, the state had taken control over city finances, a new tax had been put in place, and the city had a financial plan under which solvency could be restored. Under such circumstances, he said, a federal guarantee program "of limited scope and duration" might be established.

Simon agreed with the Burns plan but did so with the rhetoric of passionate conservatism. He told a congressional investigating committee that "the financial terms of assistance [should] be made so punitive, the overall experience be made so painful, that no city, no political subdivision, would ever be tempted to go down the same road." New York's problem was symptomatic of what was wrong with America, he later wrote. "What is happening to New York, therefore, is overwhelmingly important to all Americans, and it is imperative that they understand it . . . [or] New York's present must inevitably become America's future." Burns and others observed that New York was a special case, that no other city was in such a fiscal difficulty, but Simon seemed at least as much interested in the symbolism as the reality.

As had been the case at the beginning of the WIN campaign, Simon became the spokesman for the Administration during the New York crisis. He said the city suffered from a refusal to face up to fiscal realities, to accept responsibility for its spending programs in the form of increasing taxes. Often his arguments were cogently presented and even his detractors conceded their logic. On other occasions, he would oversimplify and state in blunt terms his contempt for the city's political leaders and their liberal philosophy. Out of all this came the famous New York Daily News headline of October 30: "FORD TO CITY: DROP DEAD."

In the end, the city did obtain outside help and management, and federal help was given. Simon might have claimed a victory in this sphere, but his proposals for microeconomic reforms were lost in the invectives hurled by both sides in the dispute. The New York crisis constituted a victory of sorts for conservative economics but did little to enhance Simon's vision of the doctrine.

Whatever else he accomplished, Simon had failed to present a unified, practical conservative economics that could meet the problems of stagflation in the 1970s. Perhaps this was too much to expect from a person with little in the way of preparation for the task. Still, he did provide half of the system—the social goals—and he was aware that microeconomics might provide the program to realize them. Of all the Ford advisors Simon was best equipped by virtue of intellect and interest to contribute to the foundation of a new conservative synthesis. Given a richer academic background, a different personality—and more time—he might have done so. As it was, he tried to ad-lib a program while in the spotlight dealing with a wide variety of complex problems. In any case, his public seemed more interested in political and social generalizations than the nuances of economics. Increasingly, he would stress the former and ignore economic reasoning. Sensing a vacuum of leadership in the Republican Party, Simon positioned himself to fill it. After leaving Washington he delivered many speeches, wrote his book and a newspaper column, and stood ready for a call to public office. By then his economic ideas had degenerated to cliches and bombast, though the forces that evoked them remained.

During the 1976 presidential campaign, Jimmy Carter often promised that, if elected, he would combat inflation with fresh men and ideas. As it turned out, Carter's ideas were quite conventional. He stressed budget balancing, microeconomic approaches, cuts in federal spending, and the modernization of the bureaucracy. There would be as much continuity between the Ford and Carter Administrations as there had been between those of Kennedy and Johnson, something liberal Democrats often noted during the next four years.

Carter brought no prominent academic economist into his inner circle. Charles Schultze, the new CEA Chairman, had been in government, on and off, for more than two decades and had also been a member of the Brookings Institution, the leading liberal "think tank." Schultze was a respected technician, especially on budget matters. Had Carter been seeking an opening to the political left, Schultze might have provided him with one. But the incoming President had other ideas, and Schultze became an invisible man in the Carter White House, rarely to be heard from during the next four years.

More than had been the case even in the Nixon and Ford Administrations, policy determination would be in the hands of bureaucrats, businessmen, politicians, and other relative nonprofessionals in economics. The most prominent of them during the first three years were W. Michael Blumenthal, James Schlesinger, and G. William Miller, each of whom appeared as spokesman for the Administration while failing to make a permanent imprint upon policy.

Blumenthal, who was Carter's first Treasury Secretary, had the best training in the discipline, having recieved a Ph.D. in the subject from Princeton and taught economics for a few years in the mid-1950s. He then spent the next two decades in big business and, during the Kennedy-Johnson years, as a State Department official concerned primarily with economic affairs. At the time of his selection, Blumenthal was chief executive officer at Bendix Corporation, a large industrial conglomerate. Generally conservative in fiscal matters, he considered defense of the dollar one of his primary duties, and the nomination was applauded by the business community.

James Schlesinger had been one of the most contentious figures in government during the Nixon and Ford years and had been eased from office as Secretary of Defense toward the end of the Ford Administration. A Harvard Ph.D. in political science, Schlesinger had served in the Bureau of the Budget and the Office of Management and Budget and so had practical experience in economic affairs. Carter was fascinated by his intellect, capacity for hard work, and puritanical approach to economic and energy matters. Schlesinger believed Americans had to make sacrifices as difficult as those in wartime in order to end the energy crisis and stagflation. Like many Carter appointees, he believed in self-reliance, balanced budgets, and fewer social programs. Schlesinger became Federal Energy Administrator in 1977 but from the first was closer to the President than most Cabinet officers. The following year he was named the first Secretary of Energy, and as such his interests overlapped into the economic sphere. Most of the time he agreed with Blumenthal's hard-line prescriptions—tight money, high interest rates, and a strong dollar.

In 1978 G. William Miller succeeded Arthur Burns as Federal

Reserve Board Chairman. Like Blumenthal, he had been chief executive officer at a large conglomerate, in his case Textron, Inc. Miller too was deemed a fiscal moderate, and Burns congratulated the President on making "a good choice." As it turned out, he was far less single-minded than Schlesinger and more pliable than Blumenthal. Equally important was Miller's ability to work smoothly with legislators and the Carter inner circle, areas in which the abrasive, independent, and often arrogant Blumenthal and Schlesinger had shortcomings. In addition, Miller was less outspoken than either man and was as much concerned with preventing a serious recession as with holding down inflation. In this regard, he clashed with Blumenthal, who continued to give top priority to defending the dollar. After a power struggle based more upon political and personal than economic considerations, Blumenthal and Schlesinger were fired from the Cabinet, and, in the summer of 1979, Miller left the Federal Reserve to assume the Treasury portfolio.

This was one of the more sensational episodes of the Carter Administration, but it had little meaning in terms of policy or philosophy. Economic analysts and journalists could uncover no ideological meaning in these shifts, in part because Schlesinger, Blumenthal, and Miller did not fit well into conventional categories. They were more technicians than ideologists, and the presence of so many men like them in such high positions indicated the failure or lack of philosophy.

In fact, the old delineation between conservative and liberal economics had become muddied in the past decade. At one time liberals generally believed in fiscal remedies of the Keynesian variety, supported federal spending programs to assist underprivileged people, and accepted unbalanced budgets and inflation as necessary prices to pay for high employment and economic growth. For their part, conservatives stressed the role of money, yearned for balanced budgets, considered unemployment a lesser evil than inflation, and distrusted government intervention into the economy. By the late 1970s liberals and conservatives alike accepted portions of Keynesianism and monetarism. On several occasions Nixon had pronounced himself a Keynesian and Friedman, agreeing, said that since all were Keynesians, no one could be categorized as such. That debate was ended, he implied; it was obsolete in the world of stagflation. Meanwhile, liberals such as Heller and Samuelson found merit in monetarist ideas, and in this period the most closely watched economic indicator became the weekly money supply figures. Samuelson spoke out against excessive government intervention in the economy. While continuing to stress the need to dissolve hard core unemployment, liberals came to see inflation as the nation's major economic problem. The clearest line of demarcation between liberals and conservatives involved energy policy, with the former favoring centralized planning and curbs on the petroleum companies, while the latter advocated free market solutions. But this did not provide a core around which a coherent philosophy could be fashioned. Pragmatism remained the rule, augmented by emotional ideological rhetoric that had little substance.

By his dramatic shifts on the controls issue, Nixon had contributed toward destroying the old battleground, and the lines between liberals and conservatives continued to fade in the mid-1970s. Nothing had appeared to take their place in the political and economic dialogue. There was little sign of a new formulation during the Ford presidency, and, three years after assuming office, Carter had failed to enunciate a clear-cut economic program or put forth a spokesman on policy on the order of Keyserling, Burns, Heller, or Shultz.

For a while it appeared that Alfred Kahn, the Administration's leading inflation fighter, might fill the gap and even contribute importantly toward the creation of a new ideological synthesis based upon what he once termed "uncommon common sense" and microeconomic policies. Of all the Carter economists, he alone possessed the right combination of training, experience, intellect, and personality capable of providing the Administration with a public philosophy.

Kahn is a natural showman, and this is an important talent in a media age. He has a dazzling smile and when about to make a pun his eyes would light up with an almost maniacal gleam. During appearances before congressional committees and at televised interviews he displayed a sharp sense of humor. At one point he described himself as a "sandlot singer," who while a senior faculty member as Cornell had often appeared in student productions of Gilbert and Sullivan operettas, and who told reporters that he would have chucked his academic and government careers to have played the lead role in the Broadway production of A Little Night Music. Almost immediately he was categorized as a "character," always good for a quote or two, a man who liked to work in stockinged feet and insisted his staff write their memos in vernacular English. But he also impressed newsmen and legislators with his intellect and talents. Rarely in the post-World War II period had there been so uninhibited and irreverent a person in such an important White House post. On one occasion he said the President was "naive" as to what constituted competition, and on another he called OPEC members "schnooks." When others in the White House complained about his predictions that the economy was headed toward recession, Kahn told reporters he would not use the word again—instead, he would speak of the forthcoming "banana," and for the next few weeks he used that word as a code message for recession. Kahn told delighted reporters that he had no intention of moderating his language. "If I have to choose between being forthright and candid and intellectually honest and keeping this job, I will select the former," adding that if things didn't work out in Washington, he could always resume his tenured professorship at Cornell.

But Kahn didn't want to return to academia, at least not before finishing his work at the White House. He enjoyed public life and relished the challenges presented. A well-known and respected microeconomist, he was given the chance to help direct the struggle against inflation, to make policy recommendations, and then help implement them. It was as though a platoon commander had been asked to lead an army, and Kahn grasped at the chance, all the while realizing that his new job would require talents different from those he had displayed in the past.

For years Kahn had honed his skills as a leading expert on the regulation of public utilities. He had been asked to find ways to maximize efficiencies in power generation and production; now he was supposed to use his experiences in this narrow field as a model for prescribing for the entire economy. Kahn told an interviewer in early 1979:

> In a sense it's a job that I've been preparing for all of my professional life. But there's an enormous change. All my life I have tried to talk about only things that I have been expert at. I would not ordinarily write something or make policy recommendations unless I thought I knew more about the subject than anybody in the whole world. Now I have to move to an almost precise polar opposite of that. I have the whole world about which I'm supposed to pontificate and make suggestions in something like zero time— I mean zero time plus whatever experience and instincts I have.

Kahn believed these would suffice for the tasks. Defeating inflation, he said, was a problem "worthy of my talents."

William Simon had started with a general philosophy, to which he attempted to append specific knowledge of how the components of the economy behaved. He would select his facts more with an eye toward theatrics and shock value than consistency and use them to illustrate his generalized beliefs and free enterprise philosophy. In contrast, Kahn is every bit as much an empirical scientist as Arthur Burns. He has a fine respect for economic complexities, paradoxes, and irregularities, and an awareness of the limited value of economic prescriptions. He combines this with a glowing view of the goodness of the American people, and, while this was not evident at first, it remains the core of his doctrines. Kahn is an unusual combination of the scientist and romantic, and he carries it off better than anyone of his generation.

Kahn was born in Paterson, New Jersey, in 1917, ten years before Simon would be born in that city. His father, a Russian-Jewish immigrant, worked in silk manufacturing and managed to keep his family afloat during the Great Depression. The Kahns moved to New York, where Fred attended a public high school and then went on to New York University, from which he received his B.A. in 1936 and M. A. the following year. After a brief stay at the University of Missouri he enrolled at Yale, and while working for his Ph.D. supported himself as a researcher at the Brookings Institution and the antitrust division of the Justice Department.

Kahn considered himself a New Deal liberal. He had not been bitten by the Keynesian bug, however, and even then was skeptical of attempts to describe a complex economy in systematic, ideological terms. Rather, he was critical of businessmen who tried to stifle competition and, through agreements between themselves, prevented the free exercise of classical economic laws. Government's role in his view should be to clear the channels of supply and demand, to enforce antitrust laws, and be on guard to prevent collusion. Kahn was at the Department of Justice at a time when that bureau was still basking in the afterglow of Thurman Arnold's massive antitrust crusade, and along with others he was swept along by Arnold's enthusiasm for free markets. His later criticisms of government for having cooperated with businessmen to hinder competition had their origins in this prewar experience.

Kahn was awarded the Ph.D. in 1942 and four years later a version of his dissertation, *Great Britain in the World Economy*, was published by Columbia University Press. Most such first efforts are earnest, plodding, and heavily annotated, designed more to advance the author's academic career than to make a contribution to knowledge. But while Kahn's book is dated, it is clearly written and jargon-free, and in the work can be found many examples of his distaste for barriers to competition. Kahn described "the progressive ossification of British business organization" before the war, a condition that had to be altered drastically if that nation's industries were to have hopes of recovering their earlier vitality. "There has been an almost unanimous abandonment of price competition, and scarcely less widespread are schemes, in endless variety, for output control, cooperative marketing, and restriction against the entrance of outsiders." More than three decades later he would describe the American airlines in much the same way.

After receiving his degree Kahn served briefly in the Army and then took posts at research organizations in New York. In 1945 he accepted an assistant professorship at Ripon College, and two years later, at the age of 30, he joined the Cornell economics department, which has been his base of operations from that time to the present. More than most leading academics, he became involved in the operations of the school, accepting the chairmanship and becoming a member of the board of trustees. Kahn was dean of the College of Arts and Sciences from 1969 to 1974, and all the while he turned out books and articles, participated on panels, and acted as consultant for such entities as American Telephone & Telegraph, the Federal Trade Commission, and the Federal Energy Commission, among others. He also took a leave to serve as a senior staffer for Eisenhower's Council of Economic Advisors.

Kahn's principle area of expertise, the economics of regulation, is a fairly narrow one, more of interest to corporate and government lawyers and bureaucrats than to macroeconomists. His studies and proclivities led him to the conclusion that American businessmen were being harassed by complex and overlapping regulations, shifting government policies, and uncertain interpretations of antitrust laws, all of which stifled and discouraged initiative and added to the prices of goods and services. But he also criticized businessmen who, like the British, sought protection against market forces by allying themselves with bureaucrats and politicians. In a coauthored book, *Fair Competition: The Law and Economics of Antitrust Policy* (1954), Kahn called for a more coherent, less ideological antitrust approach.

It made little sense to penalize firms if by virtue of superior products and marketing they became giants in their industries. "The antitrust laws cannot be turned into a statute for the structuring of all markets in the direction of purer competition." Not should the Justice Department or the courts embark on crusades either to assist or penalize companies. Rather, both should try to provide businessmen and union leaders with clear and consistent rules under which they should operate. Government intervention in the economy may be necessary on occasion but always should be undertaken with caution and in as limited a fashion as possible. Well-intentioned attempts at eliminating unwholesome practices result in the creation of still greater abuses and disharmonies. It follows, said Kahn, that government should not enter into alliances with labor or businesses in order to make public policy. Thus, he opposed government attempts to set wages in the construction industry, and also criticized government-business alliances to regulate markets.

Kahn was especially critical of the way the Texas Railroad Commission acted to protect markets, maintain prices, and eliminate competition in the petroleum industry. This regulatory body, which exercised jurisdiction over firms that produced more than 40 percent of the nation's oil, used its powers to exclude the foreign product from domestic markets by means of quotas, in this way contributing to higher prices and erecting barriers to trade. In a co-authored book published in 1959, *Integration and Competition in the Petroleum Industry,* Kahn observed that "the crude-oil price structure, both within the United States and outside our borders, is artificial in the sense that it is set by policy and maintained by administrative action, rather than determined by competitive adjustment to costs." He urged abolition of all quotas on the importation of foreign oil, even if this meant the temporary shut-down of some American wells. This action, he said, "should provide the catalyst for a highly desirable reinvigoration of competition at home."

Kahn would eliminate the Texas Railroad Commission, which he considered the political arm of domestic producers who sought unfair protection against competition. But he also realized the petroleum industry was critical to the nation's well-being and so could not be permitted to function with no regulations at all. "More than anything else there is needed at the national level a body charged with the responsibility to think through these problems of government-industry relations, including the special tax inducements thus far extended, to formulate a coordinated policy toward crude oil and an effective method of realizing it."

Integration and Competition in the Petroleum Industry established Kahn as one of the nation's foremost experts in the field of energy regulation, and it was a subject he continued to pursue during the next decade. In 1970 he published the first volume of a two-volume study dealing with *The Economics of Regulation,* which contained an extended analysis of rate determination in the utilities industry. Now he became a consultant to and critic of the New York State Public Service Commission, and in 1974 he took a leave of absence from Cornell to become chairman of that body.

Kahn transformed an agency that in the past had been somewhat moribund and dull into one of the most imaginative and interesting parts of state government. Among his innovations were the introduction of lower rates for electric power use during off-peak hours and insistence that the power companies introduce efficiencies to hold down rates. He obliged New York Telephone to allow customers to use their own equipment rather than requiring them to lease from the company. In return for permitting Telephone to charge for the use of directory assistance, Kahn insisted upon credits for those who did not utilize the service. In these and other instances, he demonstrated a willingness to restudy established practices and if necessary abandon them, to innovate in order to rationalize and economize, and, wherever possible, simplify and clarify regulations. Little of this fit in with any established economic ideology. Rather, Kahn prided himself on helping fashion an efficient structure that resulted in better services at lower costs.

Kahn considered this approach one of the best methods for combating inflation. He recognized the need for fiscal and monetary medicines and in general favored balanced budgets and automatic increases in the money supply. He deplored the use of wage and price controls and preferred free market operations. Kahn was not a Friedmanite, however. Instead, he shared with Leontief and Houthakker a belief that many price boosts resulted from bottlenecks in production and distribution, harmful government regulations, and structural diseconomies. The elimination of these was no less important in the fight against inflation than balancing budgets and controlling the money supply. As Kahn saw it, government mismanagement in all three areas had contributed greatly to current problems. In a 1975 essay on "Market Power Inflation," he wrote, "It remains true that here can be no inflation that is not validated by public policy. And that, consequently, it is faulty government policy that is, in a sense, 'responsible' for all inflation."

This government-sponsored and tolerated inflation was compounded by business, union, and consumer psychology. In an inflationary environment all feared "falling behind" and seeing their profits, incomes, and purchasing power diminished. Thus, businessmen advance their prices in order to include the future costs of inflation, unions demand large wage increases in anticipation of higher prices ahead, and consumers buy more and save less, believing that prices will be higher tomorrow at which time the dollar will be worth less. Their actions, based upon anticipation of future inflation, in themselves result in price rises, and so we have the phenomenon of self-fulfilling prophecy.

Kahn believed the inflationary spiral would slow down if all ceased playing this game of "catch-up." Galbraith had said as much and claimed that wage and price controls would dampen inflationary pressures. Kahn agreed in part but also felt that businessmen and unions would find ways around the regulations, which in any case would distort the economy and create additional problems. The economist who for years had criticized the federal government for setting down regulations that often added to inflationary pressures hardly could be expected to advocate the creation of a new, major bureaucracy of this kind in the expectation that somehow it would be able to hold prices down.

Kahn's views were similar to those of the President. During the campaign Carter had criticized the Washington bureaucracy and had pledged to cut red tape and end waste if elected. Kahn appeared to be doing just that in New York, and he was marked down for a future federal assignment. In May 1977, he was named to the chairmanship of the Civil Aeronautics Board (CAB), a post which in the past was hardly deemed glamorous or exciting.

Like many such agencies, the CAB was considered a captive of the very industry it was supposed to regulate. The major carriers preferred fixed prices, set routes, and as little competition as possible. From the first Kahn indicated that he intended to alter this situation. Shortly after taking office he told airline executives that he would welcome applications for discount and special fares, and he pressed successfully for legislation making it easier for new carriers to enter the industry. When several of the weaker lines protested, Kahn observed that "no businessman protected from competition ever believed that competition is anything but destructive," and, in any case, his job was "to protect competition, not companies." When warned that several companies might be obliged to leave the industry, Kahn responded, "Some may drop to the wayside, but those managements that learn to adjust are going to do very well."

Within a few months Kahn was able to claim, with justification, that prices were down and efficiencies increased. "There are already signs that price competition is eliminating a lot of slovenliness in route planning," he told a reporter. Now Kahn prepared to go even further. On accepting the CAB post he had quipped, "I will consider it some measure of success in this job if there *is* no job when I leave it." In late summer he advocated the phasing out of the CAB and did so in such a way as to suggest that other, similar regulatory agencies might also be scuttled. Partly as a result of his skillful lobbying, a bill embodying this recommendation was passed and signed into law in October 1978.

Kahn's reputation seemed secure. He was now described as the best of Carter's more than 600 appointees and the only man in the Administration who seemed to know how to bring prices down. In addition he was one of the few White House figures with good relations on Capitol Hill, and he remained a favorite of reporters. Asked if he meant to continue his crusade, he said something to the effect that "Rome wasn't destroyed in a day."

In late October the President elevated Kahn to three new positions. Now he would be a member of the Economic Policy Group and chairman of the Council on Wage and Price Stability, in addition to serving in the White House as counselor for inflation. This placed him in effective command of the Administration's struggle against rising prices; he would be the most prominent and influential economist in government and Carter's chief spokesman in this area.

There was little surprising in Kahn's initial plans to restore a measure of stability to the economy. As he had in other posts, Kahn would push vigorously for deregulation in order to free petrified channels of competition; there was talk of a "new day" in such agencies as the Federal Trade Commission, the Food and Drug Administration, the Occupational Health and Safety Administration, and the Federal Communications Commission. But even more important than this was an assumption regarding the population that Kahn shared with Carter. Both men believed the people were better than their institutions and that reforms in the latter would free the latent energies and sense of community in the former. Even before the President called for "the moral equivalent of war" in dealing with the energy crisis, Kahn asked for as much in the struggle against inflation. There would be no attempt to impose wage and price controls, but instead a new try at jawboning. Kahn would appeal to the patriotism of union leaders and businessmen when asking them to keep wage demands and prices down. If this failed, he would speak out against the offenders and hope that the pressure of public opinion would force them to back down from inflationary practices. Given an aroused public opinion, such an approach had a good chance of working. Clearly it was in line with the Carter Administration's penchant for moral exhortation.

On accepting his new assignment, Kahn said, "We either demonstrate that we are an American people, or that we are just 200,000,000 people at war with one another." In the same vein, Carter drew an analogy between the public's behavior during inflationary periods and the way crowds acted at football games, when everyone was standing, craning their necks to see over the heads of people in front of them. He suggested the same results could be obtained if everyone sat down at the same time. Again, this was what Galbraith had been saying for years, but Carter and Kahn clearly believed that they could obtain results with volunteerism.

Kahn indicated he would accept wage increases on the order of 7 percent and price increases of 5.75 percent. If these limits were adhered to there would be a period of discomfort followed by a steady decline in the inflation rate. Economies realized through deregulation and a concomitant increase in productivity would further contribute toward making possible a period of relative price stability, and this in turn eventually would reverse the psychology of inflation. "The fight against inflation requires an attack on all sources of government-induced inefficiency in the economy," said Kahn. "I become not Mr. Wage and Price Regulator, but Mr. Efficiency in Government, Mr. Deregulator, or Mr. Minimizer of Coercion."

Kahn received cooperation from Federal Reserve Board Chairman Miller; from September 1978 to March 1979, the money supply actually shrank by close to 1 percent. Treasury Secretary Blumenthal tried to cut spending and assure the Europeans and Japanese the United States truly intended to buttress the dollar and bring an end to chronic inflation. True to his past utterances, George Meany characterized the guidelines as "inequitable and unworkable" and proclaimed they would not be adhered to in upcoming union-management contract negotiations. Kahn reacted by taking to the stump to seek public support. Unless inflation were checked, he said, "sooner or later we will have such a total breakdown of the organization and morale of our economy that we will have a deep, deep depression."

This kind of warning led to a rift between Kahn and Carter. The President had been saying there would be no decline, and he now dismissed Kahn's warnings as just "idle talk." Rebuked, Kahn told reporters that he would continue to speak his mind, and as has been noted, it was then that he announced that in the future he would substitute the word "banana" for "depressions" to sooth ruffled feelings at the White House. "I am using 'bananas' very freely these days," he said ruefully.

The Iranian Revolution, which disrupted world oil markets and set off another round of price increases, gave added credence to Kahn's predictions of a recession and also crippled his program to bring down the inflation rate. He received little credit for the slowing of the price advance in early 1979; monetarists said the cause had been tight money, while others thought such behavior normal at the onset of an economic decline. As fuel shortages were felt on the consumer level and prices advanced, Kahn became one of the Administration's scapegoats. Unions and managements ignored the guidelines, and he could do nothing to punish them. By midsummer, the inflation rate stood at 14 percent. Unemployment was close to 6 percent and rising. The economy was growing at a rate of less than one half of one percent, which was the lowest in the industrialized world. America was experiencing stagflation with a vengeance, and Kahn was in eclipse.

One day in late spring a visitor to his offices pointed out three dead plants on the terrace. "Oh yes," said the inflation fighter. "The first one is the pay standard, the second is the wage standard, and that one over there is regulatory reform." While freely conceding defeats, he remained optimistic that volunteerism would be effective given a stable international situation. "It was an impossible job and any economist that took it was bound to have his reputation ruined," said one business economist, who added, "We've been Kahned."

Little was heard of Kahn that summer. Although he had more experience in the energy field than most White House figures, he was not visible at the President's Camp David energy meetings, and, while not dismissed in the general reorganization, his influence in Washington was diminished. In August, when it appeared the fight against inflation had been lost, Kahn continued to issue his by-now familiar exhortation. "We are calling on all the American people for an act of faith." Clearly no such gesture would be forthcoming. The nation's mood was sour, its optimism crushed, and the sense of community Kahn had hoped to recreate was no longer there.

The Kahn prescriptions might have worked if applied during a simpler and better period. One can imagine them being quite effective in the 1950s or even as late as the mid-1960s. But not during the Great Inflation, a time which called for drastic surgery, not simple medicines. *Newsweek* observed that Kahn's defeats spoke volumes about the malaise of the American people toward the end of the 1970s. The alternative now would be a turning away from volunteerism and toward controls. The failure of his strategy might turn out to be the last stand for center-of-the road economics in this generation.

That July, *New York Times* economics commentator Peter Passell asked readers to consider what this meant. "Remember Fred Kahn, the witty Cornell economics professor who presided triumphantly over the deregulation of the airlines industry? Since he took the job of chief inflation fighter, the bloom has faded from Mr. Kahn's checks." Passell went on to observe that along with the entire economics profession, Kahn had lost a measure of credibility, and he suggested this was not completely fair. Perhaps economists, like other people, have become prisoners of their preconceptions. The old Keynesian and monetarist solutions hadn't worked in the fight against stagflation, because they were inadequate and out-dated: "They must await a conceptual breakthrough—presumably by some yet unknown genius."

Or it could be something else. Economists knew how to deal with inflation, but recourse to self-interest and appeals to patriotism no longer worked well. Sacrifices were required, said many within the profession, but in a free society they lacked the power to extract them. Passell suggests the problem is more political than economic. Perhaps coercion is needed to bring prices into line. What may be required is an overall program derived from an activist philosophy, with leadership from a strong, charismatic President assisted by a political economist. Attempts on the part of Kahn and others to infuse the old system with a new vigor apparently haven't been effective. The professionals have failed, not so much because their medicines are weak but rather that the patient they have been designed to help has so radically changed. "The fault lies not in our economics," says Passell, "but in ourselves."

Critical junctures seem to appear in years divisible by four—just in time for presidential campaigns. On such occasions commentators often suggest the nation is either at a turning point or a dead end. Much of this is pure or diluted hyperbole, but as Kahn thought about packing his bags for the return trip to Cornell it appeared evident that Americans yearned for a change, not only in politics but in the economic approach to solving problems as well. They seemed to want an energy policy that will be clear-cut and easily understood, medical protection that will safeguard them against rising hospital and physician costs, and relief from what they deem to be oppressive taxes. More than anything else, perhaps, they sought an end to stagflation, that phenomenon that is for this generation what the depression was to that of the 1930s. To obtain all this, they may be willing to relinquish some of their freedoms, to bestow upon a strong leader the power to act and be responsible for results.

The nation may be at the edge, in somewhat the same way it was in the early 1930s. We could be about to see the creation of what for the lack of a better term might be called the "newer economics." And this matter of terminology is significant. In the early years of the Great Depression John Maynard Keynes became a rallying point and symbol for a new generation of economists prepared to deal with problems of stagnation and unemployment, as well as a target for others who opposed his prescriptions. The young Keynesians and anti-Keynesians of the 1930s are now in their sixties and seventies. Many of their proferred solutions to problems appear outdated and in any case ineffectual.

Leon Keyserling continues to talk of the need for expanding productivity. This is, to be sure, a major problem. Productivity growth, which as recently as 1975 was 5.2 percent, fell to below 1 percent in 1979 and actually dipped into the negative figures for 1980. Some have argued that this is to be expected in a mature capitalist economy, while others observe that businessmen hardly can make meaningful plans in an inflationary environment. As for investors, they seek safety in "collectibles," gold, paintings, and other tangible items. Given a period of intense inflation, they liquidate savings and go into debt in order to maintain standards of living they had become accustomed to in more secure times. It may be that without entrepreneurship and private investment, economic growth in the American context cannot be expected, and both have been crippled by the surging inflation. Alfred Kahn, who in attempting to cut back on regulation thought to increase productivity and ease inflation, has conceded defeat, and he fears for the future of democracy. He observes that a people accustomed to real, noninflationary growth may not stand still when this no longer seems possible. Inflation "seems to generate a sense of outrage and injustice even on the part of people who are holding stable or even improving their situation. There's a tendency to set group against group." To which he adds, ominously, that "revolutions come at the end of periods of prosperity." German economist Günter Schmölders agrees: in a study of the behavior of world economies during the 1960s and 1970s he concluded that they tend to abolish or limit democratic institutions once the inflation rate reaches 15 percent or so.

In such periods the analyses of many of the economists discussed in this work appear more akin to nostrums or placebos than effective, believable prescriptions. The new economists, led by Heller, no longer talk of such things as fiscal dividends and tax cuts as though they would solve current problems, and in fact they have become scapegoats for the present stagflation, which most believe originated in Lyndon Johnson's attempt to maintain both the Vietnam War and the Great Society programs. The Arthur Burns of today seems more like his mentor, Wesley Clair Mitchell, than was the case during the Eisenhower and Nixon years; he is long on analysis and short on solutions. The same is true of Paul Samuelson, who in recent years appears to have arrived at an ideological dead end. Both Burns and Samuelson devote an increasing amount of their writings to celebrations of the past rather than discussions of the present and future. As for Milton Friedman and his followers, they continue to press on for monetarist and free market solutions, and there are reasons to believe that these indeed may work—over a very long period of time, say five to ten years. But there is far less evidence that the American people are prepared to wait that long, and endure necessary sacrifices along the way, to obtain a more secure and stable economy. John Galbraith has said that time is short and it perhaps is impossible to put a cap on consumption. The American people demand prosperity, and will settle for nothing less. His prescription, now as before, remains wage and price controls. There is no evidence, either in the American or the European experiences, that controls work over a long period of time. Rather, they tend to create black markets, result in shortages of goods, distort the economy, and encourage cheating while breeding cynicism. "Controls attack symptoms rather than causes," concludes economic journalist Robert Hershey, Jr., and are "rather like corking a whistling teapot instead of turning down the steam."

Our more famous worldly economists are easy to criticize, but uncovering a better prescription than what each offers is another matter. It would appear that the time is ripe for the appearance of a "new Keynes," an economist with a doctrine that could become the beacon for this generation of graduate students, the men and women who will help establish national policies and priorities for the rest of the century. Most commentators seem to believe that there is yet no such person or ideology lurking in the wings of history. Hence, the lack of even a name for any new school, or a banner that it could carry into battle.

The politicians who will lead the nation during the 1980s will have to deal with an economy that is troubled by seemingly irresolvable problems and sharply conflicting demands upon limited resources. They will select gurus from among men and women whose prescriptions no longer appear as certain of success as they had been in earlier times. Under the circumstances their rhetoric is likely to be conservative, even Friedmanesque, for such has been the style since the perceived failure of the new economics. Besides, Americans appear more concerned with keeping what they have than with growth and innovation. Given the nature of the problems, however, it is probable that any new approach will involve more controls and regulations than most Americans are accustomed to. This appears more suitable to an era in which politicians have become more concerned with the problem of slicing the pie equitably than with making it increase in size. Even the conservatives will have to bend to this, as Nixon did in his time.

Given our present circumstances, the 1980s may well turn out to be the long-anticipated Age of Galbraith, though it would be administered by individuals who might appear more centrist than he. Whether we will be able to stop at this level of regimentation could turn out to be the decade's most important economic and social question.

SELECTED
BIBLIOGRAPHY

WITH THE EXCEPTION OF WILLIAM SIMON, all of the political economists featured in this work have written many scholarly articles and reviews. Once in the public spotlight they were interviewed, profiled, and analyzed. The appended bibliography does not list the articles and journalism by and about these men, for two reasons: the selection has been made with an eye toward further reading, not research, and to include all of them would require many scores of pages. Similarly, some of the men have presented their ideas in the form of pamphlets and monographs, not books. Keyserling, for one, had turned out approximately 50 such publications, and these contain many of his most illuminating ideas regarding the economy. Others—Burns, Samuelson, Friedman, and Galbraith—have contributed interesting prefaces to books by other economists. Not all of these have been listed. Thus, this "selected bibliography" is not meant to be exhaustive.

ADAMS, SHERMAN. *Firsthand Report: The Story of the Eisenhower Administration.* New York, 1961.

ALLEN, ROBERT, and SHANNON, WILLIAM. *The Truman Merry-Go-Round.* New York, 1950.

AMERICAN BANKERS ASSOCIATION. *Proceedings of a Symposium on Economic Growth.* New York, 1963.

AMERICAN ECONOMIC ASSOCIATION, ed. *Readings in Monetary Theory.* New York, 1951.

ARNOLD, THURMAN. *Fair Fights and Foul.* New York, 1965.

ASHMAN, CHARLES. *Connally: The Adventures of Big Bad John.* New York, 1974.

AULETTA, KEN. *The Streets Were Paved With Gold.* New York, 1979.

BAILEY, STEPHEN. *Congress Makes a Law: The Story Behind the Employment Act of 1946.* New York, 1950.

BREIT, WILLIAM, and RANSOM, ROGER. *The Academic Scribblers.* New York, 1971.

BROOKS, JOHN. *The Go-Go Years.* New York, 1973.

BURNS, ARTHUR. *Production Trends in the United States Since 1870.* New York, 1934.

——. *Wesley Clair Mitchell: The Economist Scientist.* New York, 1952.

——. *Prosperity Without Inflation.* New York, 1957.

——. *The Management of Prosperity.* New York, 1965.

——. *The Business Cycle in a Changing World,* New York, 1969.

——. *Reflections of an Economic Policy Maker.* Washington, D. C., 1978.

——, and Mitchell, Wesley Clair. *Measuring Business Cycles.* New York, 1946.

——,and Samuelson, Paul. *Full Employment, Guideposts and Economic Stability.* Washington, D.C., 1967.

——, and Watson, Donald. *Government Spending and Economic Expansion.* Washington, D. C., 1940.

CHILDS, MARQUIS. *Eisenhower: Captive Hero.* New York, 1958.

COLM, GERHARD, ed. *The Employment Act: Past and Future.* Washington, D. C., 1956.

COLSON, CHARLES. *Born Again.* Old Tappan, N.J., 1976.

DALE, EDWIN, JR. *Conservatives in Power.* New York, 1960.

DAVIS, J. RONNIE. *The New Economics and the Old Economists.* Ames, Iowa, 1971.

DE CHASEAU, MELVIN, and KAHN, ALFRED. *Integration and Competition in the Petroleum Industry.* New Haven, 1959.

DIRLAM, JOEL, and KAHN, ALFRED. *Fair Competition: The Law and Economics of Antitrust Policy.* New York, 1954.

Dirlam, Joel, and Kahn, Alfred. *Fair Competition: The Law and Economics of Antitrust Policy.* New York, 1954.

DONOVAN, ROBERT. *Eisenhower: The Inside Story.* New York, 1956.

EISENHOWER, DWIGHT. *Mandate for Change, 1953-1956* New York, 1963.

EPERNAY, MARK [JOHN KENNETH GALBRAITH]. *The McLandress Dimension.* New York, 1964.

EVANS, ROWLAND, and NOVAK, ROBERT. *Lyndon B. Johnson: The Exercise of Power*. New York, 1966.

———. *Nixon in the White House*. New York, 1971.

FLASH, EDWARD, JR. *Economic Advice and Presidential Leadership*. New York, 1965.

FRIEDMAN, MILTON. *Essays in Positive Economics*. Chicago, 1953.

———. *A Theory of the Consumption Function*. New York, 1957.

———. *The Demand for Money: Some Theoretical and Empirical Results*. New York, 1959.

———. *Capitalism and Freedom*. Chicago, 1962.

———. *The Interpolation of Time Series in Related Series*. New York, 1962.

———. *Price Theory*. Chicago, 1962.

———. *Dollars and Deficits*. New York, 1968.

———. *The Optimum Quantity of Money and Other Essays*. Chicago, 1969.

———. *An Economist's Protest*. Glen Ridge, N.J., 1972.

———. *Money and Economic Development*. New York, 1973.

———. *There's No Such Thing as a Free Lunch*. LaSalle, Ill., 1975.

———. *From Galbraith to Economic Freedom*. London, 1977.

———, and FRIEDMAN, ROSE. *Free to Choose*. New York, 1979.

———, and KUZNETS, SIMON. *Income from Independent Professional Practice*. New York, 1945.

———, and ROOSA, ROBERT. *The Balance of Payments: Free vs. Fixed Exchange Rates*. Washington, D.C., 1967.

———, and SCHWARTZ, ANNA. *A Monetary History of the United States, 1867-1960*. New York, 1963.

———, et al. *The Business System: A Bicentennial View*. Hanover, N.H., 1977.

FUSFELD, DANIEL. *The Age of the Economist*. Glenview, Ill., 1966.

GALBRAITH, JOHN K. *A Theory of Price Control*. Cambridge, Mass., 1952.

———. *American Capitalism: The Concept of Countervailing Power*. Boston, 1952.

———. *Economics and the Art of Controversy*. New York, 1955.

———. *The Affluent Society*. Boston, 1958.

———. *Journey to Poland and Yugoslavia*. Cambridge, Mass., 1958.

———. *The Liberal Hour*. Boston, 1960.

———. *Economic Development*. Cambridge, Mass., 1964.

———. *Economic Policy Since 1945*. New York, 1965

———. *How to Get Out of Vietnam*. New York, 1967.

———. *The New Industrial State*. Boston, 1967.

———. *Ambassador's Journal: A Personal Account of the Kennedy Years*. Boston, 1968.

———. *The Triumph: A Novel of Modern Diplomacy*. Boston, 1968.

————. *Who Needs the Democrats and What It Takes to be Needed.* New York, 1970.

————. *Economics, Peace and Laughter.* Boston, 1971.

————. *A China Passage.* Boston, 1973.

————. *Economics and the Public Purpose.* Boston, 1973.

————. *Money: Whence it Came, Where it Went.* Boston, 1975.

————. *The Age of Uncertainty.* Boston, 1977.

————. *Annals of an Abiding Liberal.* Boston, 1979.

————, and JOHNSON, G. G., JR. *The Economic Effects of Federal Public Works Expenditures, 1933-1938.* Washington, D. C., 1940.

————, and SALINGER, NICOLE. *Almost Everyone's Guide to Economics.* Boston, 1978.

GAMBS, JOHN. *John Kenneth Galbraith.* New York, 1975.

GOODHART, C. A. E. *Money, Information, and Uncertainty.* New York, 1975.

GORDON, ROBERT, ed. *Milton Friedman's Monetary Framework.* Chicago, 1974.

GRAYSON, C. JACKSON, JR., with NEEB, LOUIS. *Confessions of a Price Controller.* Homewood, Ill., 1974.

GRESSLEY, GENE, ed. *Voltaire and the Cowboy: The Letters of Thurman Arnold.* Boulder, Colo., 1977.

HAMBY, ALONZO. *Beyond the New Deal.* New York, 1973.

HEATH, JIM. *John F. Kennedy and the Business Community.* Chicago, 1969.

HELLER, WALTER W. *New Dimensions of Political Economy.* Cambridge, Mass., 1966.

————. *The Economy: Old Myths and New Realities.* New York, 1976.

————, et al. *Fiscal Policy for a Balanced Economy.* New York, 1968.

————, ed. *Perspectives on Economic Growth.* New York. 1968.

HESSION, CHARLES. *John Kenneth Galbraith and his Critics.* New York, 1972.

HICKMAN, BERT. *The Korean War and the United States Economic Activity, 1950-1952.* New York, 1955.

HORWICH, GEORGE, and SAMUELSON, PAUL, eds. *Trade, Stability, and Macro-economics: Essays in Honor of Lloyd A. Metzler.* New York. 1974.

HOWARD, NATHANIEL, ed. *The Basic Papers of George M. Humphrey as Secretary of the Treasury, 1953-1957.* Cleveland, 1965.

HUNT, E. K., and SHERMAN, HOWARD. *Economics: An Introduction to Traditional and Radical Views.* New York, 1978.

HUTHMACHER, J. JOSEPH. *Senator Robert F. Wagner and the Rise of Urban Liberalism.* New York, 1968.

JOHNSON, HARRY. *Further Essays in Monetary Economics.* Cambridge, Mass., 1973.

Johnson, Lyndon B. *The Vantage Point: Perspectives of the Presidency, 1963-1969.* New York, 1971.

Kahn, Alfred. *Great Britain in the World Economy.* New York, 1946.

———. *The Economics of Regulation.* 2 vols. New York, 1970.

Keyserling, Leon H. *Toward Full Employment and Full Production.* Washington, D. C., 1954.

———. *National Prosperity Program for 1955.* Washington, D. C., 1955.

———. *Consumption—the Key to Full Employment.* Washington, D. C., 1957.

———. *The "Recession"—Cause and Cure.* Washington, D. C., 1958.

———. *Inflation—Cause and Cure.* Washington, D. C., 1959.

———. *Key Policies for Full Employment.* Washington, D. C., 1962.

———. *Progress or Poverty.* Washington, D. C., 1964.

———. *Wages, Prices and Profits.* Washington, D. C., 1971.

———. *The Scarcity School of Economics.* Washington, D. C., 1973.

———. *Full Employment Without Inflation.* Washington, D. C., 1975.

———. *The Humphrey-Hawkins Bill: "Full Employment and Balanced Growth Act of 1977."* Washington, D. C. 1977.

———. *Goals for Full Employment and How to Achieve Them Under the "Full Employment and Balanced Growth Act of 1978."* Washington, D. C., 1978.

Knight, Frank. *The Ethics of Competition and Other Essays.* New York, 1951 ed.

Koster, Marvin. *Controls and Inflation.* Washington, D.C., 1975.

Kraft, John, and Roberts, Blaine, eds. *Wages and Price Controls: The U.S. Experiment.* New York, 1975.

Laird, Melvin, ed. *Republican Papers.* New York, 1968.

Lekachman, Robert. *The Age of Keynes.* New York, 1966.

———. *Inflation: The Permanent Problem of Boom and Bust.* New York, 1973.

Levin, Maurice; Moulton, Harold; and Warburton, Clark. *America's Capacity to Consume.* Washington, D. C., 1934.

Linder, Marc. *Anti-Samuelson.* 2 vols. New York, 1977.

McCracken, Paul. *Economic Progress and the Utility Industry.* Ann Arbor. 1964.

———, et al. *Fiscal Responsibility: Tax Increases or Spending Cuts?* New York, 1973.

———, moderator. *The Energy Crisis.* Washington, D. C., 1973.

———, and Benoit, Emile. *The Balance of Payments and Domestic Prosperity.* Ann Arbor, 1963.

Mancke, Richard. *Squeaking By: Energy Policy Since the Embargo.* New York, 1976.

Means, Gardiner, et al. *The Roots of Inflation.* New York, 1975.

Meigs, A. James. *Money Matters.* New York, 1972.

MITCHELL, LUCY SPRAGUE. *Two Lives: The Story of Wesley Clair Mitchell and Myself.* New York, 1953.

MITCHELL, WESLEY CLAIR. *Business Cycles and their Causes.* Berkeley, 1950

———. *Business Cycles: Memoirs of the University of California.* Vol. 3. Berkeley, 1913.

———. *Business Cycles: The Problem and its Setting.* New York, 1927.

———. *What Happens During Business Cycles: A Progress Report.* New York, 1951.

MORGAN, BRIAN. *Monetarists and Keynesians.* New York, 1978.

MYERS, CHARLES, and SHULTZ, GEORGE P. *The Dynamics of a Labor Market.* New York, 1951.

NATIONAL BUREAU OF ECONOMIC RESEARCH. *Conference on Business Cycles.* New York, 1951.

———. *Economic Research and the Development of Economic Science and Public Policy.* New York, 1946.

———. *The Frontiers of Economic Knowledge: Essays by Arthur F. Burns.* New York, 1954.

NESSEN, RON. *It Sure Looks Different from the Inside.* New York, 1978.

NIXON, RICHARD. *A New Road for America.* New York, 1978.

———. *RN: The Memoirs of Richard Nixon.* New York, 1978.

———. *Setting the Course: The First Year.* New York, 1970.

———. *Six Crises.* New York, 1962.

NORTON, HUGH. *The Employment Act and the Council of Economic Advisors, 1946-1976.* Columbia, S. C., 1977.

———. *The Role of the Economist in Government.* Berkeley, 1969.

———. *The World of the Economist.* Columbia, S. C., 1973.

NOURSE, EDWIN. *Economics in the Public Service.* New York, 1953.

OKUN, ARTHUR. *The Political Economy of Prosperity.* Washington, D. C., 1970.

———; FOWLER, HENRY; and GILBERT, MARTIN. *Inflation: The Problem it Creates and the Policies it Requires.* New York, 1970.

OSBORNE, JOHN. *White House Watch.* Washington, D. C., 1977.

PATINKIN, DON. *Studies in Monetary Economics.* New York, 1972.

PHILLIPS, CABELL. *The Truman Presidency.* New York, 1966.

PRATSON, FREDERICK. *Perspectives on Galbraith.* Boston, 1978.

PROCHNOW, NORBERT, ed. *Dilemmas Facing the Nation.* New York, 1979.

RATHER, DAN, and GATES, GARY PAUL. *The Palace Guard.* New York, 1974.

ROWEN, HOBART. *The Free Enterprisers: Kennedy, Johnson, and the Business Establishment.* New York, 1964.

SAFIRE, WILLIAM. *Before the Fall.* New York, 1975.

SAMUELSON, PAUL A. *Economics.* New York, 1948, 1951, 1955, 1958, 1961, 1964, 1967, 1970, 1973, 1976.

———. *Foundations of Economic Analysis.* Cambridge, Mass., 1955.

——. *Stability and Growth in the American Economy.* Uppsala, Sweden, 1962.

Schlesinger, Arthur M., Jr. *A Thousand Days.* Boston, 1965.

Sharpe, Myron. *John Kenneth Galbraith and the Lower Economics.* New York, 1973.

Shultz, George, and Dam, Kenneth. *Economic Policy Beyond the Headlines.* New York, 1977.

——, and Weber, Arnold. *Strategies for the Displaced Worker.* New York, 1966.

——, and Aliber, Robert, eds. *Guidelines, Informal Controls, and the Market Place.* Chicago, 1966.

Silk, Leonard. *The Economists.* New York, 1976.

——. *Nixonomics.* New York, 1972.

Simon, William. *A Time for Truth.* New York, 1978.

Solomon, Ezra. *An Anxious Economy.* San Francisco, 1975.

Sorenson, Theodore. *Kennedy.* New York, 1965.

Stein, Herbert. *The Fiscal Revolution in America.* Chicago, 1969.

Sternsher, Bernard. *Rexford Tugwell and the New Deal.* New Brunswick, N. J., 1964.

Stevens, Robert. *Vain Hopes, Grim Realities: The Economic Consequences of the Vietnam War.* New York, 1976.

Stiglitz, Joseph E., ed. *The Collected Papers of Paul A. Samuelson.* 3 vols. Cambridge, Mass., 1966, 1972.

Szulc, Tad. *The Energy Crisis.* New York, 1974.

Tanzer, Lester, ed. *The Kennedy Circle.* Washington, D. C., 1961.

Temin, Peter. *Did Monetary Forces Cause the Great Depression?* New York, 1976.

Theobold, Robert, ed. *Social Policies for America in the Seventies: Nine Divergent Views.* New York, 1968.

Tugwell, Rexford, and Keyserling, Leon, eds. *Redirecting Education.* 2 vols. New York, 1934.

Truman, Harry S. *Memoirs: Years of Decisions,* Vol. 1. New York, 1955.

——. *Memoirs: Years of Trial and Hope,* vol. 2. New York, 1956.

United States. Joint Economic Committee. *Economic Report of the President. 1947-1978.* Washington, D. C., 1947-1978.

Warburton, Clark. *Depression, Inflation, and Monetary Policy: Selected Papers, 1945-1953.* Baltimore, 1966.

Weber, Arnold. *In Pursuit of Price Stability.* Washington, D. C., 1973.

Wiegand, G. Carl. *The Menace of Inflation.* Old Greenwich, Conn., 1977.

Weintraub, Sidney. *Keynes, Keynesians, and Monetarists.* Philadelphia, 1978.

Whittaker, Edmund. *Schools and Streams of Economic Thought.* New York, 1960.

INDEX

255